D0777217

A DEATH ON

W STREET

A DEATH ON W STREET

The Murder of Seth Rich and the Age of Conspiracy

ANDY KROLL

PUBLICAFFAIRS

New York

PublicAffairs
Hachette Book Group
1290 Avenue of the Americas, New York, NY 10104
www.publicaffairsbooks.com
@Public_Affairs

Printed in the United States of America

First Edition: September 2022

Published by PublicAffairs, an imprint of Perseus Books, LLC, a subsidiary of Hachette Book Group, Inc. The PublicAffairs name and logo is a trademark of the Hachette Book Group.

The Hachette Speakers Bureau provides a wide range of authors for speaking events. To find out more, go to www.hachettespeakersbureau.com or call (866) 376-6591.

The publisher is not responsible for websites (or their content) that are not owned by the publisher.

Print book interior design by name.

Library of Congress Cataloging-in-Publication Data has been applied for.

ISBNs: 9781541751149 (hardcover), 9781541751156 (ebook)

LSC-C

Printing 1, 2022

For SES

Contents

Good name in man and woman, dear my lord,
Is the immediate jewel of their souls:
Who steals my purse steals trash; 'tis something, nothing;
'Twas mine, 'tis his, and has been slave to thousands:
But he that filches from me my good name
Robs me of that which not enriches him
And makes me poor indeed.

  —*William Shakespeare,* Othello

Prologue

California's sun-beaten Central Valley stretched out ahead of me as I drove south on Highway 99, trying to reach Los Angeles before sundown. The horizon line dissolved into a distant pool of glass as the temperature nosed past ninety degrees. I was traveling for a story and had spent the day interviewing people. I was replaying those conversations in my head when my phone chirped with a message. A friend had sent me a link to a news story.

"Holy shit . . . ," my friend wrote.

Keeping one eye on the road, I clicked the link. "A twenty-seven-year-old man who worked for the Democratic National Committee was shot and killed as he walked home early Sunday," the article began. The victim's name was Seth Conrad Rich.

I read the words again, then a third time, then a fourth. I tossed my phone onto the passenger's seat and stared blankly at the road ahead, processing what I'd just learned.

I was stunned. I knew Seth Rich. Not well, we weren't close, but we had friends in common. We both lived in Washington, DC, and had crossed paths at parties and different bars around town. I had filled in on his weekend soccer team when they needed extra bodies.

For days afterward I read everything I could find about Seth and his murder. It turned out we'd had more in common than I'd known. We both grew up in the Midwest and remained fierce partisans for our home states, Nebraska for him, Michigan for me. We'd both moved to Washington after college with dreams of leaving our mark on the world, him in politics, me in journalism. When I read that he'd been shot walking home from a bar and heard the police describe the crime as an attempted armed robbery, a tragic case of wrong time, wrong place, I remembered all the times I'd wandered home late at night on those same streets. I thought to myself, *That could've been me.*

I kept up with the coverage for a few weeks, reading about Seth's funeral in Omaha and the memorial organized by some friends at his favorite bar in Washington, the one he'd gone to on the night he was killed. Soon enough, though, the story would recede from view. As a journalist, I knew how the news business worked. The presidential race between Hillary Clinton and Donald Trump consumed so much of the public's attention, mine included, that there was little oxygen for anything else. The media would move on to the next outrage or tragedy. Seth's name would fade from the headlines and social media.

And that, I figured, was a good thing. Seth's family would have the peace and privacy to grieve. The police would carry out their investigation and hopefully arrest the killer. Friends and family would gather on the one-year anniversary to remember him. Life, in other words, would go on. We would all do what we were taught as children: let the dead rest in peace.

But that isn't what happened. The story of Seth Rich's life and death didn't go away. Instead, it mutated into something else entirely. Hashtags. Memes. Conspiracy theories that spread around the world. In the hands of a small band of opportunists and operatives, the conspiracy theories about Seth would become political weapons. In the minds of many more people, these theories would become an article of faith and modern folklore. They would help elect a president and birth a new online religion. They would reach as far as the CIA headquarters and the halls of the White House. They would pit his unassuming parents against the world's most powerful news network in a legal battle with implications for truth, fact, and decency. They would reveal the flaws and breakdowns in American society unlike any story that had come before it.

———◦———

The book you are now reading began with a simple question, a product of basic human curiosity more than any journalistic instinct: How did this young man's death grow into something so huge and hideous?

Almost five years ago, I set out to answer that question. Put another way, I was trying to understand how a normal guy not so different from me became the obsession of millions, his name and face strewn across the internet, his life story exploited and contorted until it was unrecognizable to those who knew him, his family forced to put aside their grief and wage a battle first in the court of public opinion and then in the court of law to clear his name and defend his memory.

What I've come to believe is that Seth's story is a skeleton key to the past half-decade in America, unlocking so much about how this country ended up at this strange point in our history. Where a large percentage of society believes conspiracy theories like those about Seth Rich. Where millions of people believe that a secret cabal of pedophile elites runs the world, or that the last presidential election was stolen, or that the deadly coronavirus pandemic was a bioweapon unleashed by one of our foreign adversaries. A time when it feels like truth is whatever the loudest and most extreme voices say it is, not where the evidence leads, what the data show, or what the facts reveal. A moment when people can say whatever they want about anyone else, dead or alive, famous or obscure, and in the wrong hands, that information can take on a life of its own.

Think of this book as a true-crime story for the post-truth era. It's the story of a crime, an unsolved murder, but also the second crime that was a consequence of the first—how the failure to find those who committed that crime opened a void into which the gullible, the dangerous, and the deluded poured their misbegotten ideas and political ambitions and so created a maelstrom of deception that undermined every important institution in the country.

But it is also the story of a young man's life that was both normal and extraordinary. It begins with that young man, Seth Rich, on the brink of fulfilling a dream.

ACT I
Viral

1

Striver

"THEY'RE READY TO bring you up."

When Seth Rich heard those six words, he almost couldn't believe them. It was early July 2016. Seth sat across from his boss, a lawyer named Pratt Wiley, in an office on the second floor of the Democratic National Committee (DNC) headquarters, a pink-tan building within walking distance of the US Capitol building. It was a moment of flux at the DNC. Many colleagues had scattered across the country as the election ramped up. Others had gone to Philadelphia to prepare for the national convention in two weeks' time. In the row of grubby cubicles used by the Voter Expansion department, Seth and a group of interns were the last ones left.

If the DNC were a high school cafeteria, Voter Expansion was the chess club, a team of brainy lawyers and wonky data analysts devoted to protecting and expanding the right to vote. It wasn't considered a sexy department like Communications or Digital; its corner of the building didn't have a cool nickname like Tech's did, which was christened the "thunderdome." But the people on Voter Expansion felt a higher calling to safeguard the lifeblood of a democracy. Seth had an impressive title—Voter Expansion Data Director—but in practice the work was far from glamorous. The only non-lawyer on the team, he wrangled huge databases of messy voter data and parsed the arcane election laws of hundreds of cities, counties, and states. Yet when opportunities arose

3

to move to a different department, he chose to stay, committed to a cause that couldn't be more important to him. In the back of his mind, he always hoped the day would come when he would get the chance to fulfill his dream of working on a presidential campaign.

In the head-down, grind-it-out culture of the DNC, Seth stood out. He was a social creature, someone who lived for an audience, and he eagerly supplied comic relief in a workplace wired for tension and stress. On the day the Supreme Court legalized same-sex marriage, he wore a head-to-toe Stars and Stripes outfit to work. With his full beard and swoop of sandy hair, he looked like a hipster Uncle Sam. A lover of pandas, he sometimes wore a panda hoodie to work that could have worked as a Halloween costume—not your typical DNC attire, but Wiley, his boss, didn't care so long as Seth met his deadlines. He kept on his desk a stuffed panda named Bamboo, and Wiley and the others would steal Bamboo and hide it around the office. With Wiley as his audience, Seth waxed on about his ambitions and his love life, his political prognostications and his beloved University of Nebraska Cornhuskers football team.

Wiley, who had hired Seth, had grown fond of his young colleague, coming to view him like a kid brother. On paper, the two of them couldn't have been more different. Wiley, a Black man in his forties with salt-and-pepper stubble and an unflappable bearing, came from a prominent Boston family and had been active in politics for decades, volunteering on campaigns and working full time on Barack Obama's 2012 presidential run. Seth, a white guy in his late twenties, hailed from Omaha, Nebraska. His dad helped run the family printing business, and his mom worked most of her life in sales for the Yellow Pages. Having grown up in an overwhelmingly Republican state, Seth never operated under the illusion he could convince everyone to vote Democratic; what he cared about most was making sure everyone who could vote did. For a lifelong political junkie like Seth, working at the DNC signaled that he had arrived. He was so proud when he got the job that he took a friend on a tour of the building.

Like any kid brother, Seth could also be a pain in the ass. He was never on time, rolling in to work at noon after pulling an all-nighter. He would drop in uninvited at other people's desks, announce his presence with a schmoozy, "Heyyyyy, buddy," and proceed to bombard his helpless victims with a litany of questions about their work. While Wiley liked to play jazz at a low volume during the workday, Seth donned his headphones and streamed episodes of *The West Wing* on a spare monitor, letting Aaron Sorkin's hit 2000s show about a heart-of-gold president and his crackerjack staff serve as the soundtrack to his workday. He wouldn't even notice when Wiley walked up behind him. That was Seth.

But by the summer of 2016, Seth was struggling. The previous six months had left the DNC's employees exhausted and defeated. The committee existed to elect Democrats of all stripes, young and old, centrist and liberal, from the lowliest state legislator to the next president of the United States. But the battle for the party's presidential nomination in 2015 and 2016 between the establishment favorite Hillary Clinton and the left-wing insurgent Senator Bernie Sanders had nearly ripped the party in two. The only thing the warring camps agreed on, it seemed, was their disdain for the DNC. The Clinton campaign treated it like a useless appendage; the Sanders campaign and its die-hard supporters accused it of rigging the race against their candidate, even suing the DNC over a disagreement involving the party's voter list. Death threats and other abuse were a regular occurrence. Wiley reminded his charges that the DNC represented the establishment in an inherently antiestablishment party. All the incoming vitriol and animosity—well, it came with the territory.

For as long as Seth could remember, he had hoped to work in politics. But the stress of the 2016 campaign made him question if he really wanted that life after all. He and Wiley had discussed grad school programs, with Wiley encouraging him to pursue a degree in data science after the election. Seth had also applied for jobs that weren't overtly political; he had an interview scheduled for one position the following week. A few days before the interview, at the end of a hectic week in July, Wiley delivered the exciting news: the Clinton campaign wanted Seth. Wiley wasn't sure what the pay or the title would be, but they would need him up in Brooklyn soon.

What Wiley didn't say was that he thought time away from Washington might do Seth some good. He knew Seth was having relationship trouble with a woman he loved, leaving him conflicted and heartbroken. A new job in a big city could take his mind off these problems. *Go be a stag in Brooklyn,* Wiley wanted to say, *and then if things work out, you come back and you guys reconcile. And if not . . .* He let the thought trail off. Instead, he told Seth that everything he had done so far—all the work he had put in, the late nights and weekend shifts, the daily indignities of working at the DNC—had led him here. "This is what you've been waiting for," Wiley said.

———◆———

Joel Rich liked to say his youngest son had politics in his blood. The way other kids memorized sports statistics, Seth learned the name and state of nearly every one of the 535 members of Congress. He watched C-SPAN for fun. Seth was the unrivaled political junkie in the Rich family, and no one was quite sure where he got it from.

Joel was an Omaha native, a gentle bear of a man with springy curls and a sneaky sense of humor. His family ran a print shop that supplied menus and signs to restaurants, bars, and other small businesses. He felt a quiet pride when he sat down at a nice steakhouse and picked up his family's handiwork. The other dominant force in Joel's life was his faith. The Riches belonged to Omaha's small, tight-knit Jewish community, attending Beth El, one of the city's larger synagogues on the west side. He attended college in Des Moines and stayed there for work after he graduated. That was where he met Mary.

Joel's secretary at the time was Mary's high school best friend. On the night they met, before Joel could say a word, Mary berated him for the fact that his company didn't give business cards to secretaries. Blond-haired and fair-skinned, Mary grew up in small-town Iowa. She was bighearted and hot-tempered, just like her mother. "You pissed my mother off," Mary liked to say. "She'd have ripped you a new one in a heartbeat, and then she would have had a joke and laughed." Mary sprinkled her sentences with "fucks" and "bullshits" like salt on a tough steak. One time, she went out to a fancy Italian restaurant with her first husband. He was "acting like an ass," Mary remembered, and disrupting other patrons with his behavior. When she couldn't take it any longer, Mary picked up her plate of spaghetti and dumped it on his head, topping it off with the rest of her diet soda. The entire place erupted with applause as the maître d' politely offered his arm and escorted her to the exit.

Joel loved that story even though he could never imagine doing such a thing. Unlike Mary, he never swore and hated confrontation. He was the smooth to Mary's spiky. But on the night they met, he noticed Mary's eyes light up when he mentioned his Saint Bernard dog. She demanded they drive to the kennel and spring the dog loose even though it was eleven o'clock at night. (Joel was such a good customer the kennel obliged.) Joel's first marriage hadn't worked out, and Mary was finalizing her own divorce with the pasta guy. They both wanted a family. Four months after meeting, they got married and soon welcomed their first son, Aaron.

The new family eventually moved back to Omaha, buying a two-story house with a big yard on the west side not far from the Beth El synagogue. Joel's faith was so important to him that Mary converted to Judaism. When Aaron informed Joel and Mary one day that he would like a sibling, preferably a brother, they told him they couldn't guarantee it. They tried for months to have a second child and had almost given up when Mary learned she was pregnant.

At just past four in the morning on January 3, 1989, weighing seven pounds and fourteen ounces, Seth Conrad Rich was born. He squatted in this funny way when Mary held him, so she nicknamed him Froggy. Later, she called him Roo, short for Kangaroo, because he loved to bounce through the house. When he was about two weeks old, Aaron asked Mary if they could take baby Seth to school for show-and-tell. He had cried for most of his brief existence up to that point, but when Mary brought him to the front of the class that day, he turned calm.

———◆———

When Seth was in the ninth grade, a teacher gave him and his classmates an assignment: create a "memory book," a kind of mini-autobiography about their lives so far. Seth's reflections ranged from basic personality traits—"I just plain love to talk," he wrote—to the mix of Jewish and Irish cultures "running through me." He showed a degree of self-awareness that stood out for someone his age. He was competitive, "no matter how much I try not to be," and believed that the simple act of making someone laugh left the world a better place. His biggest goal for the future, he went on, was to be famous. He had already done some modeling as a kid and had shown an interest in acting. "I just want to be known for something," he wrote. "I don't care what for, but I just want to be famous."

Even as a teenager, Seth knew he couldn't be summed up with a few pithy sentences. "So there you have it," he wrote. "I'm a nice, funny, kind, athletic, pretty, hot, ghetto, handsome, talkative, smart, energetic, hyper, cute, studly, blonde, modeling, weird, creative, friendly, spontaneous, strange, argumentative, coordinated, expressive, sharing, happy, outgoing, honest, self-assured Jewish guy."

To his friends and family, he was also a schemer and a prankster. At summer camp in northern Wisconsin, he made friends easily and tried his best to make everyone feel included, but at times found himself scrubbing trash bins with a toothbrush after breaking one rule or another for the umpteenth time. On phone calls home, he and Mary schemed about how to send him contraband—candy, a mini-cooler, not one but two George Foreman grills (one for dairy and one for meat)—without the camp counselors intercepting the goods. Mary, ever the coconspirator, hid sweets in emptied-out toothpaste boxes to evade detection.

Seth never met a stranger, Mary liked to say; he charmed anyone who crossed paths with him. When Aaron graduated from high school, some of his classmates invited Seth, a lowly sixth grader, to their graduation parties—not as a courtesy but because they genuinely wanted him there, he was *that* entertaining. On a summer trip to Israel organized by his camp, he taught a group of young soldiers roofball, a game he had played back at camp; at the end of the trip, Seth gave the Israelis a ball signed by all the Americans, posing for a photo with his companions like a foreign ambassador. At the age of fourteen, he enrolled at Central High in downtown Omaha, a half hour's drive each way. He could have gone to the big public high school up the road from his house, but Joel and Aaron had both gone to Central, and Seth also loved how diverse Central's student body was, with more than seventy native languages spoken and the hallways filled with Black, brown, and white faces. He sang a cappella, performed in musicals, and joined the debate team, where he won two state titles in national competitions.

Politics was a natural next step. He got his first campaign job working as a field coordinator for US senator Ben Nelson's 2006 reelection campaign. Friends grew weary of Seth's incessant emails pleading with them to take a shift knocking doors. ("To volunteer, or to volunteer a lot is the question!") He urged them to ditch school on Election Day to help with the final push, and if their parents had a problem with it, he wrote, "you can have them call me, or anyone at the office, and we'll help them see that it is a good decision."

For college he enrolled at Creighton University, which was practically across the street from his high school. The school had offered him a scholarship, and he felt drawn to the Jesuit ethic of social justice and service. He also didn't mind the feeling of being an outsider in his backyard, a Jew surrounded by Catholics, many of them more conservative than he was. That was true of his college girlfriend, a woman from Texas named Allison Villalobos. Coming from a conservative Catholic family, Allison disagreed with Seth on plenty of issues, and even though he served in student government and helped run the university's Young Democrats chapter, he never pushed his views on her. The only time he pressured her was when he insisted she vote in the 2008 presidential race. He knew she would probably vote a straight-Republican ticket, and he didn't care. "I just want you to vote," he told her.

Allison was his first real love, and he took it hard when she broke up with him near the end of college. He said he wanted to move to Washington, DC, to work in politics; she had no plans to follow him there. After graduation he sent his résumé to dozens of consulting firms, nonprofits, and congressional offices in Washington, DC. A well-known Democratic polling firm named Greenberg Quinlan Rosner wrote back and offered him a job. Elated, he rushed to tell Mary. She was thrilled for him, but she feared he couldn't live on what the firm had offered and, Mary being Mary, told him as much.

Seth was undeterred. Rather than decline and look for something better, he researched rent costs, grocery prices, and bus and subway fares; plugged the numbers into a spreadsheet; and sent it to the polling firm. The math didn't add up, he argued.

He was right, the manager wrote back. The firm countered with a little more money, even throwing in a small stipend for moving costs. Joel was told no one at GQR could remember another junior associate— an *associate*—who had bargained for more money and pulled it off.

———◦———

They crowded the cheap bars and the subway cars, dressed in their starter suits and boxy skirts, freshly issued ID badges dangling from their necks. Usually they had arrived here from somewhere else, anywhere else, and each year delivered a new class of them, hundreds of twentysomethings moving to the center of the political universe. They were big deals back home, student body presidents and decorated debaters, editors of college newspapers, valedictorians of their graduating class. Here they toiled as receptionists and legislative assistants, interns and tour guides—anything to get a toehold. They moved in packs like citizens of some awkward tribe, and while they might be liberal, conservative, libertarian, or socialist, they had made their way to Washington, DC, for the same reason: to make a dent in the world.

Most of them wouldn't last more than a year or two. They couldn't take the long hours or the woeful pay, the Napoleonic bosses or the degrading grunt work. The ones who really wanted it learned to survive. Work more on less sleep. Who you know matters as much as what you know. Hustle goes a long way, and shame is overrated. No one would begrudge you for cold-calling a chief of staff whose business card you plucked off the sidewalk. And when you needed inspiration, when the indignities and the grind wore you down to a nub, you searched the horizon line for the dome of the Capitol or the top of Washington Monument, symbols of power and history that fueled you, that seemed so close you could reach out and touch them.

Only a few would make it. They would outlast the rest of them, pay their dues, and find their place. A small handful of them might even go on to become a congressman or a senator one day. Either way, they knew they had what it took.

Seth arrived in this scene when he moved to Washington in March 2012. It was a heady time to be in the nation's capital. Young people worked in every corner of the Obama administration, it seemed, evidence that, if you stuck around long enough and worked hard enough, you, too, could wind up in (or at least near) the West Wing. It was an election year, Barack Obama defending his presidency against a gaggle of Republican politicians and gadfly types. Seth felt at home surrounded by fellow nerds and political junkies. As he told one of his best friends from Omaha, "When I can hit on a girl by making congressional procedure jokes, I'm in a good place." His coworkers invited him to join their historical scavenger hunt team. He found a place to live near his new office. "It's only half a mile to the Capitol, which is true of my office as well, which makes for a bit of a breathtaking moment every time I walk outside," he wrote to one of his Creighton professors.

He fit in seamlessly at Greenberg Quinlan Rosner—GQR to everyone who worked there. One of the firm's traditions held that everyone ate together, a chance for junior employees to mingle with partners and vice presidents. Still, associates and interns tended to be seen and not heard in the company lunchroom. Not Seth. He eagerly debated the senior executives who shared a lunch table with him, wheedling them about whatever was in the news, playing the devil's advocate. Seth was impish, self-assured, comfortable in his own skin. One day he showed up for work in a panda costume. Because, sure, why not? The bosses thought it was hilarious.

Along with the lunchroom salons, there was another ritual at GQR: the end-of-year bloodletting. It was the nature of the political consulting business that the firm's workload dried up after every election, and the top brass would lay off dozens of staffers. Seth made the cut in the first round of layoffs. However prankish and unserious Seth might appear, he had drive and talent. And he wanted success as badly as anyone else at the firm did.

A senior data scientist at GQR named Andrew Therriault took notice of Seth, who was hungry and ambitious, eager to learn. Therriault, who was more than seven years older, took a liking to his young colleague and became a mentor. When Therriault left GQR to build a new data team at the Democratic National Committee, the central hub for every state, county, and town Democratic Party in America, he said he would keep an eye out for any jobs there for Seth. When a position opened with a dual report to the Voter Expansion and Tech teams, Therriault put Seth's name forward, and he landed the job. Seth had always had a keen interest in voting rights and the fight to expand access to the ballot box. After he got the job, Seth sent Therriault a bottle of whiskey with a handwritten note attached. He thanked Therriault for giving him a shot at a job where he could "make the best impact possible," Seth wrote. Of the whiskey, he added, "It's not much, but hopefully this conveys a little of how much I appreciate it all."

———◆———

On a hazy summer day a few years later, Seth stepped out onto a third-floor balcony with sweeping views of the National Mall, the grand boulevard of the nation's capital. His hair was short and sculpted now, his stubble shaved clean. He wore the nicest suit he owned, a dark-blue number with pinstripes, a light-blue shirt with a crisp banker's collar, and a colorful striped tie. Off in the distance, the Washington Monument pierced the blue sky.

Seth stared into the camera for his official DNC headshot, arms folded, a faint smile on his face. He had come so far from his days volunteering for the Young Democrats in high school or passing out business cards in college that described him as a "Student with Political Ambition." He now looked like a young man in possession of the belief that he had arrived.

The camera clicked.

2

The Last Walk Home

THE WORKDAY HAD just begun on Friday, June 10, 2016, when a cryptic email appeared in the inbox of every DNC employee. All-hands meeting later that day. Attendance required. There was no call-in number, which was strange. There was no explanation of what the meeting was about. Also strange. Was Hillary Clinton's campaign about to absorb the DNC? Had the committee run out of money? Many employees feared the worst: they were all about to get fired.

At four o'clock that afternoon, the staff gathered in the only conference room big enough to fit that many people. Lindsey Reynolds, the DNC's chief operating officer and the sender of the ominous morning email, rose to speak. No employees were losing their jobs, she said. "But what I am about to tell you cannot leave this room," she warned. "You can't tell your friends. You can't tell your mother."

All employees, she explained, must hand over their laptops to the information technology staff as part of a system-wide update. Those who couldn't make it to the meeting in person would be called individually and instructed how to wipe clean and reboot their devices.

Confusion hung in the air. These were people who had worked twelve- to fourteen-hour days for the last six months, missed holidays, birthdays, and weekends. What were they supposed to do without their computers? Reynolds told them to take the weekend off. The staff gathered up their laptops and, one by one, handed them over. Each person signed their name on a checklist and received a sticker. If they didn't have a sticker, they couldn't exit the building.

The relief people felt to still have their jobs mingled uneasily with a deeper sense of concern. In the all-hands meeting, someone had asked Reynolds why they were turning over their computers. She had made an oblique reference to what James Clapper, the director of national intelligence, had recently warned at a major public event about cyberattacks and the presidential race. But Reynolds didn't give specifics.

What she didn't reveal was that several months earlier the FBI had alerted the DNC to strange activity on its computer network. A cybersecurity contractor hired by the Democrats investigated the tip and discovered that hackers had gained access to email accounts, chat messages, and private internal research. The few clues they left behind indicated that this was not the work of amateurs. To the analysts at CrowdStrike, the contractor used by the DNC, the evidence overwhelmingly pointed to two culprits. One was a team of hackers nicknamed Cozy Bear, the other was called Fancy Bear. "Both adversaries engage in extensive political and economic espionage for the benefit of the government of the Russian Federation and are believed to be closely linked to the Russian government's powerful and highly capable intelligence services," CrowdStrike cofounder Dmitri Alperovitch would later write.

Finding the hackers as they snuck through the system proved difficult enough; harder still was purging them without giving away that they had been caught. If the intruders knew they had been spotted, they might plunge deeper into the network. The DNC's tech team hatched a plan that was simple yet daunting: nuke the DNC's old network and rebuild it in a single weekend. Fueled by cheap pizza and soda, teams of information technology experts worked around the clock. Such a project normally took months to finish. They had three days.

By Monday, June 13, the job was done. They had purged the hackers. As the staff returned to work and picked up their newly rebooted devices, only a handful of senior employees knew about what had just transpired. But there was one possibility that the higher-ups at the

DNC had not considered. They had focused so intently on removing the hackers that they hadn't given any thought to whether the stolen material might be used against them. As a former senior official would later put it, "I don't think anybody was prepared for *that* inside the building."

———•———

Two days after the DNC's all-hands meeting, the British network ITV teased an upcoming interview with Julian Assange, leader of the radical transparency group WikiLeaks. Assange had explosive new developments to share related to the US presidential race.

Launched by Assange in 2006, WikiLeaks was a ragtag operation that had risen to fame and influence by publishing leaked materials revealing the inner workings of powerful governments, corporations, and militaries from around the world. The defining struggle of the twenty-first century, Assange believed, was not a contest between rival ideologies or forms of government; it was the conflict between individuals and institutions. Authoritarian regimes, corrupt political parties, or violent terrorist networks—they were all, Assange argued, conspiracies. Conspiracies to deny people freedom, truth, and happiness. The more people in on the conspiracy, the more powerful it was. And the lifeblood of any conspiracy was secrecy. Assange had created WikiLeaks to serve as a clearinghouse and a platform for whistleblowers who wished to expose large institutions by leaking their secrets. "An intelligence agency of the people" was how Assange would later describe it.

The loathing Assange felt toward big, powerful institutions was more than philosophical. Born in Australia, he was raised by his mom, a theater director, who moved the family nearly forty times before he was fourteen. He found refuge in computers, teaching himself to code on a clunky Commodore 64 and showing a preternatural talent for hacking. He and two friends formed a collective called the International Subversives. Together they broke into networks used by the US Defense Department and Los Alamos National Laboratory, where scientists had built some of the first atomic bombs in the 1940s. The Australian federal police took notice and opened a special investigation, code-named Operation Weather, into Assange's group. After they were alerted to an infiltration of the main terminal of a large telecom company, the police charged Assange with thirty-one counts of hacking and other crimes. The government would later drop some of these charges, letting him off with a small fine, but his brush with the criminal justice system as well as a vicious court battle with his estranged wife over custody of their young son left Assange scarred and angry. His naturally brown hair turned silver-white. "What we saw was a great bureaucracy that was squashing people," Assange's mother later said.

In a 2006 manifesto, Assange argued that righteous individuals must topple institutions that operated like conspiracies. Given the technological tools available, the best way to do that was by exposing how these institutions worked from within. To illustrate what he meant, he mentioned "two closely balanced and broadly conspiratorial power groupings, the US Democratic and Republican parties," and gave this example: "Consider what would happen if one of these parties gave up their mobile phones, fax and email correspondence—let alone the computer systems which manage their subscribers, donors, budgets, polling, call centres and direct mail campaigns?" All it would take was a brave whistleblower to supply the information.

In 2010, four years after launching WikiLeaks, Assange published a thirty-nine-minute video he titled *Collateral Murder*. The video, taken from an Apache helicopter piloted by US forces in the Iraq War, showed an aerial attack that killed a dozen civilians, two of whom worked as journalists for the Reuters news agency. *Collateral Murder* would amass tens of millions of viewings online; the US and international press covered it for weeks. Robert Gates, the US defense secretary, swatted away questions about the video and its implications— namely, that American forces had killed innocent civilians and possibly committed war crimes. Assange, speaking through WikiLeaks, replied that Gates was "a liar."

WikiLeaks was soon churning out a steady stream of revelations. In his manifesto, Assange had written that leaks could be especially powerful in exposing antidemocratic regimes such as China and Russia, but in practice WikiLeaks' most explosive publications focused on the US and other Western institutions. Perhaps Assange's biggest hit was a trove of a quarter million leaked classified communiqués between American officials and their counterparts abroad. "Cablegate," as it was dubbed, stripped away the empty jargon used by ambassadors and envoys and offered a harsh look at the gritty realpolitik of international diplomacy. They revealed how the US government had spied on the head of the United Nations, operated a secret bombing campaign in Yemen, and tried for years to stop the Pakistani government from developing nuclear weapons. For journalists the cables were revelatory; for the American government and especially its top diplomat, Secretary of State Hillary Clinton, they were an embarrassment. Clinton called the leak "an attack on the international community, the alliances and partnerships, the conversations and negotiations, that safeguard global security and advance economic prosperity."

Assange came to see himself as a figure of great influence. If he called a generic State Department phone number and asked to be put through to the secretary of state, he expected that to happen. But as his stature increased, so did his list of enemies and the scrutiny on WikiLeaks. A US congressman, Peter King, said he wanted Assange to be charged under the Espionage Act for releasing classified information and WikiLeaks to be designated a terrorist organization. Under pressure from the Obama administration, WikiLeaks saw its access to online servers and payment processors cut off. To remain in operation, Assange bounced from one sympathetic country to the next—Iceland, Sweden, England—only to wear out his welcome and move on.

But by the spring of 2011, he faced real legal peril. The US government had opened a grand jury investigation concerning WikiLeaks. Sweden had also issued an arrest warrant for him on suspicion of rape and sexual molestation and wanted to question him over the allegations. He believed that if he returned to Sweden, he would be extradited to the United States. His best hope for staying out of prison, he believed, was to seek asylum from a friendly government. Ecuador's president at the time, Rafael Correa, knew Assange and shared his anti-imperialist worldview. Still, if Assange boarded a plane to Ecuador, he risked arrest and extradition to the US or Sweden. And so one summer day in 2012, he disguised himself as a motorcycle courier and rode a motorbike to the Ecuadorian embassy in a posh precinct of London. He presented himself to the embassy staff and asked for political asylum on the spot. President Correa granted it several weeks later.

———◦|◦———

Assange cultivated a rakish look. He dressed for his ITV appearance in a dark blazer and a white dress shirt unbuttoned at the top, his tufted silver hair swept back. Yet he also looked unwell. His skin had a pale, sickly quality, the complexion of a recluse who hadn't gone outside in quite some time.

For the past four years, Assange's physical existence had consisted of several small rooms that doubled as his living quarters and WikiLeaks' headquarters. In the largest space there was a small desk with a chair and DVDs of *The Simpsons* and Kubrick films; laptops and cords snaked across the tables and floors. His only tangible connection to the outside world was a small balcony. And yet his refuge-turned-captivity fed into the mythology and celebrity that surrounded him. Crowds gathered outside the embassy to show their support and demand the Swedish and American authorities drop their probes. On occasion he addressed his fans from the balcony like an ailing royal, thanking them for their support.

While the threat of prosecution hung over his head, he felt he had no choice but to remain inside the embassy. His spartan accommodations felt increasingly like a prison. What kept him going was the fact that as long as he had an internet connection, he could keep WikiLeaks in operation. New sources were coming forward all the time. And if there was one major geopolitical event he hoped to influence, it was the upcoming US presidential election. To Assange, Hillary Clinton embodied all that was wrong and evil in the American body politic. In a private chat conversation in late 2015, he described Clinton as "a bright, well-connected, sadistic sociopath." He didn't think much of Donald Trump either, but he preferred any Republican to Clinton and her crew of arrogant imperialists. "We believe it would be much better for GOP to win," he wrote to the same group of WikiLeaks supporters.

"With Hillary in charge, GOP will be pushing for her worst qualities. dems+media+neoliberals will be mute."

Assange made it a priority for WikiLeaks to obtain whatever damning materials it could about Clinton, her tenure as secretary of state, and her private business dealings. Now, on June 12, he told ITV's Robert Peston that WikiLeaks had "accumulated a large cache of information" about Clinton. The material was explosive, he added, and "could be used to bring an indictment against her." He refused to say what the documents said or where he had gotten them. Assange added that the documents would be published soon and that their impact on the US election would be substantial. "WikiLeaks has a very big year ahead," he said.

What Assange did not yet know was that he was about to open a line of communication with a potential source of Clinton-related leaks who went by the name Guccifer 2.0. The name paid homage to a Romanian-Hungarian hacker who in 2013 had targeted prominent Americans including former secretary of state Colin Powell, *Sex and the City* author Candace Bushnell, and other well-known Americans. Guccifer 2.0's identity was unknown—the original Guccifer, Marcel Lazar, was serving a four-year prison sentence—but based on what the new Guccifer had already published, Assange had good reason to cultivate them as a source.

In mid-June, Guccifer 2.0 had released internal records—opposition research, campaign data, policy memos, and private donor files—evidently stolen from inside the Democratic National Committee and published them on a basic blogging website. Breaking into the Democratic Party, Guccifer 2.0 wrote, was "easy, very easy." In another release of what he said were stolen documents, Guccifer signed off, "Fuck the lies and conspirators like DNC!!!"

Reporters voiced skepticism about the value of news coming from an anonymous hacker. Seeing the leaks get little traction, Assange sent Guccifer 2.0 a message. "Do you have secure communications?" he asked. "Send any new material here for us to review and it will have a much higher impact than what you are doing."

Assange and Guccifer 2.0 messaged back and forth dozens of times as they tried to arrange a file transfer to WikiLeaks. The file was quite large, and the transfer kept failing. Finally, it went through to WikiLeaks. "Ping," Guccifer 2.0 messaged Assange. "Check ur email."

———◆———

Near the end of June, Seth flew to Kansas City. Each summer he and his closest friends from college picked a city with a big-league baseball team and reunited there for a long weekend. They took in a few games, drank the bars dry, and caught up on one another's lives. Since graduating, they had met in Minneapolis to see the Twins and in Chicago to watch the Cubs. The Chicago trip had nearly gone off the rails when Seth realized he had bought tickets to the iconic rooftop bar across the street from Wrigley Field for the wrong day. Somehow he convinced the bar's staff to let him and his friends in anyway. For 2016 they chose Kansas City because one of the friends lived there and offered to host.

Seth's best friends couldn't remember how they met him; he was just always there, a fixture from the start of college. Many of them rushed the same fraternity, Phi Delt, which was known as the nerdy, good-guy frat on campus. Seth was the loudmouth of the group, whose interviews with new pledges lasted hours instead of the usual fifteen minutes and who gave long-winded speeches at weekly frat meetings. He also threw himself into his friendships. He handed out mock business cards at his senior fraternity speech that read, "I'd like to have a beer with you! Present this card at a future date for one beer on me! Rain checks may be issued by Seth." When James Perry, Seth's friend and roommate, feared he had blown his chance to date a woman he liked, Seth delivered a Churchillian pep talk late one night and demanded Perry go back to the woman's house and ask her out on a date. Perry took Seth's advice, which turned out to be a wise decision: years later, Perry married the woman.

It was now Perry's turn to counsel Seth. During their weekend in Kansas City, Seth was distracted, his mind off somewhere else. He spent most of a Royals game walking the concourses of Kauffman Stadium, brooding. Perry knew that some of Seth's anxiety had to do with his job. By that point the DNC had gone public with the news that it had been the victim of a sophisticated cyberattack by what experts concluded were Russian-affiliated hackers. Perry felt chills when he read about the hack, as he remembered Seth making several comments months earlier about his work computer acting in strange ways, like someone else was inside of it. Perry wasn't sure how to respond. But he never forgot Seth's anger when he believed that a foreign nemesis had hacked his workplace and declared cyberwar on the political party he had belonged to and worked for since he was in high school.

Far outweighing any concerns about work, though, was the end of Seth's relationship with his girlfriend of several years. They had met each other's parents and talked about moving in together; Seth brought her to Perry's wedding and introduced her to his closest college friends. Mary thought of her as a member of the Rich family and hoped Seth would soon propose. But in recent months the relationship had frayed to the point where she and Seth were no longer dating. Seth's friends hoped the Kansas City trip would take his mind off the subject for a few days. Instead he paced around the baseball stadium and weighed whether to call her, which his friends urged him not to do. He hadn't gotten the formal Clinton campaign job offer yet, but Pratt Wiley had told him it was a possibility, and that only added to the weight he felt about the future.

When the friends said their goodbyes in Kansas City, Perry felt like Seth was in a somewhat better headspace than when he had arrived a few days earlier. He and Seth texted back and forth in the days ahead, rehashing stories about the trip. But still there were signs Seth was in a low place. When a mass shooter in Dallas killed five police officers in early July, Seth posted on Facebook, "Too much pain to process. . . . A life is exponentially valuable. I have family and friends on both sides of the law. Please, stop killing each other."

———— ✦ ————

A few weeks later, Seth walked through the doors of Lou's City Bar, his favorite drinking spot. By then Pratt had delivered the good news: the Clinton campaign wanted him. Seth had to decide what to do next. He'd started writing his acceptance email: "All my life I wanted to be in a position that I can make a difference," it began. The email sat in his drafts folder, unfinished. Though he and his girlfriend had broken up, they still talked. Maybe they could reconcile. Moving to Brooklyn, he feared, would end things once and for all.

Seth plopped onto his usual stool at Lou's and ordered the first of several rounds. The bar thrummed with the sound of tipsy customers yelling over loud music and sports playing on the TVs. Lou's was your standard-issue sports bar with its sticky floors and cheap well drinks. Seth had found Lou's shortly after he had moved to Washington and soon became a regular. They knew him by name, knew his favorite beer—Bell's Two Hearted—and knew to hold the bleu cheese when he ordered his wings because he had a dairy allergy. "Do it Seth-style," the bartender would yell back to the kitchen. He sat on the same stool in the crook of the L-shaped bar. On weekends he would hang around till closing time and join the bartenders and managers for a late-night drink. He listened as much as he talked—about politics, sports, romantic advice, whatever happened to be on the bartender's mind.

Joe Capone, a manager at Lou's, knew Seth well. Capone was friendly with all of the regulars, but Seth he genuinely liked, considered a friend. When Capone's daughter was writing her college application essay, Seth helped edit it. Now and then the bartenders would slide Seth a beer on the house; if this place was Cheers, then he was their Norm.

But on the night of Saturday, July 9, Seth drank one beer after another and kept to himself. The employees working that night could sense something was off. Seth was quieter than usual. When a country song came on the bar's overhead speakers, Seth asked a bartender if he could skip to the next track.

It was almost closing time when Seth finished his last beer and settled up. A manager watched his friend steady himself as he headed for the exit. A few of the bartenders stood outside on the sidewalk patio. One asked if Seth wanted a ride home. He said he might go to a different bar, the Wonderland Ballroom, a few blocks away, and headed off into the night.

Rather than calling a Lyft or an Uber, Seth decided to walk home from Lou's. This was another habit of his. He got a bit of exercise and used the time to call his parents or his college buddies. Mary, who also stayed up late, always enjoyed Seth's late-night check-ins. With a few beers in him, Seth tended to divulge more about the particulars of his dating life.

There was no record of Seth showing up at another bar after leaving Lou's. Twice he called his parents, but on this particular night they had already gone to bed. He tried Aaron, also with no luck. An old fraternity brother picked up and chatted for a few minutes. And then he dialed his ex-girlfriend, who was visiting family in Michigan.

By the time he was almost home, he and his ex had talked for more than two hours. He paused midsentence. She would later say she thought she heard voices in the background.

"I gotta go," he said and hung up.

3

A Hideous Parade

MARK MUELLER HAD a routine. More accurately, his cat, Boo, did. In the middle of the night, the cat would yowl until Mueller woke up. Half asleep, he rolled out of bed and let the cat out onto his roof-deck, where it liked to run around. Mueller was still orienting himself in the darkness of his bedroom when he heard two sharp pops outside. He checked the time: 4:19 a.m.

Mueller's first thought was *Not again*. A researcher at the National Institutes of Health, he had lived in the Bloomingdale neighborhood for more than a decade. On a map Bloomingdale fits snug against North Capitol Street, a six-lane thoroughfare used by people who commuted into DC from Maryland. Despite its proximity to such a busy street, Bloomingdale felt like a private enclave of narrow, tree-lined streets and elegant brick rowhouses. From the rooftops of the tallest houses, the ivory-colored dome of the Capitol building looked close enough to touch.

In the time he lived there, Mueller had watched older generations of Black Washingtonians move out and developers swoop in, flipping properties and reselling them to buyers with million-dollar budgets. New college graduates counted themselves lucky to rent a room in a neighborhood so close to the Capitol and brimming with new bars and restaurants. The median home value was 40 percent higher than the national average; the rate of robberies was four times higher.

Residents of Bloomingdale learned to live with the carjackings and muggings. But they would remember the summer of 2016 as a particularly nerve-wracking time.

The neighborhood flooded after major rainstorms, and the problem became so bad that the water utility decided to build a new underground tunnel system. The project tore up the roads and transformed whole blocks into massive construction zones blocked off with cement barricades and tall fencing wrapped in tarps. Residents complained to the utility company that the lights it had installed to illuminate the sidewalks at night had burned out and not been replaced. To Mueller, parts of Bloomingdale felt like a maze. It was a mugger's dream.

By midsummer there had been more than a dozen armed robberies in the area. Bloomingdale's residents were on edge. At a neighborhood civic association meeting, Mueller and several others pleaded with district police chiefs for help to stop the robberies. "What do we have to do?" Mueller asked. "Do we have to get killed before you'll pay attention?"

The police agreed to send a crime suppression unit into Bloomingdale. Officers would patrol the narrow alleys behind the row houses. Mueller started noticing a squad car parked overnight on the street corner by his house.

When he heard the two gunshots, Mueller ran to his bedroom window. The squad car wasn't there. He ran downstairs and out the front door just as the police arrived from a nearby precinct. There, in the crosswalk, he saw a man's body, bent over and facedown.

Several officers stood on the scene as EMTs delivered treatment. An officer approached Mueller. "Is he conscious or something?" Mueller asked. He was awake, the officer said, but badly injured. The victim also seemed to be so drunk that he didn't realize what had happened to him. As the paramedics prepared to load him into a waiting ambulance, the officer asked if Mueller would try to identify the man when the EMTs wheeled him by.

"He said his name's Seth," the officer said.

As a treat, Joel and Mary took themselves out for breakfast. It was Sunday, July 10. When they returned home, they noticed something on the front door of the house. A note from the Omaha police department. It had a phone number on it with instructions to call a detective in Washington, DC. The note mentioned Seth but gave no specifics.

Joel called the number. A detective answered. He said he couldn't talk right then and promised to call back. Joel wondered if Seth had had too much to drink and needed to get bailed out of jail. He and Mary called Aaron and asked if he had heard from Seth lately. Aaron said he hadn't. Joel waited ten minutes and called the detective again.

The detective asked if Joel and Mary were alone.

"Is this bad?" Joel asked.

"Yes."

"How bad?"

The detective said Seth had been shot several times early that morning. He had gone into emergency surgery for his wounds, but he had died at the hospital. The detective said he thought Seth had been the victim of an attempted robbery.

Mary crumpled to the floor in shock. She sat there, sobbing. She realized someone had to tell Aaron. She mustered just enough fortitude to call her other son.

"We lost Seth," she told him, her voice ragged.

"What do you mean he's lost?" Aaron said. "I can find him."

"No, we lost him."

"I can ping his phone. I'll find him, Mom."

"No," Mary blurted out. "He's dead."

Aaron's mind flashed back to the previous night. Seth had called him while he was waiting for his luggage at the airport. It had been almost midnight in Denver, close to two in the morning on the East Coast. Aaron was tired after his flight and didn't want to have a long late-night conversation with Seth. He would call him tomorrow.

Now Aaron knew that either he or his parents had to tell Seth's friends and coworkers about what had happened before they read about it in the news. He couldn't bear the thought of Joel and Mary making those calls, so he said he would do it. When he told Seth's ex-girlfriend what had happened, she realized she was the last person to speak with Seth before he was killed. "Everything was fine," she said. "This can't be possible."

———◆———

The Riches felt that the DNC should make an official announcement about Seth's passing. In a statement released the next day, Monday, July 11, Rep. Debbie Wasserman Schultz, the party chairwoman, described Seth as "a dedicated, selfless public servant who worked tirelessly to protect the most sacred right we share as Americans—the right to vote." The statement urged anyone with information about the murder to contact the DC police.

Aaron's wife hadn't returned yet from vacation, so his brother-in-law and an uncle came over to offer support. They wanted to see what the reaction online and in social media would be once the DNC's announcement went live. Dozens of news outlets ran stories, and many accompanied their coverage with Seth's official DNC headshot, the one of him standing on the balcony with the Washington monument behind him.

Stand them next to each other and you wouldn't peg the Rich boys for brothers. Aaron was tall and clean-cut, more traditionally good-looking. Even when Seth was biking several miles a day to work and back, he could never get as lean as Aaron. Whereas Seth talked as if he were paid by the word, Aaron spoke with maximum economy. He was a gifted engineer, someone who had realized at a young age that he preferred the company of computers to most people. He spent so much time thinking in code that he and the English language "aren't friends," he joked. Which didn't mean Aaron was afraid to speak his mind: one time during a college visit, he and Joel sat in on a freshman math course, and Aaron corrected the professor in front of everyone for giving an overly complicated explanation about using a graphing calculator. (Needless to say, Aaron picked a different university.) Still, there were times when Aaron would hear about Seth's latest feat on the debate stage and feel a twinge of jealousy, wishing he had one-tenth the social

ease that Seth did. He would even try to channel Seth in a work pre-
sentation by thinking to himself, *What would Seth do in this situation?*

Aaron never cared much for politics. On the few occasions when
they debated over the dinner table, Aaron played the role of needling
contrarian, arguing the opposite position of whatever Seth said no
matter how absurd it was, just to get a rise out of his brother.

The seven-year gap between them meant they were never rivals—
Seth was ten when Aaron finished high school—but they also had little
in common growing up. They never overlapped at school, didn't share
any friends, listened to different bands, and watched different TV
shows. Aaron went off to college in Colorado to study math and computer science and loved his new home so much he rarely came back to
Omaha. It wasn't until Seth graduated college that his and Aaron's lives
reconverged. When Seth first moved to Washington, Aaron coached
him on how to live cheaply in a big city. Aaron's job at a defense contractor required periodic visits to the DC area; he and Seth would go out for
beers and talk like old friends. For his wedding in 2015, Aaron asked
Seth to be his best man. There's a photo of them at the wedding, wearing
tuxes, arms around each other, grinning wide. Aaron loved the photo so
much he had it framed and hung it in his house.

The initial responses to the DNC's announcement were kind and
sympathetic. "Seth Rich was one of the good guys," one person tweeted.
"Warm, funny, happy, extremely talented and creative," a second person chimed in. Sean Spicer, then the communications director at the
Republican National Committee, shared his condolences: "Despite the
political differences, prayers of @gop go out to our counterparts at @
TheDemocrats for their loss."

Within hours, though, a different kind of reaction started to
appear. Unfamiliar Twitter accounts speculated about whether Seth's
murder had anything to do with his job.

> Creighton grad & DNC employee Seth Rich mysteriously shot & killed
> in DC. Hmmm I wonder if he knew too much?

The first wave of speculation about Seth's murder originated on the far-
left end of the political spectrum. Many supporters of Bernie Sanders

were primed to suspect the worst about the DNC. The national party had undercut Sanders, they believed, rigging the primary to ensure that Clinton, the chosen candidate of the corporate class, won the party's nomination. Sanders's fans shared a cartoon during the 2016 campaign that shows Sanders dressed like Shaggy from the Scooby-Doo cartoons surrounded by a gaggle of young people and a van called "The Millennial Machine." Sanders has just ripped a mask off of "Hillary" to reveal a robot stamped with the logos for Citibank, JPMorgan Chase, and other corporations.

Some liberal diehards wouldn't accept that this young DNC employee had died in an armed robbery gone wrong, as the police suspected. If it *had* been a robbery, why had nothing been taken from him, they wondered. To show their solidarity, Sanders supporters began using the hashtag #IAmSethRich, an allusion to the climactic scene in the classic 1960 film *Spartacus*.

> DC police, the world watches you investigate the death of Seth Rich, murdered at 27 for the crime of ensuring fair elections. #IAmSethRich

With each retelling, Seth's title and stature seemed to grow. One tweet labeled him a "DNC official," another called him a "top U.S. Democratic Party official," and then a third described him as the person at the DNC "in charge" of preventing election fraud. (Along with the duties of his job, the only people Seth managed were the summer interns on the Voter Expansion team.) Whether these were honest mistakes or intentional deceptions, Aaron felt like he was watching reality crumble in real time, right before his eyes.

Aaron's brother-in-law was looking at Reddit, the popular online forum. Organized by topic into so-called subreddits, Reddit, which had several millions of users, was like an endless rabbit hole, a place you could go, with the promise of anonymity, to indulge your interests, fantasies, and obsessions, no matter how weird or dark. There were subreddits for world news, sports, and politics. Subs for fans of Pokémon and World of Warcraft. Subs for just about every sexual kink and fetish imaginable. Some subs were just plain bizarre. R/

WtWFotMJaJtRAtCaB, short for "when the water flows over the milk jug at just the right angle to create a bubble," was mostly photos of people pouring water over milk jugs. R/WolvesEatingWatermelons was, well, exactly what it sounded like.

R/Conspiracy was one of the larger subs on Reddit, with some 365,000 followers. It was there Aaron's friend saw a thread about Seth. It would be the first of many to appear on r/Conspiracy, which soon became a hub of speculation about what really happened to Seth.

———————◦◦———————

"SETH RICH was a young Washington D.C insider," the Reddit post began, "hired by the Democratic National Committee/Convention, who was assassinated early this morning, July 11th." It had taken mere hours for the theories about Seth to evolve like a new variant of a virus. Seth's murder was now an assassination, as if he had been targeted for his views or his job. The author, a user named "kurtchella," had combed through Seth's LinkedIn page for clues and pieced together a story of murder, corporate influence, and political skullduggery. It read like the internet version of a spider wall with photos and red string webbing outward in every direction.

In real life "kurtchella" was Kurt Ramos, a college freshman and Bernie Sanders supporter who lived in central Florida. A shy kid with thick dark hair and a soft, airy voice, Ramos had nurtured a contrarian streak since he was young. He felt drawn to outsiders, perhaps because he felt a bit like one himself. He remembered seeing a TV ad for libertarian Ron Paul's 2012 presidential campaign and liking some of what Paul had to say. When he watched one of the early Democratic debates, he felt drawn to Sanders and later drove two hours to attend a Sanders rally in the city of Kissimmee. On a family trip to Washington, DC, he proudly wore his "Sanders for President" T-shirt during a tour of the Capitol.

When Ramos wasn't studying, hanging out with friends, or attending his classes, he spent time on Reddit and YouTube, wading through long discussions about stolen votes and rigged primaries and all the other ways the Democratic Party was screwing Sanders over. He preferred to get his news from independent sources like the anti-war program *Democracy Now!* or the feisty left-wing show *The Young Turks*. They covered stories the mainstream media didn't or wouldn't touch. When he watched episodes of these shows on YouTube, the algorithm suggested other independent voices he should seek out. One was H. A. Goodman, who devoted hours of his show to the DNC's efforts to thwart Sanders's bid for the presidency. Goodman predicted violence if the DNC prevailed and Clinton clinched the nomination.

Now Ramos was watching the corruption play out right before his eyes. When he heard about Seth Rich's murder, Ramos thought back to H. A. Goodman's warning. He saw the conspiracy theories about the Clintons in a whole new light. Maybe those theories were right all along.

He decided to research who Seth Rich was and distill the story in a Reddit post. He wanted to put forward his own theory of the case before the mainstream media swooped in to set the narrative and possibly cover up the truth about the death of this fellow Sanders supporter. He noted Seth's job at GQR and pointed out that Stan Greenberg, one of the firm's founders and the CEO, had once worked as Bill Clinton's pollster. *Had the Clintons worked through Greenberg?* The firm had once advised British Petroleum. Kurtchella drew a line from BP to the controversial Keystone XL pipeline, even though the pipeline was not a BP project. Keystone was "one of the MANY positions on which Hillary Clinton has flip-flopped on." *Was Big Oil implicated?*

The post went on like this for thousands of words, a mishmash of conjecture and speculation with no actual evidence to support the theories presented. But that didn't prevent kurtchella from seeing a vast and nefarious plot at work. "It gives me no joy to post this," he wrote, "but given his position & timing in politics, I believe Seth Rich was murdered by corrupt politicians for knowing too much information on election fraud."

———— ◦ ————

Aaron's friend read the responses to kurtchella's post. The first page was split between people expressing sympathy for the Riches and those who saw sinister forces at work. But by the second and third pages, conspiracy theories dominated the discussion.

> Add another one to the list of "suspicious" Clinton deaths.

> What's the over under on how many people the Clinton's [*sic*] have had murdered? I'd set it at about 350.

> I don't think his killing needs to be attributed to Clinton to be a part of a conspiracy. I think it's enough that he was killed in DC holding the position that he did.

Aaron dismissed the people who made these comments as idiots. He knew his brother spent time on Reddit; he also knew that Seth, like a lot of people, couldn't resist a good conspiracy theory, marveling at how far some people could venture into the absurd.

Seth would've found this absurd and hilarious, Aaron thought. Here he was, the subject of lengthy Reddit threads and viral hashtags. Seth would have pictured all this attention like a parade of people, his friends and family on one side of the street, the conspiracy theorists on the other. What Aaron never imagined was that this parade would become a riot.

———— ◆ ————

When the plane transporting Seth's body landed at the Omaha airport, Mary, Joel, Aaron, and Molly, Aaron's wife, waited on the tarmac to greet it. The airport usually didn't allow this, but Mary had demanded to see her son one final time before his funeral, and Joel called in a favor to make it happen. The airport workers took off their hats as a plain pine casket was carried off the plane. Mary stood over it and had one final conversation with her baby boy, her Froggy, her Roo.

The funeral took place at Beth El Synagogue. Friends, family, old teachers, and neighbors filled the sanctuary. Until that moment, Joel and Mary hadn't realized how many people Seth had touched. There were friends from summer camp and old buddies from Central High. Former US senator Ben Nelson, whose campaign had hired Seth for his first real job in politics, attended; the Jesuit president of Creighton University read a psalm in perfect Hebrew. "There are no answers for a young man gunned down in the prime of his life," Rabbi Steven Abraham said in his remarks. "All we have is questions of what could have been, what should have been, and talk of potential greatness for which we will never bear witness."

At the gravesite, after the pallbearers had lowered the pine casket into the ground, the rabbi asked everyone to deposit a small amount of earth on top with the back of a shovel. In Judaism this is a final act to honor the dead, a favor that can never be repaid. Normally, mourners add just enough dirt to cover the casket and then depart, leaving the cemetery's grounds crew to finish filling the hole.

Seth's high school friends and fraternity brothers stepped forward and insisted they would do it themselves. They took off their suit jackets, loosened their ties, and took turns shoveling until they had filled Seth's grave with fresh earth.

———◆———

Seth's DNC coworkers thought of their own way to honor him. The day after his death was announced, Clinton and Sanders were scheduled to make their first joint appearance since Clinton had effectively won the nomination. The animosity between Clinton and Sanders supporters threatened to tear the party apart, and so as a gesture of party unity, Sanders agreed to officially endorse his erstwhile rival on the campaign trail shortly before the Democratic convention.

Someone at the DNC passed a request to the Clinton campaign: Could she mention Seth in her speech? Media from around the world had descended on Portsmouth, New Hampshire, to cover the rally. It was hard to envision a bigger stage on which to remember Seth.

Backed by an enormous American flag, Clinton and Sanders took the stage on the morning of Tuesday, July 12. As Clinton worked through her stump speech, DNC employees waited with anticipation. "From Sandy Hook to Orlando to Dallas, and so many other places, these tragedies tear at our soul," she said, referring to several tragic mass shootings, "and so do the incidents that don't even dominate the headlines. Just this past Sunday," she went on, "a young man, Seth Rich, who worked for the Democratic National Committee to expand voting rights, was shot and killed in his neighborhood in Washington. He was just twenty-seven years old. Surely, we can agree that weapons of war have no place on the streets of America."

Seth's coworkers watched Clinton's speech, holding back tears. It meant so much to them—and to Joel and Mary and Aaron—to hear one of the most recognizable people on the planet pay homage to Seth. But as Clinton kept speaking, one of Seth's old colleagues started to feel uneasy. She remembered all the people out there who hated Hillary Clinton and obsessed over her every word, forever in search of a hidden motive or a sinister plot. Many of those people probably hadn't heard the name Seth Rich until it came out of Hillary Clinton's mouth.

"I had a moment when I watched her say it on TV," the colleague would later say, "and then the next thought was, 'Oh, dear God, what have we done?'"

4

The United States of Sheeple

ALMOST NINETEEN YEARS to the day before Seth Rich's murder, the police opened a homicide investigation in northwest Washington, DC. At 5:15 a.m. on Monday, July 7, 1997, an employee at a Starbucks coffee shop in the Georgetown neighborhood had arrived for work and found the bodies of three colleagues, all of them shot to death.

The victims were Mary Caitrin Mahoney, Emory Allen Evans, and Aaron David Goodrich. Mahoney, who went by "Caity," was two weeks short of her twenty-fifth birthday; Evans was twenty-five; and Goodrich was eighteen. A triple homicide in one of Washington's most affluent neighborhoods terrified DC's citizens and made national news. Howard Schultz, the CEO of Starbucks, cut short his vacation and flew to Washington to meet with the store's employees. The newspapers described the murders as "execution-style slayings"; it later emerged that Mahoney had been shot once in the chest and four times in the head. There were no witnesses, no fingerprints, no physical evidence apart from shell casings found at the crime scene. No money had been taken from the store's safe.

The working theory put forward by DC's Metropolitan Police Department was an armed robbery gone wrong. Months passed and no arrests were made. On the one-year anniversary of the murders,

Mahoney's mother told a *Washington Post* reporter that she doubted whether the case would ever be solved. "We gave the police six months and didn't hear a word from them," she said. "We're not sure they even have anyone in mind." An assistant police chief insisted that the investigation remained active, telling the *Post*, "We're very optimistic we'll close this case."

As law enforcement agencies continued their search for the Starbucks killer, Mahoney's name began appearing on a list that circulated in emails, newsletters, take-home videos, and bare-bones online message boards. The list, titled "The Clinton Body-Count," claimed to be a roster of nearly sixty people "who have recently met their demise in suspicious circumstances who appear to have some connection to the Clintons." There were well-known names on the list, such as Vincent Foster Jr., the former White House lawyer who had died by suicide during Bill Clinton's first year as president, and Ron Brown, Clinton's commerce secretary who died in a plane crash in 1996. It also featured the names of bodyguards who had worked for Bill and Hillary Clinton, supposed mistresses of Bill's, and old friends, associates, and journalists from Arkansas. One version of the list even included Abbie Hoffman and Nicole Brown Simpson. All of these people had died, the authors of the Clinton Body-Count surmised, because of their proximity to the Clinton family. "Arkancide," some called it.

The origins of the list were murky and contested. Some said it grew out of a 1993 movie, *The Clinton Chronicles*, that put forward a number of conspiracy theories, including that eight people were mysteriously killed for knowing too much about an international drug-smuggling ring run by Bill Clinton during his time as the governor of Arkansas. *The Clinton Chronicles* was a smash hit among conservatives, with Jerry Falwell, Rush Limbaugh, and Pat Robertson all peddling it on their respective shows. Others attributed the Body-Count list to Linda Thompson, a fringe lawyer who had put together a list of thirty-four deceased people in the Clintons' orbit and titled it "The Clinton Body Count: Coincidence or Kiss of Death?"

Caity Mahoney's connection to the Clintons was slight. She had interned for a few months in the Clinton White House, scheduling tours for visitors. She was not a friend, rival, or spurned lover of either Bill or Hillary; she didn't know them at all. But in the minds of a small but passionate group of Clinton obsessives, Mahoney's death reeked of suspicion. Conspiracy theorists pointed out that just a few days before Mahoney's murder, a *Newsweek* reporter had dropped a hint that a "former White House staffer" would soon speak out about sexual harassment she experienced working for the president. The reporter did not reveal the ex-staffer's identity and referred to her as "M," the first initial of her first name. The conspiracy theorists speculated that perhaps the Clintons had ordered Mahoney's killing to silence her before she could speak out about what she had gone through in the White House.

As the world would soon learn, "M" was shorthand for Monica, as in Monica Lewinsky, the former White House intern who'd had an affair with Bill Clinton. Then, on March 6, 1999, the DC police announced that they had charged twenty-nine-year-old Carl Cooper with the murders of Mahoney, Evans, and Goodrich. Cooper told police investigators that he had planned to rob the Starbucks two days after July 4 because he thought the store's safe would be flush with cash after the holiday. He entered the store after closing time and demanded that Mahoney, the assistant manager, give him the keys to the safe. When she refused, he shot her multiple times and then shot Evans and Goodrich. He fled the store without taking any money and ditched his guns in a different part of DC. More than a year later, a woman whose boyfriend knew Cooper called in a tip after seeing an episode of *America's Most Wanted* about the case. Cooper would later plead guilty to forty-seven counts, including the Starbucks murders, several additional killings, and the attempted murder of a DC cop, as well as conspiracy and racketeering.

Yet long after Cooper had confessed to his crimes and a judge had sentenced him to life in prison without parole, the belief that Caity Mahoney's death was somehow tied to the Clintons lived on. No amount of evidence could convince a hardened crew of believers that the hidden hand of the Clintons wasn't in some way present in Mahoney's murder. In the years that followed, Mahoney remained on the different versions of the Clinton Body-Count, which circulated online like an organism that never died, fueling one of the most enduring conspiracy theories of modern times.

———◦|———

Americans have indulged in wild speculation and paranoid fantasies about their leaders and their countrymen for as long as the country has existed—and even earlier. The radical Samuel Adams mobilized support for the American Revolution by stoking fears about a British conspiracy to enslave the colonists and make them property of the empire. There was no truth to this theory—and it was grimly ironic given the many enslaved people who'd been brought to the colonies—but Adams's ploy nonetheless helped lead America into war. Ever since, Americans have turned to conspiracy theories to explain what they believe to be inexplicable.

For the first 150 years of our history, the subjects of these theories tended to be outside forces—Catholics, Masons, Jews—who were trying to infiltrate the nation and its government. But after the First World War and the explosive growth of the federal bureaucracy in the twentieth century, conspiracy theories turned inward: now the threat facing America wasn't coming from outside but from within. JFK's assassination, UFOs, Waco, Oklahoma City, 9/11, Sandy Hook: a subset of Americans saw the hidden hand of government behind these tragedies, scandals, or cataclysms. So it was easy for them to believe when it was revealed that the government actually *did* engage in conspiracies, like the FBI's domestic spying campaign known as COINTELPRO, Watergate, and Iran-Contra. Conspiracy thinking flourished on both ends of the ideological spectrum. And in the case of the 9/11 truth movement, the left and right converged on the belief that two passenger airplanes alone couldn't have toppled two of the tallest buildings in the world and that, despite all the evidence, the government must have played a role and then covered it up.

In 2005, three filmmakers released a documentary they had made on a laptop for a few thousand dollars. Dylan Avery described himself and his two collaborators Korey Rowe and Jason Bermas as "three kids from a hick town in upstate New York." What those three hick kids had in common was a lot of questions—and suspicions, and doubts—about the seminal event of their young lives, the September 11 terrorist attacks.

Their movie was called *Loose Change*. Avery had set out to write a screenplay about a pair of friends who uncover the chilling truth about September 11. As he researched his screenplay, scouring US military archives, reading blogs, and replaying the coverage from that tragic day, he realized a feature film was the wrong format. "I was supposed to be making a fictional story about me and my friends discovering that 9/11 was an inside job, and doing something about it," he told an interviewer years later, "and basically that happened in real life."

Narrated by Avery, *Loose Change* presented an alternate history of the 9/11 attacks. It raised questions that, at first glance, created intrigue: How was it that the black boxes for American Airlines Flight 11 and United Airlines Flight 175 were never recovered, but one of the hijackers' passports was found intact near ground zero? Why did a third tower, WTC 7, crumble to the ground even though no plane hit it? Could two commercial jets bring down buildings so large?

The central premise of *Loose Change* is that the US government not only knew about the 9/11 attacks but played an active role in them. Perhaps explosives brought down the towers, the so-called controlled demolition theory. Or the US engineered the attacks as a pretext to go to war in the Middle East. The movie was riddled with errors; its critics created entire websites devoted to pointing out the movie's many factual mistakes and logical fallacies. Still, those who watched *Loose Change* were left with a foreboding sense that they hadn't received the true story of one of the worst acts of terrorism in the history of America. And it popularized the idea of a "false flag," a cover-up operation used to hide the real source and responsible party.

There was no glitzy premiere for the release of *Loose Change*. Fans uploaded the hour-long film to Google Video, the search giant's competitor to YouTube, and hoped somebody would notice it. What happened next would mark a turning point in the history of conspiracism:

The film was a hit. It tapped into an already fervent community of 9/11 "truthers," then spread far beyond that. *Vanity Fair* called it "the first internet blockbuster." Years later Avery would estimate that more than one hundred million people had watched his movie, which, if true, would make it one of the most successful independent documentary films of all time.

———◆———

The September 11 attacks surely rank among the most-watched events in human history. We saw with our own eyes, first in real time and then in endless replays, as United Airlines Flight 175 hit the second tower and then, an hour later, as both towers crumpled to the ground. Which made the success of *Loose Change* so staggering and perplexing. What was it about that horrific day that led people to distrust the official story? Why did we search for our own answers instead of believing what we saw? What made the conspiracy theories so attractive?

The usual answer to these kinds of questions goes something like this: The human mind seeks comfort in the face of uncertainty, order from chaos, patterns in the rubble. Our minds can't handle the complexity, let alone the unknowns, of a terrorist attack or a global pandemic. Conspiracy theories organize the world. Better yet, they simplify it: inside job, false flag, cover-up. A conspiracy theory is concise and clear when the world is not.

That's the easy answer for why we believe conspiracy theories. It is not, however, the full picture. After all, some conspiracy theories complicate the world—a random act of violence becomes a well-orchestrated plot, a stray bullet turns into an assassination. Where the 9/11 Commission faulted the Bush and Clinton administrations, Congress, and US intelligence agencies for bureaucratic ineptitude and a failure to heed repeated warnings, *Loose Change* and the 9/11 truther movement saw a carefully planned and masterfully executed covert operation, an epic fraud perpetrated on the American people that made real conspiracies like the Bay of Pigs look like a clerical error.

Throughout American history you can find instance after instance of some political scholar or cultural observer declaring his or her era uniquely deranged. The most famous is Richard Hofstadter's 1964 essay "The Paranoid Style in American Politics," a perceptive piece of writing for its time but one that is now cited so easily and often it has entered the realm of cliché. The reality about conspiracy theories, if we dare to face it, is that they have existed for as long as we have. From the Puritans to the present day, conspiracy theories have flourished every step of the way.

And yet, in the canon of conspiracism, the massive success of *Loose Change* merits a special place. A decade and a half later, it's fair to say that *Loose Change*'s release in the mid-aughts marked the dawn of a golden age of conspiracy theorizing. In the past, the tools available to a conspiracy theorist were newspapers, pamphlets, short-wave radio—technologies that were slow, expensive, and inefficient. One famous anarchist from the early 1900s flung his leaflets out the window of a New York City high-rise, hoping people might pluck one from the sky and read it. The paranoid anti-communists of the John Birch Society relied on books and magazines to reach their membership, which peaked in the mid-1960s at around one hundred thousand people. Milton William Cooper, perhaps the most famous ufologist in American history, sold more than three hundred thousand copies of his underground classic book, *Behold a Pale Horse*, an impressive total for any author let alone one published by an obscure independent press.

Loose Change wasn't an especially convincing movie. Its production values were dismal. It matters because of the technological moment it heralded: by 2005, a cheap laptop and an internet connection provided all the tools necessary to reach millions. You didn't have to sit back and absorb someone else's theories; you could now do your own research, create your own alternate theories, and share them with the world. YouTube was in its infancy and Twitter didn't exist when Dylan Avery released the first cut of *Loose Change*, but as social media grew to occupy a central place in American culture, it ushered in a new generation of conspiracy theorists who had means of communication their predecessors could only have dreamt about.

Dylan Avery saw the early potential of the internet to get the message out. But he showed little interest in turning his hit movie into a money-making enterprise, giving away thousands of copies and eventually receding from the public spotlight. It would take another skeptic to realize the enormous potential of the business of conspiracy theories.

———•|•———

As a teenager in the early 1990s, Alex Jones obsessed over the fifty-one-day standoff between government agents and the Branch Davidian sect in the small town of Waco, Texas. Jones watched C-SPAN for hours at a time as federal agents launched a violent raid on the Branch Davidian compound, leading to the deaths of more than eighty people. He didn't trust the official story of what happened at Waco and began to seek ideas and theories outside the mainstream. He discovered *Alternative Views*, a weekly show on Austin's public access station that had a liberal slant and covered topics ignored or poorly covered by the mainstream media, such as the CIA, alternative energy sources, labor unions, and US foreign policy.

A college dropout whose father ran a successful dental practice, Jones eventually got his own show on the public access station. He was a local gadfly, known for showing up at political events and staging guerilla interviews with politicians. He had a blunt, in-your-face style, with a voice that sounded like sandpaper dragged over asphalt. But he had no hesitation about saying things other people wouldn't, and the shock value of that skill, if you could call it that, would take him far. He parlayed a weekend hosting gig at a local radio station into his own talk radio show just as the medium was taking off, thanks to the massive popularity of right-wing talk radio. A familiar nuisance to the citizens of Austin, Jones broke through on the national stage after the September 11 attacks. Six weeks earlier he had said on his public access show that the Bush administration would stage an attack on American soil and blame it on Osama bin Laden. After the attacks happened, Jones was called the man who "predicted 9/11." He was invited to speak at 9/11 truther conferences and treated like an oracle and a hero.

The "truth" about September 11 was just one of many conspiracy theories Jones championed. He made a movie, *Dark Secrets*, about the private Bohemian Grove retreat where, in his telling, world leaders gathered to engage in bizarre and occult rituals and even—maybe— human sacrifice. Another go-to bogeyman was the New World Order, which he once described as a "demonic high-tech tyranny" of Satan-worshipping elites led by Bill and Melinda Gates, who, through their foundation, using a mix of fabricated crises and eugenics, were slowly seizing control of the entire planet. Jones long believed that the government controlled the weather, weaponizing tornadoes and hurricanes. Glenn Beck, the Fox News host, was a CIA plant. The 2012 mass shooting at Sandy Hook Elementary was a false flag, the grieving parents "crisis actors," and the entire tragedy a "giant hoax" intended to strip away the right of Americans to bear arms.

But as long as he operated in the analog era, there would always be a limit to Jones's reach. The viewership for Austin public access TV was miniscule. The audience for his syndicated radio show numbered as high as two million listeners a week—impressive but far behind Rush Limbaugh or Sean Hannity. His breakthrough came when he launched the website Infowars in 1999, and another site called Prison Planet. Now he had the ability to take his rage-filled diatribes and wild-eyed theories to the masses.

Behind the bluster, it turned out, was a savvy businessman. Infowars opened an online store that hawked everything from "Made in 1776" T-shirts and "Don't Tread on Me" Gadsden flags to nutritional supplements called Super Male Vitality, an endurance supplement, and Brain Force Plus, a pill to "supercharge" your cognitive abilities. He sold survivalist gear including iodine drops, cases of freeze-dried meals ready to eat, and handbooks for "nuclear war survival skills," all of it aimed at the "prepper" movement, people who want to equip themselves for societal collapse or World War III. There was an entire section of the store devoted to seeds: for $179 (on sale from $231), an Infowars fan could buy the "Deluxe Emergency Seed Bank," which included fifty-some varieties of "non-hybrid," "non-GMO" seeds. (Genetically modified organisms were another bugbear of Jones's and a popular topic on the show.) Under the reasons someone should buy the seed packet, the website said, "When disaster hits, it is to [*sic*] late." You watched his show, heard him plug his products, and clicked over to his store to buy them. Alex Jones was the first vertically integrated conspiracy theorist of the internet era.

It made him a very rich man. In 2014 alone he brought in revenue of $20 million across the business and reported profits of $5 million. Milton William Cooper, the proto-Jones who popularized the phrase "wake up, sheeple," had lived in a ramshackle house on the side of a mountain in rural Arizona. As the money poured in, Jones moved into a massive house with a pool in a gated Austin neighborhood. He bought four Rolexes on a single day in 2014 and spent $40,000 on a saltwater aquarium. A list of his and his wife's assets filed with the court during their acrimonious divorce included a $70,000 grand piano, $50,000 in firearms, and $752,000 in gold, silver, and other valuable metals.

Despite pressure from advocacy groups and victims of Jones's conspiracy theories, like the parents of the children killed at Sandy Hook, his audience grew. Social media platforms took a hands-off approach when it came to moderating the content that appeared on their platforms. They allowed Jones to broadcast more or less whatever he wanted, day after day, and as he did his online following rivaled that of mainstream news organizations. The 2016 election sent Jones's audience soaring, leading to 1.8 million subscribers on YouTube—a larger subscriber base on the platform than the *New York Times*, the *Wall Street Journal*, and the *Washington Post* combined. Ten million people visited the Infowars website each month, which surpassed the online readership of *Newsweek* or the *Economist*. The money kept pouring in: between 2015 and 2018, Jones's store brought in $165 million, according to court records.

Despite his massive audience and financial success, the US political establishment kept Jones at a distance. Few elected officials agreed to appear on Infowars, not wanting to be associated in any way with Jones's deranged views. This was not surprising: for most of the twentieth century, the Democratic and Republican parties had policed the line between the real and the conspiratorial. There were always going to be a few crank types yelling at the fringes, people like the perennial political candidate and extreme conspiracist Lyndon LaRouche, but mainstream politicians ignored those people and kept them far away from the microphone.

The 2016 presidential race would obliterate that line. The first inkling of this came on December 2, 2015, when the real estate mogul turned presidential hopeful Donald Trump made an appearance on Infowars. Alex Jones said he couldn't be more thrilled with Trump's entry into the race, adding that "my audience, 90 percent of them, they support you." Trump returned the love. "Your reputation is amazing," Trump said. "I will not let you down."

———◆———

By the time Trump ran for president in 2016, he had established his conservative bona fides by championing the Obama "birther" conspiracy theory—the false notion that the country's first Black president had a fake birth certificate, wasn't born in Hawai'i, and thus was ineligible to serve as president. In TV appearances and interviews, Trump tossed off claims like "nobody ever comes forward" from Obama's childhood or hometown to say they knew him, when several people had. He insisted no one had signed or certified the birth certificate Obama had released in 2011, even though a signature was clearly visible on the document. Trump called Obama's birth certificate "one of the great cons in the history of politics" and pledged to write a $5 million check to Obama's charity of choice if the president handed over records related to his citizenship.

His role as the chief spokesman for the birther smear led to invitations to speak at conservative galas and in front of local Republican parties. When he arrived at the 2011 Conservative Political Action Conference (CPAC), the Woodstock of right-wing politics, hordes of fans and reporters trailed him everywhere he went. One political consultant compared the scene to "Michael Jackson coming out of a Japanese airport."

As a presidential candidate, he used conspiracy theories to discredit his Republican rivals. He floated the idea that Ted Cruz's father, Rafael, had spent time with Lee Harvey Oswald before Oswald assassinated John F. Kennedy. He pointed out that Ted Cruz was born in Canada and questioned *his* eligibility to run for president. (Cruz's mother was American, which made him a US citizen.) He even had his own version of a 9/11 conspiracy: he said he remembered watching footage of Jersey City, New Jersey, that showed "thousands and thousands" of Arab people "cheering" as the twin towers fell. "It did happen. I saw it. It was on television," he said. But there was no available footage anywhere of the incident.

Trump represented a new style of conspiracy theorist. Unlike those of Alex Jones or the Birchers, his theories didn't attempt to explain the world. They didn't connect any dots or try to make sense of seemingly disparate events. He couched his attacks by attributing them to an "extremely credible source" who had given him information, or he began the statements with the vague claim that "a lot of people are saying . . ." or "some people think . . ." As Trump himself once said, "Even if it isn't totally true, there's something there." Used this way, conspiracy theories aren't a misguided attempt to make sense of the world; they're a blunt-force instrument that dehumanizes one's enemies and dog whistles to one's followers.

As Trump pushed the birther conspiracy theory, or lavished praise on Alex Jones, or implicated Ted Cruz's father in the JFK assassination, mainstream Republicans looked the other way or dismissed him as a buffoon, while the grass roots propelled him on to clinching the Republican presidential nomination.

At the 2016 Republican National Convention in Cleveland, the language of Alex Jones had already infiltrated the convention festivities. One of the convention's speakers was Pat Smith, the mother of a State Department employee who had been killed in the 2012 attack on a diplomatic facility in Benghazi, Libya, when a group of violent extremists overran the compound and set fire to the main facility with several Americans still inside, including Ambassador J. Christopher Stevens. Ambassador Stevens, Pat Smith's son Sean, and two American private security officers died defending US facilities. At the end of her speech, Smith said she blamed Hillary Clinton, who was secretary of state at the time, for the death of her son.

At the foot of the stage, a man dressed in a suit and a Stars and Stripes hat held up a sign with the words "Hillary for prison" on it. "That's right," Smith said, holding back tears as she pointed to the sign in the crowd. "Hillary for prison. She deserves to be in stripes." The crowd rose to its feet and cheered. Alex Jones didn't need a floor pass to the convention. His candidate had won the nomination. The paranoid fringe was fringe no longer.

————◆————

The rest of July passed in a fog of grief for Joel, Mary, and Aaron. *Good Morning America* interviewed them about Seth. Visitors dropped by to pay their respects. In early August, Joel and Mary traveled to Washington to pack up Seth's belongings and attend a memorial organized by some of Seth's friends. Nearly 150 friends and colleagues, many wearing "Vote for Seth Rich" stickers from one of his Creighton student government campaigns, drank pints of Bell's Two Hearted and traded stories. Joel and Mary laughed so hard they hurt afterward.

The next day they held a press conference close to Seth's house. Surrounded by reporters and television cameras, Mary pleaded with anyone who had information about the murder to come forward. "If you saw anything, if you saw anyone in the area at this time, if you know of people that came home after 4:30 in the early morning," she stressed, please call the police. Joel and Mary had also met in private with Cathy Lanier, the DC chief of police. The key to solving the case, Lanier told them, was keeping the case in the public eye. The higher the reward for information and the more public attention on the case, Lanier said, the more likely it was someone would come forward with a tip or a lead. The police had announced a $25,000 reward for information, which was typical for an unsolved homicide. Joel and Mary couldn't afford to put up that kind of money, so they resolved to do whatever they could to keep the press interested in the case.

After their press conference, Joel and Mary talked again with Chief Lanier. Before she left, Lanier, who was in a cruiser, reached through the window and grabbed Joel's arm. "We're going to find the bastards who did this," she told him.

The online conspiracy theories continued to spread. Now, not even a month after Seth's still-mysterious death, there were different rival theories about what happened. One strange website, WhatDoesIt-Mean.com, which claimed to be run by an order of nuns but was really the work of a retired chemical plant control room operator and prolific conspiracy theorist who lived near the Smoky Mountains in Tennessee, claimed that Seth had been on his way to give testimony to the FBI about Hillary Clinton's corruption when he was killed. The site credited an intercepted Russian intelligence bulletin; how the site obtained the bulletin was left to the imagination. Stories had also started to appear in more prominent outlets, like the *Daily Mail* tabloid. Raw with grief, Joel and Mary didn't notice.

5

Our Sources Take Risks

EELCO BOSCH VAN Rosenthal snuck a final look at his notes before the cameras rolled. Trim, early forties, with piercing blue eyes, van Rosenthal was an anchor for *Nieuwsuur*, a highly popular news show in the Netherlands. He had been a correspondent for the network and had reported from all over the world, including six years in Washington covering the Obama presidency. He spoke fluent English and had a reputation as a dogged interviewer, and he knew he would need to be on his game for the guest now dialing into the studio.

Van Rosenthal had dealt with Julian Assange before, once spending a maddening week in Iceland, where WikiLeaks had a temporary base of operations, trying to report on some of the leaked US diplomatic cables released in the Cablegate publication. He knew Assange to be a prickly character and a tough subject—evasive, combative, quick to reject the premise of a question or launch into a self-righteous lecture.

WikiLeaks had just published the "DNC Leaks," an archive of nearly twenty thousand internal emails, strategy memos, and other documents from inside the Democratic National Committee. By Assange's standards the emails were far less powerful than the *Collateral Murder* video or any one of the many revelations brought to light in Cablegate. But the DNC documents did offer a rare look at the inner workings of a major political party, a place where sharp elbows and testy arguments were the norm. They depicted a world more like the dark satire *Veep* than the feel-good drama *The West Wing*. The emails also revealed a level of antipathy voiced by some DNC employees toward Sanders and his campaign. In one email senior DNC employees suggested hurting Sanders's candidacy by saying he was an atheist (he was Jewish). In another Chairwoman Debbie Wasserman Schultz called a top Sanders aide a "damn liar." The leaked messages seemed to confirm some of what Sanders's supporters had suspected all along—that the DNC, or elements of it, hated Sanders and wanted Clinton to win.

WikiLeaks timed its release of the emails for the eve of the Democratic National Convention, when the political press corps was primed to write about them. Until that moment the mainstream media had mostly ignored Sanders's claims that the DNC had it out for him. But with the emails to prove it, news outlets couldn't resist covering the story, plunging the party into chaos just before the convention. The outcry led to the resignations of Wasserman Schultz and Amy Dacey, the DNC's chief executive. The convention was meant to be a chance to heal the rift between the pro-Sanders progressive left and the establishment camp that backed Clinton. Instead Sanders's supporters staged a revolt on the convention floor in protest.

Assange was inundated with interview requests to discuss the DNC Leaks. He was asked often about the provenance of the emails. Wasn't it true that Russian hackers had stolen the emails, as cybersecurity experts who reviewed the data from the DNC's network concluded? Assange bristled at the suggestion that a hostile state actor had used WikiLeaks to launder the emails. WikiLeaks, Assange said, never confirmed or denied the identities of its sources. "We like to create maximum ambiguity as to who our sources are," he said.

In the interviews, he dropped what appeared to be small clues—or were they feints?—about the provenance of the emails. "It's, I think, interesting and acceptable to speculate who our sources are," he said in one TV interview. "But if we're talking about the DNC, there's lots of consultants that have access, lots of programmers." He claimed the

DNC had been hacked dozens and dozens of times but gave no evidence to support this claim. He remarked that it was up to the sources themselves to reveal their identities and their role. "Perhaps one day the source or sources will step forward, and it might be an interesting moment," he said. "Some people will have egg on their faces."

Van Rosenthal, the *Nieuwsuur* anchor, had studied the recent interviews Assange had given and noted the irritation in Assange's voice when asked about the Russian hacking allegations. When it was his turn to question Assange, he pressed the WikiLeaks founder on the Russian connection. How could a self-proclaimed believer in democracy and transparency accept stolen emails from Russia, a country where dissidents were imprisoned, defectors poisoned, and independent journalists murdered for reporting the truth about powerful elites?

"Well, that's false," Assange replied. The Russian hacking story was nonsense, he said, ginned up by the Clinton campaign "to try and distract from the revelations of rigging the nomination process." By screaming "Russia, Russia, Russia" all the time, he added, WikiLeaks' critics were engaging in a modern form of McCarthyism.

But if a foreign government *were* interfering in an American election, van Rosenthal asked, didn't the public deserve to know? Couldn't what WikiLeaks was doing be considered interfering with an election? The DNC Leaks had nothing to do with his distaste for Clinton or help from Russian hackers, Assange insisted. The principle behind every one of WikiLeaks' publications was to expose how power truly worked, and now the organization had given American voters valuable information for when they cast their vote in November.

Van Rosenthal changed subjects. He mentioned Donald Trump's sinking support in the polls. At that point, it seemed, only a so-called October surprise could save Trump's campaign. Did WikiLeaks have any such bombshells in its possession?

"WikiLeaks never sits on material," Assange said. Doing so would be a disservice to the sources who risked their jobs and sometimes their lives to get information to WikiLeaks. "There's a twenty-seven-year-old works for the DNC," Assange went on, "[who] was shot in the back, murdered just two weeks ago for unknown reasons as he was walking down the street in Washington."

Van Rosenthal felt a prickle of recognition. When he lived in DC, he had read the *Washington Post*'s Metro section every day. He continued to read it after he had moved back to Amsterdam. He had followed the paper's coverage of Seth Rich's murder.

"That was just a robbery, I believe. Wasn't it?" he interjected.

"No. There is no finding," Assange replied.

"What are you suggesting?"

"I'm suggesting that our sources take risks, and they are—they become concerned to see things occurring like that."

"Was he one of your sources, then?"

"We don't comment on who our sources are."

"Then why make the suggestion about a young guy being shot in the streets of Washington?"

Assange repeated what he'd already said—that it was concerning to WikiLeaks' sources to know that a political aide had been gunned down in the middle of a contentious presidential campaign. The murder only underscored the "serious risks" those sources faced.

Van Rosenthal wasn't buying it. "But it's quite something to suggest a murder," he said. "That's basically what you're doing."

"Others have suggested that," Assange said. "We are investigating to understand what happened in that situation with Seth Rich. I think it is a concerning situation. There's not a conclusion yet. But we are concerned about it."

When the interview was over, van Rosenthal spoke with his editor. They had a decision to make. Van Rosenthal was stunned that Assange had implicated Seth in the DNC leak without any evidence to back it up—at the very least, it was reckless, and possibly worse. Because the interview was conducted in English, it was taped an hour before *Nieuwsuur* went live in the Netherlands so it could be translated and captioned in Dutch. Should they edit out Assange's comments about Rich? His editor argued that Assange had made real news, hinting at his possible source, and the clip would surely get a good deal of attention. They decided to keep Assange's comments about Seth. "To be honest," van

Rosenthal would say years later, "I'm not completely sure that was the right decision."

———◆———

In the days after the murder, it had unnerved Aaron to watch his brother's name and photo ricochet around the internet. Aaron treated the theories about Seth like a temporary annoyance. It was a presidential campaign year; people were riled up. With enough time this brief fit of madness would fade away. People would move on.

Just when it felt like the initial frenzy after Seth's murder had subsided, Aaron noticed a surge in activity on the morning of August 9. It didn't take much searching to find out why: WikiLeaks had announced on Twitter a $20,000 reward for information about Seth's murder. But why? What did WikiLeaks want to do with Seth? Aaron eventually found his way to a short clip of Assange's interview with a Dutch news anchor about the DNC leaks. "There's a twenty-seven-year-old works for the DNC," Aaron heard Assange say. "Our sources take risks."

There were, by that point, several versions of the theories about Seth circulating on social media. The far-left Bernie fanatics claimed he'd been murdered for trying to expose corruption at the DNC, possibly at the behest of the Clinton family. A few fringe websites speculated that unknown hitmen had killed him for discovering the hack-and-leak operation as it was happening. But Assange's comments ignited a new version of the theory, one that would take hold in far-right circles. The appeal of this story to Donald Trump's supporters was obvious: if a disgruntled young Democrat had stolen the emails from his employer and provided them to WikiLeaks, then the culprit for that brazen cybercrime, a Watergate for the digital age, was not Russia. The allegation that Russia had interfered in the election to help Trump and damage Clinton, or that Trump's campaign had somehow conspired with Russians—all of it was bunk. Trump had been right the whole time when he called the Russian interference story "fake news."

On social media Trump's followers mobilized around this theory. More than eighty thousand tweets with the hashtag #SethRich appeared on Twitter within hours of the *Nieuwsuur* interview appearing online. You could trace the start of that viral surge to anonymous pro-Trump accounts that urged coordination. Take the Twitter account @Nimble-Navgater. Soon after Assange's interview went live, the account issued a rallying cry to its followers:

TWEET USING HASHTAGS #SethRich and #HisNameWasSethRich !!!

On the surface, @NimbleNavgater had all the hallmarks of a diehard Trump supporter. The account's bio said she was "DANI THE DEM DESTROYER" who lived in Boston, Massachusetts. She joined Twitter in March 2016 and spent nearly all of her time on the platform pushing pro-Trump messages and memes while attacking anyone who said a mean word about him—Barack Obama, Hillary Clinton, Ted Cruz, feminists, Cher. She reveled in any setback for Clinton's campaign ("FBI recovers 30 new Clinton emails dealing with Benghazi!") and ran interference with every new Trump-related scandal. What you couldn't find in @NimbleNavgater's tweets was any confirmation that she was who she said she was, or that she was a real person at all. @NimbleNavgater could have been a working mom in Boston, a fifty-year-old lawyer in Fresno, a bratty teenager in Brazil, or a bot—and there was no way to know in the moment. At any one time, thousands of fake accounts mixed in with real ones promoted certain hashtags, gaming the algorithm to make a topic go viral, creating buzz and critical mass.

Seth Rich is one of SEVEN Clinton affiliates murdered this month. This is no coincidence people. #HisNameWasSethRich

Julian Assange Suggests That DNC Staffer Shot To Death Was A WikiLeaks Source #SethRich #HisNameWasSethRich

An American patriot saw corruption in his own party and decided he wouldn't help hide it. #HisNameWasSethRich

The hashtags #SethRich and #HisNameWasSethRich trended for several hours, which caused conservative influencers with much larger followings to take notice. Curt Schilling, the former Boston Red Sox pitcher turned belligerent right-wing podcaster, shared one of @NimbleNavgater's Seth Rich tweets to his 160,000 Twitter followers. Mike Cernovich, a leading voice in the misogynist alt-right, sent this tweet to his eighty thousand followers: "Was Seth Rich, the source of #DNCleaks, murdered?" The Gateway Pundit, a fringe blog, included these tweets and Assange's *Nieuwsuur* interview in a story titled "WOW! BREAKING=> Julian Assange Suggests Seth Rich – Who Was MURDERED in DC – Was Wikileaks DNC Source!"

From there the Assange-fueled conspiracy theory landed on the front page of The Drudge Report, one of the most visited websites on the English-language internet. Drudge's title read, "It Wasn't the Russians . . . Julian Assange Fingers Murdered DNC Staffer." The *Daily Mail* covered Assange's comments, as did *Sputnik News*, the English-language propaganda site funded by the Russian government; the Ghana News Agency; Iran's Fars government news service; and newspapers from France to New Zealand. The Twitter account for the Chinese Communist Party's youth wing told its four million members, "The sources of the Hillary leaked emails were murdered, one after another? This is the truth of Western democracy!"

This was how a conspiracy theory went viral: a vaguely worded insinuation by a well-known figure found an eager audience on social media; fringe blogs and websites grabbed a few of those posts and compiled them into a story; aggregator sites shared the stories to millions; and mainstream outlets saw the aggregation and treated it like national news. The surest sign that the theories about Seth had reached a critical mass was when Fox News picked them up. For an entire day, from *Fox & Friends* in the morning to Megyn Kelly and Lou Dobbs at night, Fox aired wall-to-wall coverage of Assange's interview and the WikiLeaks reward. Eric Bolling, who was filling in for primetime host Bill O'Reilly, didn't hold back. "There wasn't a robbery," Bolling said. "They weren't even trying to get his information. This was a hit."

Assange's *Nieuwsuur* interview drove so much activity online that the FBI took notice and discussed how it should respond to possible inquiries. A public-affairs employee in the bureau's Washington Field

Office mentioned the widespread coverage of Assange's comments and asked if the agency had any involvement in the Rich homicide investigation. "I'm aware of this reporting from earlier this week," a colleague replied, "but not any specific involvement in any related case."

It was one thing for the claims about Seth to be a meme or a rumor. It was quite another for a national news network—at least in the minds of its viewers—to suggest that he had been murdered because he was Assange's source. Whether they were true or not, whatever dark and disturbing corner of the internet they had crawled out of, the claims had for the first time gone mainstream. And to a powerful class of political professionals, the conspiracy theories about Seth had suddenly become useful. Just as the deaths of people like Vince Foster and Caity Mahoney had been turned into conspiracy theories to be used against Bill Clinton, the baseless claim that a dead DNC staffer was in fact a disillusioned insider who gave stolen emails to WikiLeaks could now be used against Hillary Clinton. Roger Stone—the dapper-dressing, dirty-trick-loving Republican operative who had advised Donald Trump for years—tweeted that Assange's remarks confirmed Seth had a role in the "DNC heist." In another tweet, he included a photo of Seth alongside three other supposed Clinton victims:

> Four more dead bodies in the Clinton's wake. Coincidence? I think not.

———◦———

To anyone who knew Seth well or worked closely with him, the idea that he was a criminal mastermind who had hacked the DNC from the inside was laughable. He sometimes locked himself out of his own email account. A friend had to teach him how to use Twitter. Andrew Therriault had given Seth a book on how to learn a coding language known as Python, but it looked like Seth never opened the book. "He wasn't good enough to grab the data that they think he grabbed to uncover a conspiracy that could not have existed without me knowing about it," Pratt Wiley, his old boss, would later say. "I'm glad people are projecting his skills as superhuman, but that's not the Seth that I paid every week."

The supposed motive for this theoretical crime—that Seth was a Sanders supporter who wanted to expose Clinton's corruption—didn't make sense either. Seth took the DNC's neutrality so seriously he refused to tell his friends or family members which candidate he preferred. (He did make his feelings known about Trump, whom he called a "giant orange baby," according to a friend from high school.) He liked some of the policies Sanders had proposed, he told Mary, but he knew there was no realistic way to pay for all of it. Plus, if he were such a Sanders diehard, why would he have wanted a job on the Clinton campaign? In the event he did have a grievance with the DNC or the Clintons, his parents believed that Seth's patriotism—his love of country and democracy—meant he would have shared those concerns through the appropriate channels, not by committing a massive crime against his own employer.

Aaron watched the Assange clip over and over, first in disbelief, then in anger. He worked for a defense contractor, a job that required him to hold a clearance. Now, for the first time, he felt like he needed to inform his security officer about what was happening online. He feared that if he didn't, it could endanger his clearance.

Reporters from across the country and around the world wanted a reaction to Assange's remarks and the WikiLeaks reward offer. Aaron called Seth's former colleague and mentor Andrew Therriault. "This is getting to be more than we can handle," he said. "We need help." Through some of Seth's former colleagues, the Riches got in touch with a man named Brad Bauman, a PR consultant who had kicked around Democratic politics for years. Bauman had read about Seth's murder but hadn't followed the aftermath. After talking to Joel and Mary on the phone, he couldn't say no to them given what they'd gone through. Figuring he was signing up for a few weeks of pro bono work, he agreed to act as the family's spokesman, and he helped them put out a statement that responded to Assange and asked the public to "refrain from pushing unproven and harmful theories about Seth's murder."

WikiLeaks, for its part, issued its own statement in response to the outcry. "We treat threats towards any suspected WikiLeaks sources with extreme gravity," it said. "This should not be taken to imply that Seth Rich was a source to WikiLeaks or that his murder is connected to our publications." Assange himself continued to stoke the theories. "We don't disclose sources," he said in a different interview, "even dead sources."

The First Good Samaritan

THE TWO CHIPPER morning anchors for the local Fox station in Washington, DC, introduced their next segment. Video clips played showing Seth and the scene of the crime. After a brief recap of the case and reference to Julian Assange's recent comments, the anchors introduced their guest, a man dressed in a sky-blue pinstriped suit and crocodile-skin loafers. Two oversized photos of Seth appeared on the video screens behind him.

"Jack," one of the anchors asked, "why this much and why now?"

It was the morning of September 15, 2016. Two months had passed since the murder. Jack Burkman had come on the show to announce he was offering $100,000 in reward money for information leading to an arrest in the case, bringing the total reward to $145,000 if you included the DC police and WikiLeaks rewards.

"I know people react cynically," Burkman said. "They say, oh, I'm a Republican, so this is anti–Hillary Clinton." But he insisted that wasn't the case. "I'm not here to expound on any kind of conspiratorial theory about Seth Rich or how he died." Burkman said he'd taken an interest in the case because he had seen the police's call for outside help and felt a connection to Seth, saying they were both a part of what he referred to as "the DC political family." Burkman said he imagined his own mother's reaction to the news that he'd been gunned down on the streets of DC and wanted to help in some way.

Near the end of the segment, the anchor asked about Assange's intimation that Rich was WikiLeaks' source. "I don't think you can rule out any theory at this point," Burkman said, "and when you have no theory of the case, how can you rule out any theory of the case?"

———◦———

On a typical day, Burkman could be found in the bar of a drab Marriott hotel in Arlington, Virginia, just across the Potomac River from Washington, DC. He was impossible to miss—a middle-aged man dressed like a Vegas lounge singer from the 1980s, all turtlenecks and loud suits, usually cradling a chocolate Dachshund in his arms. When the dog, Jack Jr., wasn't yapping at the other patrons, he was eating whipped cream out of a bowl at his owner's feet, while Burkman looked on lovingly, cooing at his "baby" as he transacted the day's business.

If you had to guess Burkman's line of work, you might have ventured a personal injury lawyer. He gave off the vibe of someone whose face was plastered across a billboard urging onlookers to *CALL THIS NUMBER NOW!*

Burkman was a hustler of a different variety. He was a registered lobbyist. His firm, J. M. Burkman and Associates, operated out of the northern Virginia townhouse where Burkman lived. He took his meetings at the Marriott. He once bragged to a DC tabloid that he had more clients than any other lobbyist in town, and while the claim was suspect, it was undeniable that his client list was prodigious, the official lobbying records counting upward of seventy different clients as of the summer of 2016. When pressed, Burkman conceded that he erred on the side of overreporting his client base to the lobbying board. Still, if his firm, which employed only a handful of people, earned half of the $3.5 million in revenue it publicly reported in the year 2013, Burkman was doing plenty well for himself.

There were no Fortune 500 companies, trade associations, or prominent individuals on his client list. He represented more nontraditional outfits. One was Desert Lakes University, which had no working phone number and no website and whose only proof of existence was a typo-riddled Facebook page filled with stock images of happy students. The Black Moon Cooperation hired Burkman to lobby NASA and the Pentagon to fund a project that would store human genetic material in a crater on the moon. Burkman's part-time lobbying partner, Ralph Palmieri, described their clients as middle-aged businessmen with a healthy appetite for risk. "They've made some good decisions over the course of time," he said. "And they've made some terrible ones." Ostensibly, these clients hired Burkman to help them navigate the byzantine world of securing government grants and contracts, but his track record was dubious at best.

In the political pecking order, Burkman fell somewhere near the bottom. Though the promise, however elusive, of reaping federal money meant clients kept coming his way, he would never be a K Street power broker or a managing partner at one of the downtown law firms. His talent lay elsewhere—namely, in getting attention. He seemed to get a thrill seeing his name in the newspaper or splashed across the bottom of a television screen. After a brief stint working for then-congressman Rick Lazio in the 1990s, he leveraged his political experience into appearances on Fox News, Bill Maher, and other TV shows to talk about the Clintons and the Whitewater scandal. But the offers to become a full-time TV talking head never materialized, so he took his mother's advice and put his law degree to use.

But he never lost his love of the spotlight. Once he'd started his lobbying business, he launched a radio show called *Behind the Curtain* and bought airtime on a Spanish-language AM station. In 2014, when University of Missouri linebacker Michael Sam became the first openly gay football player drafted by an NFL team, Burkman called a press conference and unveiled a bill he said he was preparing to ban gay NFL players. It was a cruel ploy and a farce: private citizens can't introduce legislation any more than a turkey sandwich can run for president. But the press conference had the intended effect, leading to dozens of news stories and mentions on TV, most of them negative. (Burkman's brother, who is gay, called it "an attention grab and a media grab to pander to those folks who pay him to lobby on their behalf.") But any attention, it seemed, was better than obscurity. No spotlight was too small for Jack Burkman.

He also seemed to grasp that a fundamental change had taken place in how the news media operated. Gone were the days when reporters fought over scarce column inches in a print newspaper that came out once a day. Now, in the internet age, reporters had an endless news hole to fill and were forever in search of something to write about. At the same time, the social-media platforms directed increasing numbers of readers to news outlets whose stories generated buzz, usually by stoking outrage or fear. Burkman may not have been the most impressive lobbyist, but he understood what it took to get attention in the era of endless news.

He eventually hired a publicist, a fellow named Glenn Selig, to find more ways to get him more press clips. One day in the fall of 2016, Selig called Burkman with an idea. Selig had just read a story in the *Washington Post* about the murder of a DNC staffer named Seth Rich. Burkman had seen it too. "Listen, this is an opportunity to get in front of people and increase your exposure," Burkman remembers Selig saying. "Let's come in and offer a reward here."

————◆————

It was a journalist the Riches had come to trust, Joe Morton at their hometown newspaper, the *Omaha World-Herald*, who first mentioned Burkman to them. "An additional $100K reward is kind of inherently newsy," Morton wrote to Bauman, "but this guy Burkman has pulled some odd stunts for publicity in the past and even if he's not totally diving into the conspiracy theories he still seems to be indulging them." Having worked in Washington for fifteen years, Bauman knew a lot of people in town—it was his job to know a lot of people—but somehow, he'd never heard of Jack Burkman.

Joel ran a quick Google search for information about Jack Burkman. He turned up a few hits about his anti-gay NFL stunt and his claim to have the largest book of clients of any lobbyist in Washington.

Other than that, there wasn't much to go on. Burkman did appear to have a knack for publicity and money to spare—the two things Joel, Mary, and Aaron had been told would get them closer to finding Seth's killer and some semblance of closure.

Burkman had put the Riches in an awkward position. He had made his reward announcement without seeking out the family in any way, which meant they never had a chance to consider his offer. Still, lacking resources, cash, and political connections, they made a call that they would later realize was a terrible mistake: they invited Burkman to help with their search for Seth's killer. Burkman repeated the bromides he'd said on his TV appearance—about the political fraternity he and Seth shared, the importance of looking past Democrats and Republicans, that his reward offer had nothing to do with politics. That resonated with Mary because she knew Seth had felt the same way, that whether you were a Democrat or a Republican mattered less than if you cared about the country. He suggested holding a press conference with the family to drum up more publicity; they could also buy bus stop advertisements and distribute flyers in Seth's old neighborhood.

Bauman, the family's press rep, insisted they wait until after the upcoming election to hold any press conference. They didn't want their son's death sucked into the news cycle of the presidential race and politicized by strangers. Surely after the election the controversy around Seth's murder would subside.

7

Through the Looking Glass

Aaron sometimes felt like he was leading two lives. There was his normal day-to-day existence, the one where he went to work each day as an engineer at defense contractor Northrop Grumman, the same company he had worked for since he graduated from college. The company's employees weren't allowed to access certain websites at the office, including any social media platforms. That was fine with Aaron. Unlike his brother, who had dreamt of being famous one day, Aaron valued his privacy. He had a Facebook profile that he rarely updated. He had no interest in sharing every inane detail of his life on Instagram. The appeal of Twitter was a mystery to him, all those rants and half-baked musings tumbling past like some demented ticker-tape machine.

But as the months passed with no breakthroughs in the search for Seth's killer and as the conspiracy theories multiplied, Aaron felt he had no choice but to track what people were saying about his dead brother. Most nights, usually after his wife had gone to bed, he searched for Seth's name on the big social media sites: Twitter, Reddit, Facebook. As he scrolled through the results, his face bathed in the white glow of his oversized computer monitor, he wondered, *What new ridiculousness have they come up with now?*

The most widely circulated theory was the one Julian Assange had introduced, that Seth had hacked his way into the Democratic National

Committee's network and made off with all those emails. For now, Aaron kept this to himself. Joel and Mary were so focused on assisting the police investigation into Seth's murder that they hadn't the first clue what anonymous Trump supporters were saying about Seth online. Even if they had been aware of it, they didn't have any idea how to use Twitter and wouldn't know what Reddit was if you'd asked them about it. His parents had enough to worry about. He didn't want to burden them with the knowledge that, online, Seth's death had taken on a twisted afterlife of its own, and that a significant number of people out there, people who'd never once met his brother, were convinced Seth was a cunning cybercriminal or a brave whistleblower, the next Edward Snowden or Chelsea Manning.

The theory made no sense. But the more time Aaron spent online, the more he worried that facts and logic didn't matter. If enough people kept saying Seth had hacked the DNC and leaked the stolen files to WikiLeaks, or that he'd been "murdered" by Hillary Clinton's henchmen, the sheer repetition of such a lie would create the impression of truth. Each lie kicked up a cloud of dust, and the more the lies spread, the more dust seemed to hang in the sky, blotting out the sun, making it that much harder to see clearly.

———————◆———————

The presidential campaign had entered the final stretch. At around 3:30 p.m. on Friday, October 7, the Department of Homeland Security and the Office of the Director of National Intelligence released a brief statement. Written in government legalese, the statement declared for the first time that the American intelligence community was "confident" the Russian government had orchestrated "the recent compromises of emails from US persons and institutions, including from US political organizations." The hacked emails published first by DCLeaks.com and then by WikiLeaks, the statement continued, were "consistent with the methods and motivations of Russian-directed efforts" and were meant to interfere with the presidential election. It was the strongest indication yet that Russia had orchestrated the DNC attack and funneled its stolen goods through WikiLeaks.

Thirty minutes later another breaking news story appeared. The *Washington Post* had obtained a video of Trump bragging about committing sexual assault during a 2005 appearance on the show *Access Hollywood*. For days the cable news shows played the video over and over. Hundreds of millions of people watched it. The Trump campaign had gotten word about the *Access Hollywood* footage about an hour before the *Post* published it. Candidate Trump was preparing for his second debate with Clinton. He asked each of his top campaign advisers to tell him what chance he had of still winning. Reince Priebus, the Republican National Committee chairman, told Trump he had two choices: "You either drop out right now, or you lose by the biggest landslide in American political history."

Roger Stone had also learned about the *Access Hollywood* video ahead of time. He no longer had an official role in the campaign—Steve Bannon, the campaign chairman, had fired him for being too much of a distraction—but he remained in contact with Trump and others as an unofficial adviser. Months earlier Stone had teased the idea that WikiLeaks had a so-called October surprise in the works, tweeting that it would soon be "Podesta's time in the barrel," a reference to Clinton campaign chairman and longtime Democratic operative John Podesta. Stone had an idea for how to blunt the impact of the *Access Hollywood* tape. Stone called a friend named Jerome Corsi, a ruddy-faced columnist for far-right websites with a track record of peddling conspiracy theories. Corsi had a connection to Assange. As Corsi would later tell federal investigators, Stone wanted WikiLeaks to "drop the Podesta emails immediately."

Half an hour after the *Access Hollywood* video first appeared and an hour after the US government accused Russia of the DNC hack, WikiLeaks tweeted an announcement:

RELEASE: The Podesta Emails #HillaryClinton #Podesta #imWithHer
https://wikileaks.org/podesta-emails/

The link led to a database of what looked to be thousands of private emails stolen from John Podesta's personal email account. Reporters mined the trove for anything that might make news. The emails contained excerpts of speeches Clinton had given to Wall Street firms and big corporations for which she'd been paid hundreds of thousands of dollars. The Clinton campaign had declined to provide the transcripts of those speeches to the media, but now anyone could read them. WikiLeaks highlighted quotes that might damage Clinton—one saying she envisioned a future with "open borders and open markets," another in which she conceded that she was "far removed" from the struggles of the middle class.

For a few days, the *Access Hollywood* story and the release of Podesta's emails by WikiLeaks competed to be the top story in coverage of the campaign. The intelligence community's statement about Russian interference all but disappeared from news coverage. The Podesta emails themselves were now the story.

Rather than release the stolen emails all at once, WikiLeaks parceled them out, posting a new batch every few days during the final weeks of the campaign. Political reporters awaited the latest WikiLeaks drop with giddy anticipation, hoping to be the first to find anything newsworthy and keeping the story alive day after day. The public devoured the coverage of the Podesta emails because they fed into so many of the preexisting criticisms of Clinton—that she was secretive, hypocritical, and corrupt, an elitist who'd spent too long in the spotlight and couldn't care less about the concerns of regular people.

Political reporters weren't the only ones scouring Podesta's emails. Crowdsourced investigations of the emails appeared on Reddit subs like r/Conspiracy, r/HillaryforPrison, and r/WayoftheBern, a pro-Sanders community. On the website 4chan, an unfiltered and more vulgar version of Reddit, an army of users mobilized to launch its own investigation. These armchair sleuths pored over the emails and reported back on any morsel of information that struck them as suspicious, compelling, or just weird. Why, for instance, were there so many references to "pasta" and "pizza"? Were the words code for something else? On a subreddit called r/The_Donald, sprinkled in among the comments about Podesta's emails and the supposed corruption they revealed was a five-word refrain, a mantra meant to give thanks to the man who had exposed this skullduggery: "His name was Seth Rich."

Equal parts clubhouse, staging ground, and viral content workshop, r/The_Donald was the primary gathering place for Trump supporters on the internet—the frothy id of the Make America Great Again movement. "What I'm interested in is letting Donald Trump supporters speak among themselves," a moderator for r/The_Donald told one reporter in early 2016. "That will help them consolidate a stronger position."

Just as Trump had courted Alex Jones in his bid to win the Republican nomination, Trump's campaign saw in r/The_Donald an untapped source of support and viral content. Brad Parscale, Trump's campaign manager, said he visited the subreddit daily, and Trump participated in an "Ask Me Anything" Q-and-A open to any member of r/The_Donald.

Trump's supporters on r/The_Donald called their candidate Trump "God Emperor" and themselves "deplorables," a winking reference to Hillary Clinton's description of Trump supporters (a "basket of deplorables" were her words), and also "centipedes" or "pedes," a nod to a viral YouTube clip that spliced together footage of Trump with a nature video about the prowess of the centipede. The pedes saw themselves as foot soldiers in a "Great Meme War." They flooded online polls using a tactic called "brigading" to make it look like Trump led the race or had won the latest presidential debate. Day and night they churned out memes and videos—shitposting, they called it—that would help hurt Clinton, aka "Killary" and "Klanton." Anyone who abandoned the cause was labeled a "cuck," a play on cuckold, or a "cuckservative."

Conspiracy theories were rampant, from speculation about Hillary Clinton's declining health ("FRAIL HILLARY") to Alex Jones's belief that 9/11 was an inside job. Few conspiracy theories gained as much traction as those having to do with Seth. There were thousands upon thousands of mentions of his name. Many parroted the theory that Assange had seeded and Roger Stone had amplified. When Aaron scanned the seemingly endless list of comments on r/The_Donald, he encountered post after post:

Just a friendly reminder: this man's name is Seth Rich and he was killed by Hillary Clinton.

His name is Seth Rich and he died to hold the corrupt accountable.

REMINDER THAT HIS NAME WAS SETH RICH, AND WE WILL NEVER FORGET HIM.

His name was Seth Rich.

To the members of r/The_Donald, Seth was a martyr, their martyr. To make him into one of their own, they stripped away the facts of his actual life to create a fictional one. Members of r/The_Donald found images of Seth dressed in Stars and Stripes posted on social media by friends and family and turned them into memes with captions such as "Seth Rich is an american hero." One r/The_Donald user posted a selfie wearing an American flag polo shirt on Halloween and said he'd dressed up as Seth. "I wonder if his family has any idea about the amount of love and respect we have for their late son," another user replied. "He should receive honors like fallen soldiers do as he died to protect the country."

It was perplexing and fascinating and maddening all at once. Aaron knew Seth better than anyone else on this earth save his parents; certainly he knew Seth better than any of these Reddit commenters. Yet that didn't stop these anonymous strangers from claiming a brotherhood with Seth, didn't stop them from hoisting up Seth like some kind of hero, an icon.

On election night, Trump's online foot solidiers posted their reactions on r/The_Donald as the results trickled in. At first the mood was grim as Clinton took an early lead. But as the night wore on, the atmosphere changed from anxious to fatalistic to hopeful. By the time Trump took the stage at 2:49 in the morning to declare victory, the pedes were euphoric: in their view, they had shitposted

Trump into the White House, and they were quick to credit their fallen comrade for this stunning victory.

Reddit threads that mentioned Rich earned hundreds of comments and thousands of positive "votes," as users imagined Rich cheering Trump's 290 electoral votes from heaven. "I know we're in the middle of celebrating, but it's important to remember: His name was Seth Rich," one Reddit user wrote. Dozens of people chimed in to pay homage.

"I know your [*sic*] looking down on us," another user wrote. "Love you bro."

8

The Lives of a Few for the Lives of Many

JAMES ALEFANTIS DIDN'T hear his phone ring over the noise of the kitchen. It wasn't uncommon to dine at Comet Ping Pong, a pizzeria in a leafy neighborhood in upper northwest Washington, and spot Alefantis, a trim man in his early forties with curly gray hair and sharp features, working elbow to elbow with the employees on his payroll. Comet was a local institution. With ping-pong tables and kids' games, Comet was intended to be a welcoming place where parents could take their kids for a night out or host a birthday party. In the back of the restaurant was a small stage, where local bands played shows a few nights a week.

It wasn't until nine thirty or ten o'clock that night, November 5, that Alefantis noticed that he had a new voicemail message. A reporter with the local alt-weekly magazine wanted to speak with him. Alefantis called the guy back. "Do you know about this online conspiracy theory that you're running a child-slavery ring out of Comet with Hillary Clinton?" the reporter asked. People were calling it "Pizzagate."

Alefantis said he didn't know anything about it.

"Will you comment on it?" the reporter asked.

The reporter sent Alefantis some of the things he had found online. The posts might as well have been written in a foreign language.

71

Apparently, there were people on the internet who had found an old email of John Podesta's in which Alefantis thanked Podesta for attending a fundraiser at Comet and expressed regret that he couldn't make a pizza for Podesta. Alefantis was dimly aware of the fact that Podesta's emails had been hacked and WikiLeaks had been releasing the emails in an effort to hurt Hillary Clinton. As a native Washingtonian, Alefantis had always kept one foot in the political arena, hosting fundraisers at his restaurants and getting to meet prominent politicians, including the Clintons, through his former boyfriend of more than a decade, the Democratic political consultant David Brock. "I've been through a lot of Washington shit in my life," he would later say. "This is not my first time at the rodeo."

He called the reporter back and gave him a quote for the story. The election was a few days away, and Alefantis blamed this online nonsense on the heat of the moment. "The whole election has really just been insane," he said. "It has everyone on edge and just doing bizarre things." He said the same thing to his young employees after they came to him with their own concerns about what people were saying online about Comet, showing him disturbing online threads about pedophilia, sex trafficking, and satanic rituals. It was unsettling stuff, but it was hard to take seriously, and anyway it would all blow over after the election, Alefantis told his employees. Give it a few days and everything would return to normal.

———◆———

The disturbing theory that would later be dubbed Pizzagate took hold in some of the same places that the Seth Rich conspiracy theories had circulated in—r/The_Donald, 4chan's /pol/, alt-right influencers on Twitter. Pizzagate was a new theory that existed in the same conspiratorial universe, like the latest Marvel franchise full of winking references to earlier movies and character crossovers. To the MAGA movement, Seth was a hero of the 2016 election for leaking all those internal Democratic emails before his death. Pizzagate, in turn, weaponized those emails to spin a violent and horrific tale of a criminal operation run by Democratic Party elites.

One of the earliest seeds of Pizzagate had been sown on October 29, 2016, when a Facebook user named Carmen Katz typed out a fifty-four-word post and shared it with her friends. A few days earlier, James Comey, the FBI director, had announced that the bureau had reopened its investigation of Hillary Clinton's email server after discovering data from that server on a laptop that belonged to Anthony Weiner, the former congressman who was married to Clinton's personal aide, Huma Abedin. The FBI's announcement sent the online rumor mill into a frenzy. Weeks earlier, news had broken that Weiner had sent inappropriate text messages to a fifteen-year-old girl—the same act that had led to his resignation from Congress several years earlier, the same act he had expressed contrition for and had promised that he would never do again.

In her Facebook post, Carmen Katz claimed to have explosive information about the Weiner story, details that implicated not only Weiner but also the Clintons and the mysterious financier and sex abuser Jeffrey Epstein, who had socialized with Bill Clinton:

> My NYPD source said its much more vile and serious than classified material on Weiner's device. The email DETAIL the trips made by Weiner, Bill and Hillary on their pedophile billionaire friend's plane, the Lolita Express. Yup, Hillary has a well documented predilection for underage girls . . . We're talking an international child enslavement and sex ring.

Who was Carmen Katz? Katz's Facebook profile listed her residence as Joplin, Missouri, but there was no record of anyone with that name living in the state of Missouri. To this day, the true identity of "Carmen Katz" remains unknown. However, when *Rolling Stone* reporter Amanda Robb concluded that "Carmen Katz" was almost certainly the work of a sixty-year-old lawyer named Cynthia Campbell who lived in Joplin, Campbell claimed her Facebook account had been hacked. The "Carmen Katz" Facebook page soon vanished. But in the moment, the post was screenshotted and shared on Facebook and Twitter. @DavidGoldbergNY, a Twitter account with a bio that read "Jew, Lawyer & New Yorker," picked up on Katz's post and shared it to thousands more followers with the message, "I have been hearing the same thing from my NYPD buddies too. Next couple days will be interesting!"

@DavidGoldbergNY's tweet alone racked up 6,369 retweets, a runaway success by the metrics of Twitter. It would become one of 1.4 million tweets that mentioned Pizzagate in a five-week span before and after the 2016 election. Yet just like @NimbleNavgater, the vitriolic pro-Trump account that had urged people to amplify the hashtag #HisNameWasSethRich after Julian Assange first mentioned Seth, there was no evidence to connect @DavidGoldbergNY to a real person. No photos, no personal information, nothing.

Pizzagate grew so fast that it soon encompassed multiple strains. There was the Clinton angle, which claimed that Bill and Hillary were secret pedophiles connected to Jeffrey Epstein, the wealthy financier previously convicted of sex trafficking who knew Bill Clinton. Then there was the strain focused on John Podesta and James Alefantis. From the moment WikiLeaks published Podesta's private emails, citizen sleuths on Reddit and 4chan noticed that Podesta talked a lot about pizza; one email mentioned a pizza-themed handkerchief of Podesta's. The reason for this was simple enough: Podesta was an avid chef and foodie who loved Italian food. But knowing that pedophiles often used the phrase "cheese pizza" as code for "child pornography" to evade law enforcement, Redditors and 4channers decided that mentions of "pizza" in Podesta's emails were code for child porn. An anonymous 4chan user posted a list of other supposed code words to search for in Podesta's emails—"pasta" meant little boy, "ice cream" meant male prostitute, "sauce" meant orgy. Soon the hashtag #Pizzagate had gone viral.

Pizzagate embodied the new style of conspiracy theory. It was violent, horrific, painful to contemplate. It didn't merely accuse its targets of secret dealings; it painted them as sadistic predators guilty of the worst crimes imaginable: crimes against children. In the mind of a Pizzagate believer, stopping these evil elites was a matter of life and death.

Alefantis was targeted because of a 2008 email included in the WikiLeaks dump in which Alefantis asked Podesta if he would give a speech at an Obama fundraiser at the Comet Ping Pong pizzeria. From there the trolls began mining every detail they could find about Alefantis and Comet, concocting an elaborate theory that Alefantis,

Podesta, and Clinton ran a child-sex-trafficking ring out of the pizzeria. The claims built on themselves. The symbols on Comet's iconic sign (which had previously been used by a DC liquor store that had since closed) were linked to satanic rituals. A photo of an empty walk-in refrigerator was evidence of a secret kill room.

How much of this activity was coming from real people and how much of it wasn't? Social media experts who studied Pizzagate found that it was shared repeatedly by accounts that tweeted hundreds of times a day as well as accounts with names like @NIVIsa4031 that had amassed huge followings in a short span of time—telltale signs that automated accounts, better known as bots, had been used to amplify a message and give it the liftoff needed to go viral.

In other words, if you checked Facebook or Twitter in the fall of 2016, what you were seeing was not an organic outburst of concern and anger about sadistic activity at a pizzeria in Washington, DC. But for James Alefantis, on the receiving end of this online activity, the question of whether the flood of mentions of his restaurant were from real people didn't make much of a difference. He only wanted to know how to respond and whether the insanity would go away.

But Pizzagate did not blow over after the election as Alefantis believed it would. Instead, it got worse. Violent messages poured into Comet's Instagram and Facebook accounts:

I will kill you personally

I truly hope someone blows your brains all over comet pizza

Are you scared yet? You should be motherfucker because were [*sic*] coming for you

You need to be raped killed and tortured like you do to children u sick fuck . . . ur days of freedom are numbers u evil douche

The home addresses and phone numbers for Alefantis and his employees were published online, a form of harassment called "doxing." Strangers filmed Alefantis's house and questioned his neighbors. Photos of children that he'd shared on his personal Instagram, like his godchildren playing in Comet or eating their first slice of pizza, were turned into evidence of criminal activity, the photos copied and repurposed on Reddit threads and in YouTube videos—in the name of "protecting the children," the Pizzagate believers were publishing children's names and images all over the internet. Comet received so many menacing calls—at one point up to 150 a day—that Alefantis unplugged the phone. People wrote reviews on Comet's Yelp page claiming they'd found chopped-up baby parts in their food.

Mike Cernovich, the alt-right influencer, pushed Pizzagate on his blog and to his two hundred thousand Twitter followers. Jack Posobiec, a former Navy Reserve intelligence officer who had become a zealous Trump supporter, decided to go investigate Comet for himself one evening a few weeks after the election. Livestreaming his visit, Posobiec and a friend ordered garlic knots and beer, but when Posobiec tried to gain entry to a child's birthday party, an employee asked him and his friend to leave. Overnight Posobiec became a folk hero to the Pizzagaters, his ejection from the restaurant reaffirming their belief that something evil was going on at Comet.

Few people did more to amplify Pizzagate than Alex Jones. The 2016 election had caused the size of Jones's audience to soar. For decades Jones had raged and ranted against the Clintons and the dead enemies and lovers they had left in their wake. Pizzagate fit perfectly into Jones's disturbed worldview. Infowars published ten different videos about it in November and December 2016. "When I think about all the children Hillary Clinton has personally murdered and chopped up and raped, I have zero fear standing up against her," Jones said in one video.

As the threats directed at Comet became more violent, Alefantis called the DC police. They weren't interested, so he tried the FBI. A pleasant-sounding person answered the phone and seemed to know what Pizzagate was, but Alefantis explained it anyway. He knew he sounded crazy, talking about pizza-themed code words, satanic images, secret tunnels and basements. The FBI blew him off too. "They were essentially like, 'If you get a specific threat, let us know. Thank you. Goodbye.'"

Alefantis needed a lawyer. After calling friends, he found himself on the phone with a partner at a big Washington firm. She told him that he probably had a defamation case but that her firm specialized in *defending* clients in such cases, not bringing them. But there was one lawyer she could recommend. She had argued against him in a recent defamation suit and lost but had come away impressed with his abilities and his professionalism. "His name is Mike Gottlieb," she said. "He'll be surprised that I recommended you."

———◆———

Two weeks after the election, Mike Gottlieb was reading the *New York Times* when a story caught his eye. Comet Ping Pong, a local pizzeria, had come under "constant assault" because of a conspiracy theory about a supposed sex dungeon in the restaurant's basement. "It's like trying to shoot a swarm of bees with one gun," Comet's general manager told the *Times*. At the time, Gottlieb and his wife lived not far from Comet. He had been to the restaurant more times than he could count since moving to DC more than a decade ago. *Why would anyone start a conspiracy theory about my local pizza place*, he wondered.

But Gottlieb's interest in Pizzagate was more than personal. He had recently undergone an awakening of his own about conspiracy theories and the people who peddle them.

A month before the 2016 election, lawyers with the Democratic Party had asked Gottlieb and several other litigators at his firm if they wanted to join a volunteer legal team that was trying to stop voter suppression efforts in multiple states. Gottlieb didn't think twice. He knew that any judge would be reluctant to grant a restraining order so close to the election, so these cases presented a considerable challenge to litigate.

The legal team Gottlieb had joined chose a somewhat novel strategy to convince judges to block possible acts of voter intimidation. During the post–Civil War period known as Reconstruction, the Klan and other white supremacist groups had terrorized free Black people and their allies to prevent them from voting. Congress responded by passing the Ku Klux Klan Act of 1871, which made it illegal to deny citizens their civil and political rights through intimidation or violence under the newly passed Fourteenth Amendment. As the Klan Act evolved over time, it allowed for lawsuits against public officials and private figures who conspired to stop any citizen from exercising their right to vote.

Gottlieb was familiar with the Klan Act, as it had been his senior debate topic in college. As evidence for potential lawsuits streamed in, Gottlieb encountered what felt like a parallel universe of information and news. He discovered far-right online personalities like Mike Cernovich, who had reached hundreds of millions of people with conspiracy theories about the Clintons, Pizzagate, and Seth Rich. Gottlieb saw how, for months, Stone had raised the specter of widespread fraud or a "stolen" election should Trump lose, and an entire conspiracy theory echo chamber had revved to life around "stop the steal," with Cernovich, Alex Jones and Infowars, and r/The_Donald all promoting it.

Gottlieb lingered over one conspiracy theory in particular. It claimed that busloads of illegal voters were pouring into New Hampshire in a ploy to tip the state in Clinton's favor. To stop this crime-in-progress, people had stationed themselves at different spots along the New Hampshire–Massachusetts state line with the intention of documenting and stopping any inbound buses that looked suspicious. Gottlieb knew that stoking fears about voter fraud happened in every election, part of a game the two political parties played. The Democrats looked for ways to maximize turnout and called it "voter protection," and the Republicans tried to depress turnout in unfriendly places and called it "voter integrity." But the conservative lawyers that Gottlieb knew usually acknowledged sotto voce that while some fraud did occur, it wasn't a widespread issue and it certainly wasn't changing the outcomes of elections.

But the people posted at the New Hampshire border? They honestly believed a massive crime was about to take place. They had their cameras ready to document the busloads of illegal voters streaming into their state. That was the part that was mind-boggling to Gottlieb. He struggled to find the words for it, but he could feel it, the alternate channel of information that previously had been relegated to the tin-foil-hat-wearing fringe had gone mainstream.

Stone's Stop the Steal group had spread the message that Clinton would steal the election with voting by "illegals," while Stone himself tweeted that Democratic voters should cast their ballots "the NEW way" by texting "HILLARY to 8888." Stone's group had also put out a call online for "Vote Protectors" to stand guard at polling places and for volunteers to conduct unofficial "exit polls" in nine Democratic-leaning cities.

Gottlieb understood the challenge in trying to apply civil rights legislation about the Klan to modern election tactics. In the preinternet days, voter suppression took the form of off-duty cops with guns and two-way radios harassing Black and Hispanic voters outside of a polling place, or inner-city machine bosses pressuring neighbors on how to vote. In those scenarios you only had to find three witnesses to sign an affidavit saying they felt threatened, their rights violated. But what about a guy with twenty thousand Twitter followers who had posted a picture of a pickup truck with a cage built into the bed alongside the message "We gonna be watch'n fer shenanigans . . . & haul ya away"? "A lot of the challenge was adapting the old voter intimidation case law and statutes to this environment where so much was happening on social media," Gottlieb would later say. The federal voter intimidation laws, he concluded, were designed to prevent what Stone was doing. If Stone had been standing outside of a polling place screaming in people's faces about texting in their vote, the case would be a no-brainer. The only difference was he had chosen to spread his message online to a far larger audience.

On October 30, the DNC and the Clinton campaign, represented by Gottlieb and several others, filed lawsuits in four states against Stone, Stop the Steal Inc., Donald Trump, and state Republican parties, alleging a violation of the Klan Act and asking the courts to issue a temporary restraining order against Stone's group. The lawsuits had mixed results. They had won an order in Nevada that blocked the state Republican Party from letting its poll watchers use intimidating tactics at polling places. But in most of the states where they sued, Gottlieb encountered skeptical judges. The judges didn't disagree about the nature of the evidence, all those tweets and Facebook posts included in Gottlieb's complaints, but they also said it wasn't enough to merely use somebody's tweet as evidence of voter intimidation—there needed to be hard, physical evidence to back it up.

At one hearing in Philadelphia, Gottlieb brought forward Pastor Mark Kelly Tyler to speak to the effects of Republican voter intimidation. Tyler, who led one of Philadelphia's oldest Black churches, described the "chill" he felt when he heard Trump say the only way he'd lose the election was if "cheating goes on." But under questioning from Gottlieb and the Trump campaign's lawyers, Pastor Kelly couldn't say the rhetoric from Stone had had any personal effect on him other than leading him to decide not to bring his young daughters to the polls with him on Election Day.

Gottlieb spent the rest of the hearing facing tough questions from US District Court judge Paul Diamond about whether the injunction he sought was too broad and whether it would violate Trump's and Stone's constitutional rights. Gottlieb also had to contend with accusations from the opposing lawyers that his lawsuit was little more than a publicity stunt meant to rile up the public on the eve of a presidential election. Diamond gave Gottlieb the final word. "This is not a suit intended to inflame public opinion," he told the judge. "It is a suit intended to protect the right to vote and to make sure when people come to the polls tomorrow they are not intimidated and they are not sent away . . . by people who are out acting as vigilantes." Judge Diamond said he would issue a ruling later that day.

After the hearing Gottlieb caught a train up to New York City to meet his wife for dinner. On his way he received word of Judge Diamond's decision: the judge had refused to issue a restraining order on Stone and the Trump campaign, handing Gottlieb another defeat. The volume of online evidence was wholly unconvincing, the judge wrote, adding that the allegations put forward by Gottlieb and the other lawyers "appear intended to generate only heat, not light."

Gottlieb and his wife ate at an Italian restaurant across from Central Park. The election dominated their dinner conversation. Like many, he believed Clinton would win. But the last few weeks had left

Gottlieb despondent about the state of the country. The fact that 44 or 45 percent of the country believed Donald Trump should be president was by itself sufficiently terrifying to Gottlieb. Even if Clinton won, how could she govern after everything that had happened in the campaign? "People do not understand what has changed in this country," he told his wife.

He felt like he'd been smacked in the face in those two weeks before the election. "It was just shock," he would later say. "I didn't quite know how to explain it to people. I just don't think people appreciated at that time how much of a parallel reality there was that had been created and how impenetrable it was." He couldn't help but feel fatalistic about the election. What he had seen online left him shaken. No matter who won, the country was in a far more precarious state than a lot of people in their circles realized. "There's something fundamentally broken in our democratic system," he told his wife, "that I don't know how we get fixed."

Gottlieb spent election night in New York. A feeling of dread settled in. He recalled Trump's 2015 interview on Infowars, the one where Trump praised Alex Jones for his "amazing" reputation. *We are about to have an Infowars president*, Gottlieb thought.

———◆———

A month after the election, in early December, James Alefantis of Comet Ping Pong wandered into the lobby of Boies Schiller Flexner to meet Gottlieb for the first time. Alefantis took a liking to Gottlieb right away. He had all the credentials one could ever want in a lawyer: a two-time national debate champion in college, he graduated from Harvard Law, clerked for Justice John Paul Stevens of the Supreme Court, did two stints in the Obama White House, and made partner at a major white-shoe law firm before he turned forty.

Yet Gottlieb wore his success lightly. He had grown up in Lawrence, Kansas, the son of two professors. Harvard Law had rejected him the first time he applied and wait-listed him the second time, so when he finally got in he had a sizeable chip on his shoulder. He had almost quit law shool because he found his classmates' obsession with their perfect grades and private school credentials insufferable. But even if he didn't fit in, Heather Gerken, one of his professors and a renowned constitutional law expert, knew that Gottlieb had it "in his bones" to be a superb lawyer. And unlike so many other students before him, he didn't take it for granted, which endeared him to Gerken even more. "I loved him for his modesty and humility, that he didn't just assume he was going to be the greatest lawyer in the room, even if it was clear to me he was going to be."

Gerken helped Gottlieb get a clerkship with Judge Stephen Reinhardt, who sat on the Ninth Circuit federal appeals court in San Francisco. Reinhardt "was the greatest fighter of lost causes you've ever known," Gerken would later say. She saw in Gottlieb many of the same qualities she admired in Reinhardt. "Judge Reinhardt was a combination of a cynic and an optimist. So is Mike," she would later say. "Both of them are incredibly cynical about the world, but they still find in themselves an ability to keep fighting."

Gottlieb wasn't looking for new clients when Alefantis first called him. But after reading about Pizzagate and listening to Alefantis's story, Gottlieb thought back to what he had seen during the election lawsuits. Pizzagate was a continuation of the conspiracy theories and the sneaky disinformation that had clouded the election. This was another chance to use the legal system to counter those smears and help a victim clear his name. "Of course we'll do this," Gottlieb told him.

Gottlieb said he was leaving for Taiwan shortly thereafter for client meetings. "Let's talk next week after I get back," he said.

On his flight overseas, Gottlieb pulled out his laptop and opened a zip file full of Pizzagate videos. He recognized some of the players involved from his election litigation work. The more he read about it, the more he came to see Pizzagate as a case study of all the things he had witnessed leading up to the election. Now, after Trump's victory, he feared that people like James Alefantis would get trampled by the Alex Joneses of the world, who could say and do whatever they wanted.

Gottlieb watched one Pizzagate video after another, taking notes as he went. A lot of what Jones and his minions said was hyperbole or opinion, statements like "I think this . . ." or "Isn't that suspicious?"

Even a factual-sounding comment like "These guys are satanists" was something a court might treat as opinion. But there were dozens of statements by Jones or others that were undeniably, verifiably false. Like when they said Comet had art on its walls that showed people raping and eating babies. Or the video in which Joe Biggs, an Infowars staffer, tried to pass off a fake Comet menu from which supposed VIPs could order different types of children.

Gottlieb watched so many Pizzagate videos that they began to play tricks on his mind. He could feel himself becoming entranced by it. Maybe it was the altitude, or being stuck in an aluminum tube for what felt like forever, or the minimal access to the outside world. He started to appreciate that these videos were like a powerful drug—the more you watched, the more addictive they were. And if the viewers of these videos shut themselves off from the world and binged only Alex Jones clips on YouTube, he understood how they came to believe what Jones said.

———— ◆ ————

A few days later, on the morning of December 5, Edgar Maddison Welch loaded up his Toyota Prius and drove north on I-95. He wore a blue hoodie, a pair of jeans, work boots, and a thick wool beanie over a flop of hair. Welch was in his late twenties and lived in Salisbury, North Carolina. He'd experienced tragedy at a young age: when he was eight, his sixteen-year-old brother died in a car crash. His family's home was a welcoming one: his parents ran a no-kill dog shelter out of their house and cared for several foster children over the years. Welch attended a community college in Wilmington, an hour's drive away, but struggled with addiction and checked into rehab. He moved back to "Smallsbury," as he called it, married young, and had two daughters. But by 2016 the marriage had faltered, and Welch's career prospects were grim.

He spent more and more time online, watching YouTube videos and becoming obsessed with Pizzagate. He texted his girlfriend and told her what he was learning made him "sick." He encouraged his friends to go on YouTube and do their own research. One friend texted him, "Sounds like we r freeing some oppressed pizza from the hands of an evil pizza joint." But Pizzagate wasn't funny to Welch.

He asked a friend who'd served in the army if he had any army buddies nearby who were "down for the cause." Depended on the cause, the friend texted back. Welch responded with a long message that read like a manifesto:

> Raiding a pedo ring, possibly sacraficing the lives of a few for the lives of many. Standing up against a corrupt system that kidnaps, tortures and rapes babies and children in our own backyard . . . defending the next generation of kids, our kids, from ever having to experience this kind of evil themselves I'm sorry bro, but I'm tired of turning the channel and hoping someone does something and being thankful it's not my family. One day it will be our families. The world is too afraid to act and I'm too stubborn not to

Not one of his friends would join him. Fine, he would go alone.

On the drive to Washington, Welch recorded a message to his daughters. "I can't let you grow up in a world that's so corrupted by evil," he said. "I have to at least stand up for you and for other children just like you." He told his family he loved them and that he hoped to tell them again how much he loved them. "And if not," he added, "don't ever forget it."

Welch parked his car up the street from Comet, grabbed the AR-15 rifle he'd brought with him, and entered the restaurant. An employee was retrieving some frozen pizza dough from a freezer in the alley behind Comet when he heard three loud bangs. They sounded like gunfire, but he wasn't sure and walked back into the restaurant, where he saw Welch, his AR-15 pointing in his direction.

———◆◆———

By the time Alefantis rushed over to Comet, the entire block of Connecticut Avenue, one of the busiest streets in Washington, DC, was cordoned off with yellow police tape. Every business on the street was locked down, patrons and employees sheltering until the police gave the all clear.

Moments earlier Welch had walked out of Comet with his hands in the air and surrendered to the police in the middle of the avenue.

"What were you doing in the location?" an officer asked Welch as he lay facedown in the street, hands cuffed behind his back.

"Making sure there's nothing there," Welch replied.

"Regarding what?"

"Pedophile ring."

"Regarding *what*?" the officer asked again.

"Pedophile ring."

"*Pizzagate*," a second officer said. "He's talking about *Pizzagate*."

Alefantis's staff evacuated to the fire station up the block. No one was hurt. Many were in shock. Alefantis would later learn that Welch had fired three rounds into a locked door, perhaps believing it led to the secret basement chambers used for child sex trafficking in the Pizzagate mythology. In reality the door opened to a small closet where Alefantis stored bags, coats, and some computer equipment.

Once Alefantis had made sure his employees were safe, he wondered what he should do next. Reporters were calling him. The DC mayor and chief of police were on their way for a press conference. Alefantis felt paralyzed. Then he remembered: he had a lawyer.

9

She Who Fights Monsters

FROM THE STREETS below, the glass-and-stone office at 555 Fourth Street Northwest in Washington was an intimidating presence. If you were a criminal—whether a gang member or a crooked congressman—the US Attorney's Office for the District of Columbia was the last place you wanted to go. To the people who worked on one of the building's eleven floors, the "Triple Nickel," as it was known, held a unique distinction. Because the District of Columbia has no district attorney, the office is the only one of the Justice Department's ninety-four US attorneys' offices with jurisdiction over both federal and local crimes. Ivy Leaguers in bespoke suits working paper cases in Public Integrity or Appellate rode the elevator next to hardened prosecutors in the Sex Crimes, Domestic Violence, or Homicide Sections. On any given day, one set of lawyers might be arguing a national security case in the federal courthouse down the street while another team tried a triple murder in DC Superior Court a few blocks away.

By virtue of its location in the nation's capital, the office attracted more than its share of ambitious litigators on their way to bigger things. Robert Mueller, the future FBI director, did a stint as a line prosecutor in the Homicide Section. Eric Holder ran the office in the 1990s on his way to becoming the first Black US attorney general under President Obama.

Deborah Sines had worked with Mueller and Holder. She liked both men, knew their wives. She had no plans to follow in their footsteps. She had little patience for playing office politics to land a more powerful job. "Deb," Holder had said to her when he left the office, "you're a great lawyer and a lousy revolutionary." What she cared about most was solving murders.

Sines had worked in Homicide for nearly two decades, taking some of the toughest cases involving the grisliest crimes. She was something of a legend in the halls of the Triple Nickel, adored by some and loathed by others. She had a closet full of Converse high-tops in her cluttered office, and each day she picked out a pair to wear that matched her Brooks Brothers pantsuit. In her "fuck-me heels" that she wore to court she stood maybe five-four, but in the eyes of a jury she was a foot taller, so commanding was her presence. She listened to hip-hop to pump herself up before a trial and smoked Marlboro Golds afterward. She talked like a character out of *Law & Order* or *The Wire*. "I used to know a drug dealer named Perfect," began one story of hers. "Nothing about him was perfect. He wasn't even good at drug-dealing."

Her office's unique jurisdiction meant Sines worked closely with Washington's Metropolitan Police Department (MPD). The homicide detectives loved to hang out in her office because she talked like they did and she wasn't afraid to take cases where the evidence wasn't great and a conviction wasn't a sure thing. On the walls of her office she displayed a poster from a case she'd tried against Ku Klux Klan members and a framed *Washington Post* story about her work. When detectives interviewed potential witnesses in Sines's office, they used that story—"Killers Fear This Woman" was the title—to pressure people to cooperate.

In late 2016, she recalled, a detective came to her office. He was the lead investigator on the Rich homicide investigation. With all the rumors circulating online about the murder, the case had turned into a circus. He said he needed help. Sines listened to the detective explain what had happened. Behind her hung a plaque engraved with a Nietzsche quote: "Whoever fights monsters should see to it that in the process he does not become a monster. And if you gaze long enough into an abyss, the abyss will gaze back into you."

———◆———

Sines had seen more than her share of monsters.

Since joining Homicide in the mid-1990s, she had prosecuted some of the most notorious killers in the District of Columbia's history. There was Azariah Israel, a notorious serial murderer who belonged to a violent gang known as the Clifton Terrace University or CTU Crew that had terrorized northwest Washington for years. Israel committed his first murder at the age of fourteen, spent years in prison, and resumed killing as soon as he got out, shooting a 7-Eleven clerk with a shotgun and stabbing a man to death outside a busy nightclub. Israel and his crew hunted down and killed people whom they believed had cooperated with the authorities as witnesses. When Israel's name landed on Sines's desk, it was for the 2004 murder of a man who had testified before a grand jury about another member of the CTU crew.

One Friday evening Sines got back to her office to grab a few things and saw the voicemail light was blinking. *Shit*, she thought to herself, *I haven't checked my office phone all week*. She dialed in and heard a man's voice she didn't recognize. "Let me tell you something. We will kidnap your son today," he said. Sines felt her hands tremble as the message played. "And if you think about going to motherfucking trial, we will kill you."

She listened to the message again. She made sure not to delete it even as her hands kept shaking. After a decade on the job, she had lost count of the number of times someone had vowed to kill her, or one of her witnesses, or a detective she worked with, or one of her fellow prosecutors. In her line of work, death threats were a routine occupational hazard. But no one had ever threatened her family. They weren't supposed to know she *had* a son.

She checked the date on the voicemail message: it had been left on Thursday night. She hadn't talked to her twenty-three-year-old son

Josh since before then. She tried his phone; no answer. Then she called her boss, Glenn Kirschner, the chief of the Homicide Section. "I think they kidnapped Josh," she said. Within minutes Kirschner and several agents with the FBI and the US Marshals had crowded into her office. She reached one of her son's friends, who said he'd talked to Josh the night before. Eventually Josh answered the phone—he'd been cleaning his bathtub before a date later that night—and was quickly picked up by a pair of detectives and brought to his mother's office.

Sines, her son, the detectives, and the agents were still in her office deciding what to do when the phone rang again. She answered it and put it on speakerphone. "We are gonna get your ass," he said before hanging up. It was the same voice from the message. Sines looked around the room and asked, "Any questions?"

Not for the first time, Sines was assigned a security detail of US Marshals to guard her around the clock. Her elderly live-in mother and Josh got their own details. Sines normally rode the subway to work, but now plain-clothed agents drove her in an armored black truck with thick windows she couldn't lower. At night marshals sat parked outside her old brick row house. They put Josh up at a corporate apartment with a fireplace for a few weeks for his own protection. Josh loved it: he told his mom the marshals helped him pick up women everywhere he went. "For me it's just not conducive to getting laid," Sines said. "I'll just leave it like that."

That spring Sines won jury verdicts against Israel and one of his lieutenants in three successive trials for murder and other related charges. (It later came out that a witness in the case had hired someone to make the threatening calls to Sines.) A judge sentenced Israel to more than two hundred years in prison.

Then there was Banita Jacks, a DC mother who had killed her four daughters, stabbing the eldest one and strangling the younger three, then leaving their remains in their bedrooms. US Marshals eventually discovered the girls' decomposed bodies. Sines led the prosecution in the Jacks case. Before he sentenced Jacks to 120 years in prison, the presiding judge said the case "will probably haunt me for the rest of my life." Sines also worked one of DC's most infamous triple homicides, the execution-style slaying of three employees at the Colonel Brooks Tavern, and she secured a guilty plea in the high-profile cold case of Pamela Butler, a middle-aged Black computer specialist for the federal government who vanished in 2009.

The stress of the job and the long hours were hell on Sines's marriage. She and her husband eventually divorced, and afterward she raised their two kids mostly on her own. One time, she brought her five-year-old daughter to a crime scene. Another time, her son overheard her rehearsing before a trial in the basement bathroom and gently corrected her pronunciation of "motherfucker." "White people say it wrong," he told her. (Sines's ex-husband was Black and her children biracial.) "You have to put the emphasis on 'mother.'" He was twelve at the time.

By the fall of 2016, Sines was one of the most senior homicide prosecutors in the office. Her boss assigned her the toughest cases, the ones that were high profile and politically sensitive: homicides of three or more people, cops who killed people, people who killed cops. She had two cold cases from the '80s that no other prosecutor had managed to crack. The case that had lately consumed her was one of the most well-known unsolved murders in the country: the death of Chandra Levy, a twenty-four-year-old intern who had disappeared in 2001 and whose skeletal remains were found a year later in Washington's Rock Creek Park.

The search for Levy's killer had captivated the country. Rumors that she had had an affair with her hometown congressman, Gary Condit, gave the story a tabloid-like appeal and launched the careers of lowbrow TV hosts like Nancy Grace. (Condit publicly denied having any relationship with Levy.) An informant eventually led the police to a twenty-year-old former gang member from El Salvador named Ingmar Guandique who had admitted to attacking two other women in the same park where Levy's body was found. For more than a decade, prosecutors built their case against Guandique and then tried him in court, only for the case to fall apart because of unreliable witnesses or procedural mistakes. In 2015, Sines and a team of federal prosecutors were picked for the government's second trial against Guandique for

Levy's murder. Sines had spent much of 2015 and 2016 building her case against Guandique. But three months before the case was set to go to trial, it collapsed. A woman had come forward with hours of recordings that she had secretly made of a key witness in the prosecution's case against Guandique. On the recordings the witness, Armando Morales, said he was angling to get rich from his cooperation in the Levy case by selling his story to Hollywood.

The US government dropped its charges against Guandique and deported him back to El Salvador. "When I had to move to dismiss that case, I was so fucking angry after all that work," Sines would later say. Her bosses suggested she take some time off. She refused. They then demanded she go on a vacation, and she reluctantly agreed. Her younger brother offered up his place near Daytona Beach, and she crashed there and visited the ocean every day, trying to forget about the year of her life she'd lost preparing for a trial that now would never happen.

Refreshed, tan, and still angry about the Levy case, she reported back to work a few weeks later. The new head of Homicide, Michelle Jackson, told Sines she was giving her a new assignment. Like the Levy murder, this new one had attracted its share of cranks and conspiracy theorists. It had turned into a circus, really, and the detective on the case, a by-the-books type named Joe Della-Camera, needed help. The decedent's name was Seth Conrad Rich.

When she picked up a new homicide case, Sines liked to start her investigation with fresh eyes. She had discussed the Rich case with the primary detective, but she chose not to read any of the reports he had written so far. She wanted to see the evidence for herself.

She began with the autopsy report. It described two gunshot wounds to the lower torso, which caused internal bleeding and damage to his vital organs. The autopsy also noted bruising on Seth's hands and face. Signs, perhaps, of a struggle with his assailants. Next Sines read the ballistics report. There were no shell casings found at the crime scene. That made it more likely the murder weapon was a revolver, which typically doesn't eject spent shell casings, though it was possible the killers had scooped up the casings before they fled.

The main case file said there was no DNA evidence or fingerprints found at the crime scene. Despite the shooting happening in a densely packed urban neighborhood, there wasn't much surveillance footage to draw on. The best she had was a brief clip pulled from a security camera inside a nearby bodega. The footage was grainy. She could see the legs of a white man in shorts—Seth—step into the intersection of W and Flagler Streets. Two other men in jeans and sneakers approached him. There was a brief scuffle, then Seth fell to the ground and the two other individuals ran away. The whole incident lasted a minute or less.

Right away Sines knew this case would be a difficult one. The evidence was scant. The bodega's security-camera footage was inconclusive. And she had dealt with DC's criminal underclass for long enough to know that turning a witness, let alone securing a confession, meant puncturing the code of silence demanded by the local criminal networks. Washington didn't have big gangs like Los Angeles or Chicago. Instead it tended to have smaller, tight-knit crews that each laid claim to their own pocket of DC—the 8th and R crew, the 7th and O crew. In this world snitching to the cops could get you killed.

A decade earlier Sines would have urged the police to send a vice unit into the neighborhood where Seth was shot and arrest people caught with illegal drugs or guns. Once the vice squad was done with its interviews, the cold-case detectives would step in, advise those who'd been arrested of their rights, and ask them, "Do you know anything about any murders?" But criminal-justice activists had criticized the use of vice squads for unfairly targeting minority citizens, and then-MPD chief Cathy Lanier said she believed the vice teams had outlived their usefulness. In 2015, under Lanier's leadership, the MPD dissolved the vice units in each of the department's seven police districts and incorporated them into a centralized narcotics team. Some DC residents lamented the move, with one telling a reporter that "taking away the vice squads with ears to the ground is a detriment to our safety."

Losing the vice squads took away one of Sines's best tools for solving murders. She would have to find other ways of obtaining street-level information on who might have killed Seth. One option was retracing Seth's walk home from Lou's City Bar in the early-morning hours of July 10. Why had it taken him so long? Had someone seen him in his inebriated state and followed him? Had he wandered through a drug deal? If she could piece together Seth's route and where he might have caught the eye of an attacker, then maybe she could find a suspect.

10

Code Purple

WITH THE ELECTION over, Joel and Mary booked flights back to Washington for their press conference with Jack Burkman. As they boarded the plane in Omaha in late November, they still had questions about Burkman. Why was this stranger so invested in finding Seth's killer? How rich *was* this guy that he could put up $100,000 in additional reward money? When Burkman first suggested the idea of a press conference, Joel, Mary, and Brad Bauman feared Burkman might try to use it as a publicity stunt, tapping into the wall-to-wall coverage of the election to get his name in the news. Joel and Mary said they would agree to the press conference only if it happened after the election. To their surprise Burkman agreed. "I want to be careful to keep this out of politics," he wrote in an email to Joel. Even Bauman was pleasantly surprised.

They held the event at a park a few blocks from where Seth was shot. "Today is not a happy day, it's a somber day, and it's a day for memorializing Seth," Burkman said, speaking first. But it was a hopeful day, he continued, "in that today we really continue in earnest the search for Seth's killer." He gestured to the press in attendance. "It's only through the media—local, national, international, wherever these people may be—that someone can come forward and tell us what they know," he said.

After the press conference ended, Joel and Mary drove downtown to meet with DC mayor Muriel Bowser. She reassured them that the police were doing everything they could. "This is my city," the mayor said. Mary wasn't convinced. "You're damn right it's your city," she said. "And my son was murdered in your city."

Joel, Mary, and a small group of volunteers canvassed Seth's neighborhood. They passed out flyers with Seth's photo and the new $125,000 reward included on them and asked that anyone with information come forward and call the detectives on the case. But when Joel himself called Detective Della-Camera's phone that weekend, the voicemail box was unable to accept new messages. Upset that they might have lost out on potential tips, Joel sent a terse email to the family's liaison in the mayor's office. "I was appalled that the voicemail was full," he fumed. "The objective is to make it easy for someone to report a tip."

It was a small thing, the snafu over Della-Camera's voicemail, but it added to the frustration and despair the Riches felt about the progress of the investigation. The police had yet to announce a suspect or locate an eyewitness; the Riches didn't even know Deb Sines had taken the case. The DC police chief who had vowed to "find the bastards" had left MPD. Della-Camera kept the family updated as much as he could, but Joel and Mary knew that the chances of solving the murder dwindled the longer the case dragged on, and they couldn't help but second-guess whether the police did enough in that period of time just after the murder. Officers had distributed flyers and canvassed the neighborhood within twenty-four to thirty-six hours of the crime, but did they search a two-block radius or did they go a mile? The police knew there was a gun involved, so why weren't more gun-sniffing dogs used?

Joel and Mary were thankful for Burkman's help, but Bauman was starting to have doubts. As he replayed the press conference with Burkman in his mind, he began to have suspicions about him too. Little things like the way he had carefully spelled his name for the reporters in attendance. Or how he'd referred to the "local, national, international" media. International? Was Burkman suggesting Seth's killer had fled the country? Or that the killers weren't American in the first place? The police had always treated the murder as a local matter.

But what irked Bauman the most was the way Burkman had identified himself. "I represent, very proudly, the Rich family," he'd said at the press conference. They had not hired Burkman; he was not their lawyer or their agent; and in the weeks that followed, Burkman continued to describe himself to reporters as a representative of the family or the family's lawyer when, in fact, neither of those things was true.

These representations had also irritated Aaron, who had taken a skeptical view of Burkman from the day he'd first contacted the family. But Mary was adamant: they needed Burkman's help. She kept going back to what Cathy Lanier, the former DC police chief, had told them about the importance of reward money in the investigation. The Riches didn't have $100,000 to add to the reward; Burkman apparently did. Whether it was the money, the press conference, or the new flyers, Burkman had only been of help so far to the family, and even though she couldn't quite pin down his motives, Mary felt protective of him.

Burkman wasn't the only generous stranger to contact the Rich family. One day in mid-December, Joel spoke on the phone with a man named Ed Butowsky. He said he was a wealth manager who lived in the Dallas area and that he'd gotten Joel's information from a mutual acquaintance who attended the same Omaha synagogue that the Riches did. He said he had information that could help the Riches better understand what might have happened to their youngest son.

Joel pulled up Butowsky's personal website. A self-described "internationally recognized expert in the wealth management industry," Butowsky had worked at Morgan Stanley for eighteen years. He claimed he had once been the brokerage's top producer, managing more than $1 billion in assets and earning a place in the Chairman's Club. He went on to start his own firm, Chapwood Investments, in 2005, and grew it to manage several billion dollars. He'd lectured at Yale, New York University, and Southern Methodist University. One of his specialties was providing financial advice to current and former professional athletes. *Sports Illustrated* had featured him in a story about athletes who squander their wealth. Butowsky's website featured clips of him making appearances on Fox Business, Bloomberg TV, and CNBC talking about stocks, the labor market, and other financial news.

He had an impressive résumé, there was no question about that. But what did any of that have to do with Seth? Joel and Mary agreed to have a phone call with Butowsky, to hear him out. He told them he had heard secondhand, from someone he trusted, that Julian Assange had said in private that Seth, not Russia, gave WikiLeaks the leaked DNC emails. Joel and Mary were flabbergasted. This man had contacted them out of nowhere to tell them that their dead son was a criminal? And that their government was lying to them?

Joel and Mary told Butowsky there was no truth to that rumor. They'd given the police access to Seth's computers and phones. The authorities never said a word about Seth having anything to do with the stolen emails published by WikiLeaks. They thanked Butowsky for taking the call, said goodbye, and figured that was the last they'd hear from him.

But Butowsky wouldn't go away. On January 3—what would have been Seth's twenty-eighth birthday—he emailed Joel again. "Please call ed [*sic*] Butowsky," he wrote. "We met through Jeremy from your temple." The Riches weren't sure what to make of Butowsky, who kept pestering Joel. He called Joel and suggested that he check Seth's bank accounts for any payments from WikiLeaks. He emailed Joel from Washington one day in February to say he had a "friend" who could get Joel access to surveillance video from the night of Seth's murder. He sent Joel a recording of a conversation he'd had with the investigative journalist Seymour Hersh, who said he'd heard secondhand about an FBI report that had to do with Seth and WikiLeaks. Butowsky told Joel in an email he would try to "get my hands on the FBI REPORT."

How seriously should we take this guy, Joel wondered. At one point Butowsky told Joel to refer to him by the name "Code Purple." Joel put down his pen and stopped taking notes. When he told Bauman about it, he could hardly keep a straight face. "This is some weird cloak-and-dagger stuff," Joel said. "I think this guy thinks he's some sort of spy."

Then, in late February, about a month after Donald Trump took office, Butowsky's tenor changed. He knew the Riches were frustrated at the lack of progress in the police investigation, he told Joel, and so he proposed hiring a private investigator on their behalf to reexamine the details of Seth's murder, look for clues the police had missed, and try to kick-start the search for the killer or killers. Butowsky said he had already found the ideal candidate for the job, a former Washington, DC, homicide investigator.

"Definitely interested," Joel told him. "Let me talk with Mary."

"You will have no obligations of any kind," he emailed Joel. "As I said previously, I am certain he will get you answers, and I am footing the bill." The investigator Butowsky wanted to hire already had new information about the murder, Butowsky said. There would be "a lot more info coming as he gets involved," he added, "and we can finally, for your family, solve this."

———◦|◦———

The Riches' relationship with Burkman grew strained. Burkman would announce a new round of billboards or launch a new website—WhoKilledSeth.com—and the Riches would find out about it from a press release (there was always a press release) or from a reporter who had asked them about it. Burkman gave interviews to the *Daily Mail* and Infowars, putting forward the theory that Russian agents had killed Seth because he had discovered Russia's cyberattack on the Democratic Party and tried to expose it, calling on Congress to investigate.

Aaron pleaded with Burkman to at least give the family a heads-up whenever he had something new to announce related to Seth. Fearing that anything too aggressive would cause Burkman to withdraw his reward offer, Aaron tried to strike a balance in his email. "Don't get me wrong, the message is correct and I agree with it," he wrote. "But the means in which we are finding out is not. These surprises are hard to deal with and need to stop, please."

Burkman wrote back, "Of course so sorry."

A month later Burkman told the *Daily Mail* he had "leads and evidence of Russian involvement" in Seth's killing. He said his source was a former US intelligence officer between the ages of sixty-five and seventy whom he declined to name. "The source has claimed that [the murder] was arranged by the Russian government at a very high level," Burkman was quoted as saying.

"This is repulsive," Bauman wrote to Burkman after the story appeared.

"Oh my, do you not like the billboards my friend?" Burkman replied. Criticize me, Burkman seemed to be saying, and you can forget about the reward money.

Aaron had had enough. Any further association with Burkman, he believed, risked his family's credibility with the legitimate news organizations they needed to help publicize Seth's murder. Joel and Mary weren't as sure. They worried that, without Burkman's reward, it would be that much harder to solve the case. A few weeks later, Burkman sent a press announcement in Washington, this time without the Riches, to announce more billboards.

Joel and Mary knew they had to cut Burkman loose. In early March Mary sent a three-page letter to Burkman. She thanked him for "stepping up and trying to help solve Seth's murder" and told him he would "always hold a very special place in my heart" for his reward offer and the billboards. But she couldn't take any more of his hurtful and reckless antics. "Your statement fell right into the same category as the negative, unsubstantiated conspiracy theories already out there," she wrote. "I can't support this hearsay any more than we could support the theories thrown out earlier after Seth's passing."

Burkman was defiant. "It is true you have not seen any evidence because we have not shared it with you," he wrote to Mary. The only reason "anyone anywhere" was still talking about the case, he said, was because of his reward and media interviews. Seth's murder was bigger than just a local crime story; for him it was an international scandal too big to walk away from, and Burkman was pressing on with his search with or without the Riches' blessing.

———◆———

In light of Burkman's antics, Ed Butowsky's offer seemed more appealing to Joel and Mary. This time Joel looked into Butowsky's background in a way he never had the chance to do with Burkman. Butowsky had initially contacted Joel through a friend of a friend who attended the same temple in Omaha where Joel had worshipped for decades and had recently finished a two-year stint as president. The friend of a friend said he trusted Butowsky. Joel also called someone he knew in Texas through the Jewish community, and that person vouched for Butowsky as well. Others had encouraged the Riches to hire a private investigator, but they'd balked at the cost, which could run as high as tens of thousands of dollars. Now they had an offer from someone who said he would pay the entire bill himself.

Butowsky played up the PI's credentials. His name was Rod Wheeler. He was a former homicide investigator for the DC police and now worked as an on-air law enforcement expert for Fox News and Fox's DC affiliate. In fact, Wheeler had even provided on-air commentary about Seth's murder at the scene of the crime not long after it happened and had "already uncovered some info that he will share immediately with you," Butowsky said. The Riches hadn't yet agreed to accept Butowsky's help, but Joel replied by email that he and Mary and Aaron were "VERY appreciative." Joel also spoke with Wheeler and found his credentials impressive. In his initial proposal, Wheeler suggested that he would act as the family's press representative. That was a nonstarter, Joel said. The family would have final say over any public comments about Wheeler's investigation. "I am acknowledging and agreeing with your desire to have control over any and all comments," Butowsky replied.

Joel and Aaron spoke again with Butowsky, and they came away feeling encouraged that they might finally get the answers they desperately wanted. The following day, March 14, 2017, Joel sent back an updated contract. The contract specified that Butowsky would pay all of Wheeler's fee. Wheeler, in turn, would treat any findings as confidential; he would not share them with anyone outside of the Rich family or law enforcement without the family's permission. Joel, Mary, and Aaron each signed the contract.

Joel and Mary felt hopeful for the first time in months. Someone other than the DC police was undertaking a serious investigation of Seth's murder. The confidentiality language in the updated contract gave them the peace of mind that Wheeler wouldn't go rogue as Burkman had. Still, something about Butowsky didn't sit quite right with Aaron and Bauman, this charming stranger swooping in to pay for a PI, no strings attached. *What's he getting out of this?* Bauman thought to himself. *What am I missing?*

But he couldn't bring himself to advise Joel and Mary to reject Butowsky's offer. He had just told them to cut ties with Burkman; he couldn't insist they refuse Butowsky's help too. *Are you going to be the monster who has to tell a grieving family that they can't go down another avenue of support to try and find the murderers of their son?* he asked himself. *Because of a hunch? Because your spidey senses are going off?*

Bauman kept his mouth shut, a decision he would come to regret. "I honestly feel like this might be one of my greatest failures as a human being ever," he would later say, "because I was in a position where I could have stopped something fucking horrible from happening."

ACT II
Megaphone

11

Creature of the Green Room

ED BUTOWSKY GREW up in Chappaqua, an affluent enclave north of
New York City. The youngest of three, Butowsky revered his father,
David, who had worked as an enforcement attorney for the Securities
and Exchange Commission from 1962 to 1970. A sports junkie and a
decent athlete, Butowsky tried football at Ithaca College, only to
leave after a year for warmer climes. He enrolled at the University of
Texas–Austin and studied for a degree in advertising. He took a job in
Houston at a firm called Ogilvy and Mather. One day, Butowsky would
later recall, he complimented a female colleague on her dress. She
didn't take well to it, and Butowsky's manager told him not to do it
again. A few weeks later, he saw the colleague again. "Another hot
dress," he said. Ogilvy fired him, and his career in advertising was
finished.

Unemployed, living in a storage unit outside of Austin, Butowsky
drove to a local mall, dropped a few coins into the payphone, and called
home. His dad had told him after college that he could get him an
interview at Morgan Stanley. Butowsky asked if the offer still stood.
He would even move back to New York if he had to. "Son, I'll get you
an interview," David Butowsky said, "but you're never gonna be any
good at this."

Butowsky spent two decades at Morgan Stanley. For a few years he worked in the World Trade Center, then he moved back to Texas, where he and his wife, Dani, raised two kids, a boy and a girl. They lived in a 5,800-square-foot house in a suburb of Dallas, sent the kids to private school, and joined Gleneagles, a local country club. His clients included NBA star Kevin Durant, former all-star outfielder Torii Hunter, and professional slugger Matt Kemp.

After almost two decades at Morgan Stanley, Butowsky and a colleague left and started their own firm, Chapwood Investments, in 2005. They operated out of a modest office on the seventh floor of a glass office tower north of Dallas. Butowsky soon found a niche advising pro athletes who squandered their earnings and in some cases wound up destitute. The *Sports Illustrated* story about Butowsky's work with athletes inspired an ESPN *30 for 30* documentary, *Broke*, featuring Butowsky in a prominent role. A local magazine published a gushing profile of Butowsky, calling him "Dallas's $3-Billion Money Manager." The story touted his friendships with professional athletes and with the actor and producer Peter Berg, who produced the hit show *Friday Night Lights*. According to the profile, what made Butowsky successful was his ability to stay humble in the presence of fame despite all of this attention: "The real reason those boldfaced names flock to Ed Butowsky is simple: he doesn't care."

In reality, Butowsky relished the spotlight. In 2009, he landed his first appearance on Fox Business, the media mogul Rupert Murdoch's bid to compete with financial networks like CNBC. A booker at Fox Business was looking for someone opinionated who could pick stocks on *Varney & Co.* Butowsky's brash style and increasingly conservative politics made for a natural fit at Fox Business.

The *Varney & Co.* interview went well, and soon he was making weekly appearances on Fox Business. Between 2010 and 2017, he made hundreds of appearances on different Fox News and Fox Business programs, beaming in from the network's Dallas or Los Angeles bureaus or turning up in New York, tanned and smiling in a crisp suit and glossy tie. He liked to hang out in the green room, the lounge area where guests would mingle before and after they went on air. Butowsky's appearances in the New York office were frequent enough that he became a familiar sight. He would offer to take hosts and correspondents out to dinner. "He was a hanger-on for sure," a former Fox host says, describing him as "a big personality, a back-slappy type of guy."

Fox attracted a certain kind of overexuberant, publicity-hungry creature like Ed Butowsky. The network's audience was so large and so loyal that you couldn't put a price on the kind of exposure someone got from appearing on one of Fox's shows—it could lead to a book deal, speaking gigs, or an influx of thousands of new followers on social media. A lot of regular guests angled to be a paid contributor, but Butowsky just seemed to want the exposure—to millions of viewers and, even more important, to the Fox staff. "My whole office knew who Ed was," the former correspondent said. "Did I ever use him in a story? No. Was he famous for being around and trying to take Roger [Ailes] to lunch? Yes."

What irked the former Fox correspondent during his time at the network was how little vetting there was of the network's guests. Executives didn't offer any clear guidelines about who could and couldn't go on the air, and once guests had made a few appearances, they were assumed to be good to go. "If you want to play *Talented Mr. Ripley*, once you get inside, nobody's going to think twice about whether you should be there," a former Fox producer said. The network suffered a major embarrassment when a longtime Fox News intelligence analyst named Wayne Simmons was indicted for fraud. During his time at Fox, Simmons said he had served in the CIA for twenty-seven years when, in fact, he had never worked a day at the agency. (A judge later sentenced him to thirty-three months in prison.)

Butowsky would sometimes appear on one Fox show in the morning, spend a few hours in the green room, and make a second appearance in the afternoon. Hanging around Fox brought him into contact with influential types in Republican politics. He posted photos on Facebook of himself with Republican congressmen and with private military contractor Erik Prince at a Fox studio. Butowsky had made a donation to Barack Obama's 2008 presidential campaign, but his public comments about politics and foreign affairs increasingly sounded like

Fox's. In TV appearances he criticized Obama's plan to levy a new tax on the ultrarich, his annual budget blueprint, and his administration's health care policies. "That's what the American dream is all about, achieving what your goals are, and this administration is doing everything to squash that," he typically said. He shared a post on his Facebook page that claimed Obama's birth certificate was a fake. When a friend confronted him about the post, he replied, "I am not into the birth certificate thing . . . although it is a fraud. I am more interested in why you support this guy. I have yet to hear what you like about him."

Butowsky became fixated on the 2012 attack on an American diplomatic facility in Benghazi, Libya, a tragic event that left four Americans dead, including Ambassador J. Christopher Stevens. Among conservatives Benghazi fueled a frenzy of theories. Many were variations on the same theme—that the Obama administration, or Secretary of State Hillary Clinton herself, had given a "stand-down" order and prevented US forces from reaching Benghazi in time to save American lives. Multiple internal reviews and Republican-led investigations failed to substantiate this claim, but that did little to stop Benghazi from morphing into a rallying cry for much of the Republican Party.

In November 2014, when the House Intelligence Committee concluded its investigation on Benghazi and issued its final, long-awaited report, Butowsky noticed that a friend of his had shared a *New York Times* story about the intel committee report on his Facebook page. Above the link the friend had written, "All those carnival barkers hawking crazy conspiracy theories about Benghazi must be really disappointed at having their claims so publicly discredited."

"Your Facebook post is a joke related to BENGHAZI," Butowsky responded. "You should really know what your [*sic*] talking about prior to making comments." He offered to provide the phone numbers for "the guys that were there" and repeated a claim popular on the right that the head of the CIA had ordered two planes on their way to Benghazi to turn around, a different version of the supposed stand-down order. "If you want knowledge," Butowsky wrote, "feel free to call me."

Butowsky's interest in the Benghazi story ran deeper than Facebook posts and disputes with his friends. He had gotten to know several of the security contractors who were on the ground in Benghazi and had rushed to protect the US compound and nearby CIA facility. Over time he had become good friends with the contractors. He organized a book event for the men at his local country club; the invitation said he had "privately served as a confidante" to the contractors. In a joint TV appearance with one of the Benghazi contractors, Mark "Oz" Geist, he said he had "been involved behind the scenes" with the men. "I consider them brothers, and they consider me [a brother] as well," he said.

Butowsky joined a citizens' commission launched by Accuracy in Media, a conservative watchdog group based in Washington, DC, that had also promoted the Obama birther conspiracy theory. Butowsky would later say he spent more than $100,000 of his own money and dedicated two years of his life to unearthing what he believed to be the truth about Benghazi. He introduced another one of the contractors, Kris "Tanto" Paronto, to several Fox correspondents. Butowsky claimed he was a "consultant" to the Republican-led special congressional committee that investigated the attack and that family members of the victims had offered him access to hearings and other public events. "I have an incredibly deep relationship to that story," he would later say.

Butowsky became so entrenched at Fox that he came to be seen as a conduit of information and even a source by some of the network's reporters. He assisted Adam Housley, an on-air Fox correspondent who covered the Benghazi story, and also a FoxNews.com investigative reporter named Malia Zimmerman, who had also written about Benghazi.

———◆———

Years earlier Butowsky had met a woman in the Fox News green room named Ellen Ratner. Ratner was from an influential Cleveland family. Her older brother, Bruce, was one of the most successful New York City real estate developers of the past twenty years, building the Barclays Center and the headquarters of the *New York Times*. Another brother, Michael, was a renowned civil liberties lawyer who argued several landmark cases challenging the Bush administration's prisoner detention policies during the war on terror. Ellen had worked as a journalist in Washington for decades, and although she was a well-known liberal and Democratic donor, she was an old friend of Roger Ailes—known inside Fox as an FOR, a Friend of Roger, someone given preferential treatment by the network's hosts and employees.

Butowsky and Ratner were an unlikely pair, but they hit it off. When Ratner asked Butowsky to help revise a business plan for a small media outfit she owned in Washington, he advised her on a pitch deck and finding potential investors. Ratner subsequently invited him to the White House Correspondents' Dinner and obtained a press credential for him to attend a State of the Union address as a "correspondent" for Ratner's outlet.

Ratner's brother Michael died in 2016. Michael had represented WikiLeaks in its legal battle with the US government, and on the way back from an event in Berlin honoring Michael, Ellen and members of her extended family stopped in London to pay a visit to Julian Assange. In their meeting, Ratner later recounted, Assange repeated his claim that the DNC email leak could have come from an "internal source" or an "enemy" of the Clintons, not necessarily Russia. The day after the election, during a panel discussion at Embry-Riddle Aeronautical University, she said Assange had told her the DNC leak was from "an internal source from the Hillary campaign or from somebody that knew Hillary, an enemy. He does not think they're from Russians," she added, "and he said, 'Russia got credit for something WikiLeaks should've gotten credit for.'"

Butowsky, however, would later claim that Ratner shared with him another detail: that Assange had named Seth Rich as his source. Ratner repeatedly denied this. An ardent Trump supporter who had served as a surrogate for Trump during the campaign, Butowsky knew the value of this information. If true, if the digital break-in at the DNC was not an act of foreign interference but an inside job, it changed the story of the 2016 election and lifted the cloud of suspicion from the president-elect. Butowsky suddenly had a new cause.

Butowsky sought to confirm this groundbreaking allegation by contacting a friend named Larry Johnson, a former CIA officer who had called allegations of Russian interference in 2016 "a joke" and was perhaps best known for pushing a false story in 2008 about a recording of Michelle Obama making slurs about white people. Johnson, in turn, suggested Butowsky call the investigative journalist Seymour Hersh. Hersh, who had known Johnson since the '80s from his reporting on the CIA, agreed to talk to Butowsky. The reporter who first revealed the My Lai massacre during the Vietnam War, Hersh was now seventy-nine years old and at the twilight of his career. He still wrote stories, though with less frequency, and he'd fallen out with the *New Yorker*, where he'd broken major stories about George W. Bush's war on terror, when the magazine declined to publish a thinly sourced account he'd written that accused the government of lying about the secret operation that killed Osama bin Laden.

In conversation, Hersh was lively as ever, combative one moment and flattering the next, and he had a sneaky way of pumping you for information without you realizing it. Hersh told Butowsky he wasn't sure about the Russian hacking allegations. He harbored a deep distrust of the US intelligence community, calling CIA director John Brennan an "asshole" and the head of the NSA "a fucking moron." He said he still had someone "on the inside" who "will go and read a file for me" and that he'd heard about a "report" that said Rich had tried to sell emails to WikiLeaks. It involved a drop box and some of Seth's friends, Hersh said. Then Hersh changed tack and said it could've been the Russians. "I'll tell you right now, we and the Russians are like babes compared to the Chinese," Hersh said. "The Chinese are pinging everything."

Near the end of their discussion, Hersh cautioned Butowsky that just because he'd heard something "doesn't make it true." He hadn't confirmed any of it sufficiently to publish a story about it. But Butowsky knew how valuable Hersh's rumor could be: "There's so many people throughout Trump's four years—and maybe eight years—who are gonna fall back on the idea that he's not legitimate and the Russians got him elected. This changes all of that."

Hersh could keep reporting out the story, but Butowsky wanted to share what he'd just heard with the public. "I have a great history in getting things out there," he said, "where nobody knows that I'm the one who did it."

12

Ask Me Anything

JAMES ALEFANTIS GATHERED with his new legal team led by Mike Gottlieb, and together they tried to come up with a strategy for how to debunk Pizzagate. The shooting at Comet had not deterred the conspiracy theorists in the slightest. The hardcore believers dismissed Edgar Maddison Welch's attack as a false flag or the work of a true madman. Now, instead of sending Alefantis violent Facebook messages and making menacing phone calls to the restaurant, anonymous sleuths on Reddit and 4chan scoured public records and social media for clues about his life and the people around him. Trolls called an art gallery where Alefantis was a board member and threatened the person who answered the phone. They posted the home address of one of the managers at Comet. Neighbors told Alefantis that strange people were asking about his house or filming it.

Pizzagate soon spread beyond Reddit and 4chan to politically influential figures. "Until #Pizzagate proven to be false, it'll remain a story," tweeted Michael Flynn Jr., the son of Lt. Gen. Michael Flynn, an adviser to Trump and the soon-to-be White House national security adviser. For Alefantis and Gottlieb, this tweet captured the warped logic of conspiracy theorists: *my allegation is valid until you prove me wrong.* How, then, was someone supposed to prove a negative, especially one as absurd as Pizzagate? Should he submit an op-ed to the *New York Times* titled "No, My Restaurant Is Not a Secret Globalist Child-Trafficking Hub"?

Alefantis couldn't erase Pizzagate from the internet—that moment had come and gone, if it had ever existed. He resigned himself to the fact that his name was forever connected to a horror show of noxious lies and memes. Still, he couldn't let Pizzagate roar across the internet without trying something. More than anything, he wanted to prevent anyone from shooting up his restaurant again.

Thinking about what approach they might take to push back against Pizzagate, Gottlieb and his publicity consultant Molly Levinson had an idea: If they wanted to debunk a right-wing conspiracy theory, what about doing so in front of the audience most likely to believe the theory?

Levinson reached out to a producer she knew at Fox News who worked on Megyn Kelly's show, *Kelly File*. She pitched the idea of opening Comet's doors to a Fox News correspondent and a camera crew. They could spend as much time inside the restaurant as they wanted, go wherever they wanted to go, talk to whomever they wanted to talk to, and air as much of it on primetime TV as they wanted. Alefantis would show the Fox crew that Comet did not have a basement, that there weren't secret satanic symbols in the artwork, and that his restaurant was nothing more than that—a restaurant.

Kelly and her producers liked the idea. A few weeks later the segment aired. "A *Kelly File* exclusive tonight on the conspiracy theory that came to be known as Pizzagate," Kelly announced in her no-nonsense contralto. As footage of a SWAT team rolled, Kelly gave her viewers the thumbnail version of Pizzagate—how a "bogus news story" formed on the internet and inspired a gunman to act on that story by shooting up a pizza joint to free children who weren't real from a basement prison that didn't exist. Kelly played footage of Alefantis taking a Fox cameraman to the door Welch had fired his AR-15 rifle into. Welch had thought the door might lead to the basement where the child trafficking and satanic rituals took place. Alefantis opened it to reveal a shallow closet with coats in it. "The bullet went into our computer system," he said, pointing to an old PC tower on the floor.

The camera cut to a nervous-looking James Alefantis. "The owner of the pizzeria is talking for the first time . . . he is here on set with me," Kelly told her audience. Kelly asked him about a photo taken from his

Instagram account showing a child with her hands scotch-taped to a table. Pizzagate proponents had seized on the photo as evidence that child abuse took place at Comet. "This is a picture of my godchild," Alefantis said. She had been playing with her sister, and her sister had used the tape. Their parents were there when it happened. "I put this on my Instagram with their approval," he said. "It sits there on the internet for a year and a half and then people start building these lies and falsities about innocent people."

To a public relations professional, the interview went smoothly. Afterward, when Gottlieb went online to see what the Pizzagate believers were saying, he was surprised to see how little of an impact the segment had made.

> Boycott Megyn Kelly. Don't support this woman who covers up for pedophiles and doesn't report the truth on PizzaGate.

> I AM WATCHING PIZZAGATE ON FAME WHORE MEGYN KELLY'S SHOW AND THEY ARE LYING ABOUT THE ENTIRE THING.

Someone would later post a meme that listed all the questions Kelly should have asked if she weren't a "pretend journalist": "Why are so many businesses on your block—including yours—using FBI-verified pedophile symbols as logos?" "Why do you compulsively upload pictures of sexualized infants?" "Why are the bands who perform at your restaurant using the same pedosexual imagery?"

Gottlieb and Levinson understood that the traditional crisis communications strategy was doomed to fail. No amount of op-eds or interviews would make a difference to the people who believed in Pizzagate. Any attention was bad attention, any public conversation would be twisted and contorted and become more evidence for the theory, not against it.

Gottlieb and his colleagues tried another tack. They had found dozens of videos and pictures promoting Pizzagate, but when they asked the social-media giants to discuss the damage these materials were causing and how to remove them, the tech companies responded with a collective shrug. In public, the CEOs of these companies took the position that they were just "platforms," not arbiters of truth and falsity. Lawyers for the companies said there was little they could do unless Gottlieb and the team filed a lawsuit and won a court order to remove the allegedly defamatory content. But a defamation suit could take years to play out, and in the meantime all the false and harmful memes and videos about Alefantis would remain online.

Through a friend, Alefantis had gotten in touch with a lawyer in New York named Carrie Goldberg who represented victims of sexual privacy invasion—people whose explicit photos were hacked, leaked, or posted without their consent. To remove these images from the internet, Goldberg invoked a 1998 law called the Digital Millennium Copyright Act, or DMCA. Created to help movie studios and musicians safeguard their intellectual property, the law gave anyone the right to request the removal of something online—a photo, a video, a song—if they held the copyright to that content. It soon became known as a DMCA takedown. When a client's explicit images or videos got shared without their consent, Goldberg contacted the social media company, established that the images didn't belong to the person who posted them, and demanded that the company remove them. In essence she wiped the images from the internet.

Gottlieb took a cue from Goldberg. He and his colleagues filed takedown requests with YouTube, Facebook, Twitter, and Instagram. It was an unwieldy process: each individual tweet, video, and meme required its own takedown demand even if they used the same stolen photo. But with these DMCA requests there was a law Gottlieb could point to when he and his team asked for content to be removed. A few months after the shooting, Gottlieb enlisted a small group of associates and paralegals to help out; together they logged dozens of hours on Alefantis's case. Gottlieb was making progress. Yet when he stopped to think about it, he marveled at the amount of time and manpower required to put a small dent in a viral smear like Pizzagate. The amount of time it took to watch the videos and read the tweets, to pick out any copyrighted material that was used, and then to fill out the forms and pester the lawyers at YouTube or Facebook—how could ordinary people expect to navigate this on their own?

Copyright takedowns helped in the near term. But with a conspiracy theory as widespread as Pizzagate, Gottlieb realized, the only effective strategy had to include a legal option. And any legal demand would have to include Alex Jones and Infowars. The Comet gunman told police he had binge-watched Jones's Pizzagate videos in the days before the attack, and there was no shortage of videos to choose from.

In late February Alefantis sent a letter to Jones asking for a full retraction and an apology. The letter laid out all the ways Jones and his cohosts had defamed Alefantis and Comet. Unless Jones retracted and apologized for what he and his colleagues had said, they would find themselves in court, and if a jury sided with Alefantis, the financial penalty for damages would be steep. A full retraction and apology wouldn't undo the damage Jones and Infowars had done, Alefantis wrote, "but it would be a start." Jones responded to the letter with a bizarre and often incoherent rant delivered live and on the air. "Yes, I retract that about Ping Pong pizza," he said, standing in front of a gold backdrop. "But it's not an apology. I'm covering this giant thing going on because of the Podestas and the stuff they're involved in."

Finally, after another month of tense negotiations, Jones appeared on Infowars on the evening of March 24. He said he had "an important note to our viewing, listening, and reading audience." Reading from a statement that he also published on Infowars, Jones apologized to Alefantis, announced that he had removed past broadcasts about Pizzagate, and admitted that those stories were based on "an incorrect narrative."

Jones's statement came as part of a confidential settlement with Alefantis and Comet. The agreement couldn't remove the association of Alefantis and Comet with Pizzagate, it couldn't erase the trauma that he and so many people experienced when the shooter showed up at his restaurant, but it was a victory. One of the most infamous conspiracy theorists had publicly admitted that he was wrong, and he was now being held accountable for those lies. "Suffice it to say, we have a very happy client," Gottlieb said. For him the victory only pointed to how, in this area of the law, a great deal of work needed to be done.

13

A Nice but Somewhat Uncomfortable Message

Rod Wheeler was in his fifties, thick shouldered, with a receding hairline and a carefully groomed beard. He spoke with a nasal inflection that gave away his midwestern roots and had a signature look of dark suits with brightly colored shirts and shiny ties. By day he worked as a food safety consultant. For years he had been on the payroll as a law enforcement analyst at Fox, making regular appearances on Fox 5 DC, the local affiliate, and on Fox News, weighing in on whatever major crime story was in the news. He was typically introduced on the air as a "former DC detective" or "former homicide detective," someone with the authority and credibility to weigh in about, say, an unsolved murder.

In reality Wheeler hadn't worked as a cop in more than a decade. He joined the DC police in 1990 and spent five years there, several of those in the homicide division. Despite the on-air description of him as a former detective, he had never risen above the rank of investigator, a one-year probationary job required before becoming a full-fledged detective. During a routine physical, Wheeler submitted a urine sample that tested positive for marijuana, and the police department charged him with insubordination. Wheeler denied any wrongdoing, but the department fired him in 1995. After he'd left the force, he'd made a few guest appearances on the local Fox affiliate. He was good on camera, well-spoken and authoritative, and the Fox News executives in New York eventually offered him a paid contract.

Over the years Wheeler got to know some of the network's on-air talent. One was Adam Housley, a Los Angeles–based correspondent who covered terrorism and crime. It was Housley's name that caught Wheeler's eye when a text message from an unknown number appeared one morning in February. The message's anonymous sender said he had long admired Wheeler's appearances on Fox and that he and Wheeler had many mutual friends, including Housley and many others from the network. The message went on,

> Behind the scenes I do a lot of work, (unpaid) helping to uncover certain stories, my biggest work was revealing most of what we know today about Benghazi. I'm looking for some assistance on something that happened in Washington I would appreciate if you would give me a call . . . Of all the people you have met in your line of work you have put me right next to those you view as the most confidential. I am extremely discreet. Is there a time I can give you a call this morning?

Wheeler got random messages like this all the time—someone saw him on TV, tracked down his number, and asked for something. He wouldn't have paid any attention to this text if the sender hadn't played up their shared Fox News connection. Wheeler called the number an hour later. The man on the other end was Ed Butowsky, who told him he was looking to hire a private investigator to look into the murder of Seth Rich. Wheeler said he'd be happy to help.

A week later Butowsky and Wheeler agreed to talk about next steps over lunch at a Mexican restaurant on Capitol Hill. Butowsky had invited another guest to the meeting, Malia Zimmerman, an investigative reporter for Fox News's website. She was working on a story of her own about Seth Rich. Wheeler wasn't quite sure why Zimmerman was there, but he left lunch with the impression that she would help him with *his* investigation, sharing notes and sources, giving him access to Fox's in-house research team known as the Brain Room.

"Expect a direct call from Joel Rich," Butowsky texted Wheeler a few days later. He also included some advice. "Make sure to downplay Fox News," Butowsky wrote. "Don't mention you know Malia."

———— ✦ ————

Malia Zimmerman grew up in Kailua, on the west side of Oahu, the third largest of the Hawaiian Islands. As a kid she swam in the Pacific and learned to surf, paddle outrigger canoes, and dance the hula. It was an idyllic upbringing. From her father's work, however, Zimmerman came to see the dark undercurrents that flowed through one of the most beautiful places on earth.

Her dad, Dennis, was a clinical psychologist and college professor who worked with a nearby state hospital and a prison. He served on a panel of experts that decided whether to send criminals to prison or a mental health institution. When Zimmerman was young, her father liked to give her logic puzzles, IQ tests, and handwriting analysis assessments. They often discussed his latest cases, and in the course of this he taught her about the mind of a criminal and why people committed crimes. Those conversations kindled in her a passion for solving crimes and mysteries and a drive to seek justice for victims.

If her father had one flaw, it was his long-winded way of explaining simple concepts, often using academic jargon. Listening to her dad rattle on and on taught her not only how to listen but also how to distill complicated ideas into something a regular person could understand. That skill would come in handy as a journalist, which she'd wanted to be since she was eight. She idolized Woodward and Bernstein as well as an investigative journalist for the *Honolulu Advertiser* named Jim Dooley, who chronicled the seedy side of life and politics in Hawaii. Zimmerman got her start with an internship at the local NBC affiliate, wrote for a local business journal, and eventually launched her own news site called the Hawaii Reporter. The site received funding from a right-wing charitable foundation called the Franklin Center for Government and Public Integrity; Zimmerman identified as a libertarian, socially liberal and fiscally conservative. The issue she cared about most was human freedom. She gravitated to stories about human traffickers, labor abuses, and the sex trade. She investigated a garment factory owner in American Samoa who was holding two hundred workers against their will and was later convicted by the Justice Department. She and Jim Dooley, who came to work for her at the Hawaii Reporter, investigated underground gambling operations operating out of Chinatown. All the while she raised a son mostly on her own, juggling her kid's soccer practice and school commitments with running a small newsroom and writing her own stories.

On occasion she helped a national media outlet like *20/20* or *People* magazine cover a story set in Hawaii. When a reporter for FoxNews.com spent a few weeks there to report on Obama's birth certificate, Zimmerman showed the reporter around and the two hit it off. A few years later, when that reporter left for another job, an executive at Fox named Ken LaCorte, who was close with then-CEO Roger Ailes, recruited Zimmerman to work for FoxNews.com.

Fox News Network was divided into different divisions, which had long operated more or less independently of each other. "Fox is kind of like the [intelligence] agencies: we stovepipe," as one former reporter put it. "Dot-com doesn't work with radio, radio doesn't work with TV. There's not a lot of crossover." For a long time Fox's website was a "stepchild inside the news organization," according to former host Greta Van Susteren. "It was not Fox News Channel, it was not Fox Business—it was the dot-com. Roger Ailes wasn't interested in the dot-com."

Ailes had built the network into the ratings juggernaut it was, and he wanted stories that hit you in the gut, as a former host put it. Stories that were visceral, us-against-them, good versus evil. Stories that made people feel aggrieved about the enemy but assured that the good guys were on the way. Ailes wasn't interested in nuance or policy, and his sensibility filtered down to producers who learned to pitch stories that would elicit a particular reaction from the bosses: "Oh, that feels good. That's going to create outrage."

That ethos translated into a tabloid-like mentality for the people who worked in the FoxNews.com newsroom on the fourteenth floor of headquarters. There were a few full-time reporters on staff who did original reporting and sometimes broke major stories. Most of the staff were young editors who spent their time rewriting wire-service reports—"Foxifying them," as one former staffer put it—to fit Fox's sensibility and updating the website's front page. There was a greater focus on getting the Drudge Report to link to FoxNews.com stories than there was on consistently publishing high-quality journalism, former staffers would recall. "This was not a place where sensitive stories were vetted and edited thoroughly," one former editor would recall.

By the time Trump took office in 2017, Fox had found its heroes and villains. Trump was the defender of the common man, an outsider who vowed to shake up the political order and drain the Washington, DC, swamp of all its creatures. The villains were the Democrats who said Trump was a Russian agent and an illegitimate president, and also the faceless "deep state" operatives burrowed into the federal government who tried to thwart him. The allegation that Trump and his campaign had conspired with the Russians to win the 2016 election was, in Fox's telling, nothing more than a libelous smear campaign to sabotage Trump's presidency.

But Fox felt pressure to scale up the digital side. There were the larger trends in media to contend with, as more people got their news online via social media. Fox also faced increased competition from the right, especially the website Breitbart News. Under the leadership of Steve Bannon, Breitbart channeled the ascendant nativist wing of the Republican Party and championed Donald Trump's presidential bid long before Fox did. (Bannon, of course, would leave Breitbart to run Trump's campaign in the final months of the election.) Throughout 2015 and into early 2016, Breitbart supplanted Fox as arguably the most influential force in conservative media. According to former editors and reporters, Fox was terrified of Breitbart's influence at the start of the Trump presidency and felt pressure to reassert its dominance with blockbuster stories of its own. "Everyone's refreshing Breitbart all day at Fox," one longtime Fox observer would later say. "They're worried they're losing their edge online."

Fox hired Malia Zimmerman to regain that edge. She wrote about subjects sure to rile up readers: allegations of voter fraud in liberal

California, crackdowns on gun owners, and Muslim extremists. She broke several stories that beat the mainstream outlets, stories that often leaned heavily on anonymous sources. She had written about the Benghazi controversy, publishing a story that attempted to raise questions about Clinton's role in the attack. That story also cited the Citizens' Commission on Benghazi, the same group of disgruntled ex-military officers and conservative critics that Ed Butowsky had teamed up with to investigate the assault on the American compound.

In the late summer of 2016, Zimmerman started to look into a story that had gone viral in conservative media: the murder of Seth Rich. She emailed Bauman, the Rich family's PR rep, a list of questions about Seth's murder "based on some analysis that active law enforcement outside of DC have given me about the case." Bauman never responded. In early 2017, she emailed Joel Rich and asked for an interview.

Mary and Joel participated in as many interviews as they could, having internalized the advice given to them by the police that keeping Seth's name in the news might help generate a lead in the case. They had made time for writers from *Newsweek* and the *New York Times* as well as less reputable outlets like the *Daily Mail*. Indeed there were times when Joel might have been too forthcoming with what he knew about the murder, like when he told the *Daily Mail* that the murder weapon was likely a revolver because there were no shell casings found at the crime scene. Joel hesitated when he saw that Zimmerman worked for Fox News, but Zimmerman's pitch put him somewhat at ease. She said she wanted to write a feature story about Seth to "bring further attention to his case," adding, "From everything I've read, your son seems like an amazing person who brought a great deal of light and happiness to the world."

Joel spoke with Zimmerman by phone and shared photos of Seth for her to use. The story came out a few days later. "Six months after a Democratic National Committee staffer was gunned down on a Washington, DC street," it began, "suspicion that he may have been the source who passed incriminating DNC emails on to WikiLeaks persists despite his own parents' strong doubts." Even though Zimmerman had included Joel's denials of any WikiLeaks connection, the story focused far more on the unfounded theories about why Seth was murdered than it did on his life, which was what Zimmerman had pitched to them in the first place.

Zimmerman didn't lose interest in the Seth Rich story. And with Rod Wheeler on board, she saw a new way to get information about the murder. Within days of their meeting—but before the Riches had agreed to hire Wheeler with Butowsky's financial help—Zimmerman was peppering him with questions. Was there a warrant issued by DC police for any of Seth's belongings? If so, what did the police find? Did the FBI conduct a "cyber audit" of any electronics and find any communications between Seth and WikiLeaks? Was there a "drop box," and, if so, what was in it? Had the mayor intervened in the investigation? How many officers were assigned to the case? Was the case file locked in the chief's office? In another message she asked Wheeler if he could get access to Seth's Twitter and Facebook accounts, which the family had locked down after the conspiracy theories took off.

Butowsky asked for Wheeler's bank information so he could wire him payment. "My mother would be proud of us," Butowsky told him. "Money will be in your account on Monday."

———◆———

For the first time in months, the Rich family felt hopeful. Joel had spoken with Wheeler and came away encouraged. A former DC cop who was familiar with Seth's case—it was hard to imagine a better candidate for a PI. Even Aaron, who tended to be more skeptical than his parents, was hopeful.

Aaron's wife, Molly, a lawyer, rewrote the contract that Wheeler had sent to include strict confidentiality terms. As the Riches and Wheeler went back and forth, Butowsky sent Joel email after email. "I know [Wheeler] already has info for you and I am sure he will share regardless if he is retained," Butowsky wrote in one email. "But there will be a lot more info coming as he gets involved and we can finally, for your family, solve this." Before the Riches had signed the contract, Butowsky told Joel that Wheeler "has been officially hired and is diligently working on it." He also assured Joel, "I am acknowledging and agreeing with your desire to have control over any and all comments." The Riches took more than a week to decide whether to move forward with Wheeler. Butowsky was growing anxious. "If you don't get the agreement back this morning, I'm going to leave Joel a nice but somewhat uncomfortable message," Butowsky told Wheeler.

Finally, on March 14, 2017, the Riches returned the signed contract. The final agreement noted that Butowsky would pay for Wheeler's services and forbid Wheeler from discussing his investigation with third parties without the family's permission. Wheeler then forwarded the contract to someone who, under the terms of the agreement, was not allowed to see it: Malia Zimmerman.

She was pleased that the contract didn't limit the scope of Wheeler's investigation to a street crime, which meant he could investigate the same rumors and theories she was pursuing. "I think it's a win," she said.

14

War Room

THE RICH FAMILY had cut off contact with Jack Burkman. But if they had hoped that move would deter him, they were mistaken. He felt more emboldened than ever.

Burkman had recently gone public with the allegation that Seth had discovered the Russian hacking campaign targeting the Democratic National Committee and so the Russians had him killed. Burkman said his source for this claim was a former US intelligence officer who had served as a contractor in Iraq in the 1970s. Burkman wouldn't give his name, but he took the man's accusations straight to the first news outlet that would print them, the *Daily Mail*. "These days we all know what the Russian government is like, and because I'm concerned with my safety and my family's safety, I have to be careful about what I put on the record," Burkman told the *Daily Mail*. Those fears, however, hadn't prevented him from sending letters to the chairmen of two congressional committees asking them to investigate whether Russia was "involved" or "directly responsible" for Seth's murder. His source wouldn't talk to reporters or go public, but Burkman was undeterred: "I think this guy is credible," he told a reporter.

Burkman's theory was out there already. It also flew in the face of the entire premise of the right-wing conspiracy theory about Seth, which was that the Russians didn't hack the DNC. Burkman wasn't motivated by ideology or party loyalty. Rather it seemed he trafficked in conspiracy theories primarily to get famous.

In early March, he announced his next stunt: a filmed reenactment of Seth's murder. He said he planned to hire six to ten actors to play Seth, a few of his friends, and the killer. The production would re-create Seth's final hours alive, starting at Lou's City Bar and following him until he was shot in Bloomingdale. Burkman planned to film the reenactment later that spring. "It's a California thing," he told one local reporter about the decision. Reenactments, he went on, were "a great way to bring everything out of the woodwork," adding, "There's literally nothing better to stimulate people's minds and memories."

The next day, Burkman's team received an email with the subject line "Investigative Consideration." The sender, a man named Kevin Doherty, said he was a "former federal special agent and current forensic psychology graduate student." He encouraged Burkman to consider a different approach to cracking the Rich case. Cases like this one, Doherty wrote, get solved because "someone comes forward"—a criminal charged with unrelated crimes who wants to mitigate their sentence, a scorned ex-lover, or someone the police didn't interview. Rather than reenacting the murder, Burkman needed to analyze the series of events leading up to the crime and create psychological profiles for as many people as possible with connections to the case. "I share this not to be a nay-sayer," he wrote, "but rather to offer assistance."

Burkman was eager to accept the help. Doherty's résumé was impressive: He was a former marine who had worked as a special agent for the US Energy Department and served on the security detail for Mitt Romney's 2008 presidential campaign. More recently, he was studying for a master's degree in forensic psychology at George Washington University. Burkman and Doherty hit it off in their initial conversations. With Burkman's financial backing, they decided to launch their own private investigation into Seth's murder.

On a cold afternoon in late March, bundled up in a long blue overcoat, one hand in his pocket and the other clutching his notes, Burkman stepped up to the microphone cluster. He stood in the parking lot of a gas station in northwest Washington, not far from the site of Seth's murder. Behind him was a bus stop advertisement that he'd paid for. Featuring a photo of Seth from Aaron's wedding and the latest reward total of $130,000, the ad asked, "Do you know who murdered Seth Rich?" Over Burkman's other shoulder stood Doherty, with dark sunglasses and an expressionless face. A nearby construction project threatened to drown Burkman out, so he leaned in closer to the dozen or so reporters in attendance.

He was there to announce the latest act in his self-styled pursuit of the truth in Seth's murder, dubbed the Profiling Project. He described it as a "private investigative effort" that he would underwrite himself. The name riffed on the Innocence Project, which has exonerated hundreds of felons through DNA analysis since two New York lawyers founded it in 1992. In contrast, the Profiling Project would focus on one crime: the murder of Seth Rich. A team of thirty or so college students led by a forensics grad student at nearby George Washington University would retrace the police's steps and search for evidence the police might have missed. The Profiling Project would work out of an office just across the Potomac River, which Burkman had christened the Seth Rich Investigative War Room.

Next Burkman introduced Doherty, who would lead the Profiling Project. Doherty stepped forward and addressed the reporters. The point of the Profiling Project, Doherty said, was to provide a "new set of eyes." "We'll re-create timelines, look at statistical analysis, look at link analysis, profiling, and victimology." Their work would rely on open-source data, which meant whatever they could find in the public domain. "We're going to have far less information than even the media," he said.

In interviews Burkman declined to give the precise location of the Seth Rich Investigative War Room, saying he needed to protect the safety of his team. But he did allow a photographer to take a photo from the hallway outside the office. Stenciled in red, under "Profiling Project," next to an oversize thumbprint are the words "Funded by Jack M. Burkman." In the same photo, Doherty sits hunched over his desk, a pen in his mouth, deep in his work. Photos, diagrams, clippings, and Post-it notes cover every inch of the office space you can see. For the time being, Burkman's and Doherty's interests aligned. Doherty was happy to do the investigating, Burkman eager to keep the money flowing and the public interested.

The two men got along well, at least in the beginning. "He was a smart guy, nice guy, charming guy," Burkman would later say. "I always loved talking to him. I would've never in a million years suspected him for foul play."

———— ◦ ————

Sines tried to piece together the final hours of Seth's life. She plotted the route from Lou's City Bar to the house Seth had shared with a few roommates in Bloomingdale. On foot it should have taken him half an hour. Why, then, the two-hour gap?

Sines interviewed anyone who had seen or spoken to Seth that night. Joe Capone, a manager at Lou's, said Seth had spent much of the night there, drinking more than usual and lost in his thoughts. Seth's former girlfriend helped resolve the matter of why it had taken Seth nearly two hours to walk home. Seth was extremely drunk and kept getting turned around, she said. She asked him to mention landmarks and street signs, and she told him which direction to go. She was still on the phone with Seth when he turned onto W Street and passed the local bodega, Flagler Market, which meant he was two blocks from his house.

Next Sines watched the body-camera footage from the police officers who arrived first to the scene. She had to watch all of it, several hours' worth, playing, pausing, and rewinding, looking for overlooked evidence, faces among the onlookers, anything. In the Rich case, though, she hoped Seth's family never saw the footage. Seth was slurring his words and could barely remember his name. He was so drunk, in fact, that he didn't realize what had happened to him and seemingly didn't feel the pain of having been shot, even though his wounds would prove fatal.

In past cases Sines studied the footage and often found evidence the detectives and the forensic technicians had missed; the killer could even be in the footage, blended in with the crowd that sometimes gathered around a crime scene. But that wasn't the case here.

Sines had a saying about witnesses. "Just give me one good crackhead," she said. "They always tell the truth about a murder they've seen. And people always do murders in front of them, thinking, 'No one's going to believe them—they're a crackhead.'"

There were no such eyewitnesses to Seth's murder. The most she had from that night was a woman who told the police that she was out walking her incontinent old dog when she saw two young men running away from the scene of the shooting. There was also a bartender coming home from work who heard what sounded like fireworks.

From the autopsy and the video footage alone, Sines felt confident enough to rule out any of the wild theories about Seth's murder circulating online—that he'd been killed by a hit squad or covert government agents. Right away her mind went to something more mundane if no less tragic: a random street crime, a burglary gone wrong, a classic case of wrong place, wrong time.

This was more than a hunch. Studying the crime statistics in Seth's neighborhood throughout the summer of 2016, she saw the spike in armed robberies. What's more, some of the crimes fit a pattern. Two assailants, one taller than the other, had snuck up on people walking late at night, held them up with a handgun, and demanded their cell phones. The two assailants wore black hoodies and one of them wore a black mask, but that was common. Many of the victims described a silver handgun, but there could've also been different guns that looked alike.

There was one detail that caught Sines's eye. It was specific enough to make her think that it could've been the same two guys who carried out many or most of the Bloomingdale robberies that summer. According to victim statements to the police, the robbers demanded their victims disable the "Find My Phone" tracking app on their cell phones before they grabbed the phone and ran off. Reading the incident reports, she saw this sequence of events five or six times.

She pictured the same armed thieves demanding Seth's phone in this way. Seth, in his inebriated state, could have resisted or tried to fight them off. The band on Seth's watch was torn, suggesting a possible struggle. Thieves don't usually shoot their targets, but it was possible the killer fired out of self-defense, or the gun discharged by accident.

That the two men *didn't* take Seth's phone or any of his other possessions—a key element of the conspiracy theories—didn't surprise Sines: the moment the gun went off, whoever pulled the trigger knew there would be cops on the scene in minutes. There wasn't any time to pick the guy's pockets before escaping.

Sines noticed something else interesting in the crime data. Sometime in August 2016, the street robberies stopped. There were still muggings in the Bloomingdale and LeDroit Park neighborhoods, but the pattern of robberies near Seth's house—the silver gun, disabling the tracking app—ended. She went back and found a press release on the DC Metropolitan Police Department's website that announced the arrest of a nineteen-year-old DC resident for thirteen different armed robberies committed all over the District. A few months later, the nineteen-year-old pleaded guilty to several of those armed robberies along with a codefendant who was a few years older and also a DC resident. The robberies allegedly committed by the two men had continued after Seth was shot and killed. If Sines's theory of the case was right, and this was a case of an armed robbery gone horribly wrong, then the additional robberies made sense. Street criminals in DC didn't stop committing crimes because they learned one of their victims worked at the DNC. They stopped because they got caught.

But she had no evidence that connected the two arrested men to Seth's murder. And without something tangible, she didn't have a good reason to interview the men who were about to be sentenced to years in prison for the crimes they had already admitted to.

15

Give Us a Wink

ROD WHEELER WAS walking around LeDroit Park, trying to strike up a conversation with some guys on the street. "Hey man, who do you all know?" he asked. "Do you know anything about this dude getting killed?" If two guys really had tried to rob Seth and then panicked, shot him, and run off into the night, as the police claimed, someone in the area might know about it. A girlfriend, maybe. Or a neighbor. The people most likely to have information about the unsolved murder lived nearby. The best thing you could do as a detective, Wheeler believed, was to canvass the surrounding area. Ask people if they remembered the crime, remind them about the reward for information. That was how you solved crimes on the street.

Wheeler's phone rang. It was Butowsky. When Wheeler said he was out looking for new leads in the case, Butowsky rebuked him.

Wheeler would later recall Butowsky telling him that he was wasting time and that Butowsky wasn't going to use him if he didn't do what Butowsky told him to do.

"Am I going to do the investigation or are you?" Wheeler replied. "If I'm going to do it, I'm going to do it the way I know how to do it, which is out in the street."

After he left LeDroit Park, Wheeler replayed his conversation with Butowsky, trying to make sense of it. Weeks earlier, shortly after Butowsky had first contacted him, Butowsky had played the recording of his conversation with Seymour Hersh. Wheeler found the Hersh recording less than convincing. Moreover, he didn't see the connection between the murder he was hired to solve—that Butowsky was paying him to solve—and some old journalist passing along gossip. Now, with Butowsky chiding him for doing basic police work, he started to question what Butowsky's motives were. *What's up with this dude*, Wheeler thought. (Butowsky doesn't recall the conversation.)

Wheeler was used to people telling him how to solve a homicide because they'd watched a few episodes of *CSI*. He still believed he might find something the detectives had missed, new surveillance footage or a person with information about who shot Seth. But he also didn't want to create a rift between himself and Butowsky. It was Butowsky, after all, who was paying him for his investigative work on the Rich case. What's more, Wheeler had higher aspirations than working as a food-safety consultant and moonlighting as a PI. He knew Butowsky had connections to President Trump's political network and dropped hints about his desire to join Trump's administration. "I've got to find a way on the Trump team," he texted Butowsky. When Butowsky offered to connect him with several Trump aides, Wheeler said he wanted to join FEMA, the emergency-management agency. "Lots of senior admin positions open there."

One day in mid-April, Butowsky texted him, "Are you in Washington DC area on Thursday afternoon?" He had a meeting at the White House and wanted Wheeler to join him.

———◆——

In March, Malia Zimmerman emailed the DC police, but they had no updates to share on the Rich case. She got nowhere with the FBI: a spokeswoman for the bureau's Washington Field Office said it had no involvement with the case whatsoever. She forwarded the agency's response to Butowsky and Wheeler. Butowsky replied by adding another layer to the conspiracy he was sure was underway. "The entire case is being investigated by the DC police homicide division," he wrote, "and as we know they were told not to pursue it." He didn't explain the "as we know." He didn't offer Wheeler or Zimmerman any sources to back his claim. It was just another operating assumption: a conspiracy to explain a conspiracy.

Zimmerman asked Butowsky to use his contacts in the Republican Party to aid her investigation. "Devin Nunes needs to help us or get his guy to," she emailed Butowsky. "What we know dispels that whole narrative [sic]"—meaning the Russian hacking allegations. A Republican congressman from Fresno, California, Nunes was the chairman of the House Intelligence Committee at the time, which gave him unparalleled access to classified information. Butowsky, who had met Nunes through a friend, replied, "I will get very aggressive with Devin over the weekend."

She also enlisted Wheeler's help. She forwarded him every question she had about the case and sent him a long list of items "for us to get from police and family," which included records for Seth's cell, content from his computer hard drive, security camera footage, autopsy records, and the death certificate. In the end Wheeler was never able to gain access to any of these materials, either because the police investigation remained active or because he never gained the full trust of the family, Aaron in particular.

With Joel and Mary's permission, however, Wheeler did secure a meeting with the detective in the case, Joseph Della-Camera. Two nights before, Butowsky emailed Wheeler, "Della-Camera is either helping us or we will go after him as being part of the coverup."

Sitting across from Wheeler, Della-Camera walked him through the department's working theory of the case. Della-Camera still believed it had been a "robbery gone bad," according to Wheeler's notes. Two guys had tried to rob Seth, who fought back, and the muggers shot him. Della-Camera mentioned the partial surveillance footage from Flagler Market, and he alluded to a witness who'd seen two people running near the crime scene soon after the shooting. He talked about how the theory that Seth's murder was somehow connected to his job or WikiLeaks "threw things off with the investigation . . . I've got nothing to say or to show that the shooting was related to emails or anything other than a street robbery."

Wheeler pressed Della-Camera for answers. Could it have been a hit ordered by the DNC? Della-Camera dismissed this: a hitman would've killed his target on the spot, and Seth lived long enough to get transported to a hospital and receive emergency surgery before he died. Did Seth tell the responding officers who might have shot him before he succumbed to his injuries at the hospital? Did Seth's financial records contain any evidence that he'd received any money from WikiLeaks? What was Wheeler supposed to say if reporters came to him and asked whether he could definitively rule out that Seth's murder had anything to do with his work at the DNC? Wheeler looked straight at Della-Camera and asked, "The answer?"

Della-Camera let out a long sigh and an awkward laugh. "Look, Rod, please, please do not quote me on anything," Della-Camera said near the end of their meeting. "I don't need that shit coming back on me." He had to protect the integrity of his investigation, and if he was somehow quoted, he could be reassigned to some terrible job at the Central Cell Block downtown.

Wheeler sent his notes to Zimmerman and Butowsky (but not Joel, Mary, or Aaron). Della-Camera, even with his guard somewhat down, had never wavered from his belief that Seth was the victim of a tragic but ordinary street crime. He certainly had not made any suggestion that the chief of police or the mayor had buried the case for political reasons.

If Zimmerman seemed unusually invested in finding evidence for the more sinister theories around Seth's life and death, there was a reason: she had already written a lengthy draft of a story that named Seth as the source for the WikiLeaks Democratic email dump. The draft began, "The Democratic National Committee staffer who was gunned down on a Washington, D.C., street 8 months ago just steps from his home in the cozy Washington DC Columbia Heights neighborhood did, in fact, provide some 30,000 internal emails between DNC party leaders to WikiLeaks, Fox News has confirmed."

It would be the first time a reporter from a national news organization with huge influence had made this claim as fact, not theory. The implications of such a story would be staggering. It would reveal an even vaster conspiracy at work, a cover-up of almost unimaginable proportions that would implicate anyone in power who had blamed Russia for the attack at the DNC—the Obama White House, the biggest US intelligence agencies, the FBI, the DC police, the Clinton campaign, and many others. The story played into the larger fears held by both mainstream conservatives and the far-right fringe that the deep state was out to overthrow Trump from office—a belief in an insidious government bureaucracy that had its roots in conspiracy theories going back to Joseph McCarthy and the John Birch Society.

There was one problem: Zimmerman hadn't confirmed it yet.

She hadn't confirmed it before Wheeler got hired and hadn't confirmed it after he'd begun his investigation. On April 29, she sent Butowsky a new draft of the story. She bolded the parts of the story she had yet to nail down, which included every allegation that pinned the DNC hack squarely on Seth. On May 4, she re-sent the bolded draft with a message: "Any news on the key point?" A week later she tried a different approach. "Ed, Rod, could you please ask your sources," she wrote, followed by a list of questions about whether they knew "for sure" that Seth had transmitted emails to WikiLeaks, how much he got paid for them, and whether there was an effort to "cover up the fact that Seth Rich was the leaker."

In theory Wheeler and Zimmerman were acting on separate tracks, conducting their own investigations. But by the spring of 2017, the two tracks had merged into one. In the middle of it all was Butowsky. Cell phone records show that between December 2016 and June 2017, Zimmerman and Butowsky spoke 571 times and exchanged 480 text messages. Butowsky joined most phone calls with Wheeler and Zimmerman. He asked Wheeler for updates about the status of the investigation. Before dinner with a "senior Trump person," Butowsky asked Wheeler for a two-page summary of his findings. At one point he told Wheeler that "we are working on the case together." Far from staying away from Wheeler's investigation as he had promised Joel Rich, Butowsky acted like a team lead.

———◆———

In late April, Butowsky landed a meeting with White House press secretary Sean Spicer at the White House. He invited Wheeler to join him. They stopped in the James S. Brady Briefing

Room and mingled with the handful of reporters there—Wheeler posed for a picture behind the press secretary's podium—before they made their way to Spicer's office.

Spicer would later say he had a faint recollection of meeting Butowsky at a few fundraising events during the campaign. He was familiar with Butowsky's type. The kind of guy who had enough money to fly first class but not his own plane. He knew Butowsky had volunteered as a surrogate spokesman for Trump. He also recalled that Butowsky would email him unsolicited talking points about the latest jobs report or some other economic news. When Spicer's assistant told him Butowsky would be visiting the White House and wanted to say hi, as Spicer recalled, he said, "Sure, bring him by for a few minutes."

According to Wheeler, Butowsky and Spicer did most of the talking. Butowsky introduced Wheeler and said he was working on the Rich murder investigation. Wheeler recalled Spicer asking if there was anything he could do to help; Wheeler said he thought the DC police could use some assistance from the FBI. He knew from his days as a cop that the FBI could get information the police couldn't. Wheeler said he gave Spicer the latest version of his investigative report and the meeting ended. Spicer, for his part, doesn't remember offering to help. "It was more of a 'Good to see you, I wanted to say hi,'" Spicer recalled. "The entire conversation was five to seven minutes."

At that particular moment in time, the White House would have taken a keen interest in any investigation or story that would distract from, or better yet contradict, the steady drip of revelations and controversies about Russia and the Trump administration. Trump's national security adviser, Lt. Gen. Michael Flynn, had resigned after he lied to the FBI about conversations he'd had with the Russian ambassador to the US before Trump took office. Jeff Sessions, the attorney general, had announced he would recuse himself from any federal investigations into the 2016 election after he likely misled Congress at his confirmation hearing about his own contacts with the Russian ambassador. James Comey, the head of the FBI, had told a House committee that the bureau had an active investigation into Trump ties to Russia. At the same time, Trump himself had privately pressured Comey to shut down the federal investigation into Michael Flynn, at one point telling Comey, "I hope you can let this go."

Trump and his staff were obsessed with the allegations of Russian election interference and possible collusion between the Trump campaign and Russia, viewing them as an attack on the legitimacy of his victory. The evidence for the interference was strong, less so for the collusion accusation, but the president sought to conflate the two subjects and then discredit them both as part of a politically motivated witch hunt he referred to as "Russiagate."

The pressure bearing down on the Trump White House was about to get much worse. In early May, Trump fired Comey and soon afterward suggested in an interview he did it because "this Russia thing with Trump and Russia is a made-up story." Comey, meanwhile, had written memos that documented interactions he'd had with Trump that bordered on questionable if not illegal behavior. Sensing he wouldn't last long as the FBI changed direction under Trump, Comey had passed the memos to a friend with instructions to relay them to a reporter at the *New York Times*, which prepared to publish them as soon as possible.

Even if Butowsky and Wheeler had the support of the White House, they weren't any closer to getting Zimmerman the confirmation she needed. May was ticking by, and she was no closer to securing the confirmation she needed. Butowsky emailed Seymour Hersh on several occasions, asking him for help confirming the Seth–WikiLeaks story. "if i believed it, i would have written it," Hersh told him. "that's what i do for a living. . . and i did not write a word about seth rich." Butowsky wouldn't relent. He asked if Hersh would call his source again to confirm whether the FBI's "cyber unit" had indeed analyzed Seth's computer, adding, "I have been helping the family out on my own nickel and just want to confirm that one little piece of the story."

Reporters hear things, Hersh wrote back, they believe things, and they check those things out. And if what they hear isn't true or can't be proved, they move on to the next story. That's how journalism works. Hersh said he never had enough information to take to the FBI, so he moved on. "i did not write it, and that is all you need to know," Hersh wrote.

"I understand," Butowsky responded.

There was still another source Butowsky knew that could be in a position to help. He worked for Congressman Nunes on the Intelligence Committee. Butowsky never used his name in text messages, instead referring to him as D.O. or Dee O. Before Wheeler met with D.O. at the Library of Congress, Butowsky sent him a message intended to keep Wheeler's spirits up. "Once we get the story out, you will be one of the most recognize [*sic*] names in America," Butowsky told him. "Please call me after you meet with Dee O. The main goal with him is to get him to get the FBI record and give us a wink to go [with the] story that the emails are there."

Wheeler sat down across from Butowsky's source, who introduced himself by his first name only. "Just call me Kash," he said. He looked to be in his thirties, Indian descent, with a beard and glasses. It was only afterward that Wheeler realized "Kash" was Kash Patel, an investigator on the Intelligence Committee and an aide to Chairman Nunes.

Nunes held an outsized role at the start of the Trump presidency. He ran one of the most powerful committees in Congress and was one of the president's most loyal allies. At the time, Patel and Nunes were preparing the first of Congress's many exhaustive reports on the 2016 election and Russian interference. As the meeting unfolded, it was unclear if Patel expected Wheeler to provide evidence for the report, or if Patel planned to share intel for Wheeler's murder investigation. Over coffee Wheeler briefed Patel on his findings so far and offered to introduce Patel to the DC police. They could share files and compare notes, see if one could help the other. Patel didn't give up much about his own investigation, but he agreed to take Wheeler up on his offer to meet with the police. The meeting ended after twenty minutes.

But a few days later, on May 10, Butowsky and Zimmerman called Wheeler with exciting news: they had found a source at the FBI who supposedly confirmed that Seth had communicated with WikiLeaks. "Are you sure about this source?" Wheeler asked. "Is the source credible?"

Zimmerman and Butowsky wouldn't say who the source was or what was said. But the source was legit, they said. The only catch: this source, whoever it was, could not be named. Zimmerman needed at least one on-the-record source in the story. It had to be Wheeler.

Zimmerman then circulated a new version of her story to Wheeler and Butowsky. The crux of it was the same as in previous drafts, but now it featured a new source: a "federal investigator" who had "reviewed an FBI forensic report" about the contents of Seth's computer. That report confirmed that Seth had sent emails to WikiLeaks, the story said.

Butowsky was getting anxious. He pleaded with Wheeler in texts and phone calls to finish his investigation and help Zimmerman finish her story. On May 14, Butowsky left Wheeler a voicemail. "We have the full attention of the White House on this," Butowsky said.

"Not to add any more pressure but the president just read the article," Butowsky said in a follow-up text message. "He wants the article out immediately. It's now all up to you. But don't feel the pressure." Butowsky would later say he had "never communicated" with Trump "about any article ever published by Fox News, whether in draft form or otherwise." In the moment, though, it was possible Butowsky said this to pressure Wheeler into providing confirmation or quotes for Zimmerman's story.

The following day, May 15, Zimmerman called Wheeler and told him the "bosses at Fox want her to go" with her story. She sent him the latest draft and asked him to review several quotes in the story attributed to him. Wheeler texted Zimmerman back a few hours later: "Malia you can add [to the story] that I do strongly believe that the answers to who murdered Seth sits on his computer on a shelf at the D.C. Police or FBI headquarters!"

That evening, the *Washington Post* reported that Trump had revealed "highly classified information" to the Russian foreign minister and ambassador in an Oval Office meeting the week before. At that point anything that moved the spotlight from the Trump-Russia story for even a single news cycle couldn't come soon enough for the White House.

Zimmerman sent a brief request for comment to Joel Rich and then filed her latest draft with the editors in New York. Wheeler, for his part, texted a local TV reporter he knew and tipped her off to the big scoop Fox was set to publish. The reporter, Marina Marraco, asked Wheeler if he'd go on camera for a short segment teasing the story. He was eating dinner at a steakhouse near the Capitol and stepped outside to tape the interview. He told Marraco that it's "confirmed" Seth was the WikiLeaks source. Marraco wrote up Wheeler's remarks and published her own story that evening, preempting Zimmerman's.

Zimmerman was angry. "This could be really bad if the Fox News channel thinks you fed an exclusive we invested a lot of time and money into to a local channel just hours before we were going to publish," she texted Wheeler. Butowsky urged them all to calm down. Zimmerman's story would run the next morning, and its impact would be massive. In the early morning hours of May 16, Butowsky alerted producers and hosts at Fox News to Zimmerman's forthcoming story and emphasized the biggest takeaway: "If you have any questions about the story or more information needed, call me. I'm actually the one who's been putting this together but as you know I keep my name out of things because I have no credibility. One of the big conclusions we need to draw from this is that the Russians did not hack our computer systems and ste[a]l emails and there was no collusion like trump with the Russians."

16

Rabbits Out of Hats

EARLY THE NEXT morning, Brad Bauman, the Rich family's spokes-man, awoke at his uncle's house in Fort Lauderdale. His grandfather had just died. He had flown to Florida to attend the funeral and sit shiva with the rest of his family. He began his day like he would any other, by scanning the Drudge Report.

Above the words "Drudge Report" he saw Seth's face. It was the same photo of Seth that had circulated after the murder—wry grin, arms folded, Washington monument in the distance. An enormous, all-caps headline shouted in bright red letters, "Dead DNC Staffer 'Had Contact' with WikiLeaks." The link took him to a story on the website of a local Fox affiliate for Washington, DC. Its headline read, "Family's private investigator: There is evidence Seth Rich had contact with WikiLeaks prior to death." The story said there was "tangible evidence on Rich's laptop that confirms he was communicating with WikiLeaks prior to his death." The only source cited for this bold claim was Rod Wheeler, who, when asked by the reporter about the Seth Rich–WikiLeaks connections, replied, "Absolutely. Yeah. That's correct."

Nothing about the story made sense. Bauman had never heard of the reporter who'd written it, and there was no indication she had con-tacted him or the Riches before publication. And then there was Wheeler—why had he talked to this reporter? He wasn't supposed to talk to *any* media. Less than an hour later, a second story about Seth appeared on the front page of FoxNews.com. This time Bauman recognized the byline: Malia Zimmerman. Her story was much longer and went into greater detail than the local Fox affiliate's report. According to her story, a federal investigator, who had reviewed an "FBI forensic report" about Seth's computer, claimed Seth was the source for the DNC emails published by WikiLeaks. The federal investigator went on to assert that Seth had initially contacted WikiLeaks through Gavin McFadyen, an American documentary filmmaker and associate of Assange's. McFadyen had died in October 2016 and couldn't corroborate this story.

To support the anonymous federal investigator's claims, Zimmerman turned to a second, on-the-record source: Rod Wheeler. "My investigation up to this point shows there was some degree of email exchange between Seth Rich and WikiLeaks," Wheeler was quoted as saying. "I do believe that the answers to who murdered Seth Rich sits on his computer on a shelf at the DC police or FBI headquarters." Zimmerman identified Wheeler as a private investigator "hired by Rich's family to probe the case." Who could be a better authority on the details of the Rich murder investigation than the person hired by Rich's family to solve it?

The two articles raced across the internet, inspiring hundreds of follow-up stories in American and international news outlets. "Not Russia, but an Inside Job?" read the headline of the lead story on Breitbart News. "If proven, the report has the potential to be one of the biggest cover-ups in American political history," Breitbart's reporter wrote, "dispelling the widespread claim that the Russians were behind hacks on the DNC." Commenters on Reddit's r/The_Donald forum seized on the story as proof of what they had believed all along: "This is so huge," one wrote. "We can't let up. We have been wanting justice for Seth for a long time. We were the only ones, and now look what's happening." By midmorning, Seth's name was trending on Twitter. The allegation that he was WikiLeaks' source had gone viral.

———◆———

Minutes after Zimmerman's story appeared, the hosts of *Fox & Friends* read from it live on air. "It seems very suspicious," cohost Ainsley Earhardt said, adding, "You know what's interesting—that the parents aren't pursuing it." Laura Ingraham, the conservative media star, blasted the "frothing media" for its "aggressive lack of curiosity" in the story.

The same couldn't be said for Fox News. By 9:00 a.m., Fox had aired four different segments about the allegations. The new revelations were "breathtaking" and "bombshell new evidence." The Fox News Twitter account shared the Fox 5 interview and Zimmerman's story with its 14.5 million followers. In the week that followed, hosts, correspondents, and guest commentators at the network would push the Seth Rich story and proclaim Trump absolved of any wrongdoing related to Russia and the 2016 election. During an appearance on Fox, Newt Gingrich, the former Speaker of the House turned conservative pundit, said Seth had been "assassinated." He added, "It turns out it wasn't the Russians. It was this young guy who, I suspect, was disgusted by the corruption of the Democratic National Committee. He's been killed, and apparently nothing serious has been done to investigate his murder."

The Seth Rich–WikiLeaks story was a winner for Fox. It flipped the Russian interference story on its head, pinning the blame instead on a young political staffer who wasn't alive to defend himself. It exonerated Trump from any culpability that he knew about or encouraged Russia's meddling in the 2016 election. The cloud of scandal that had settled over Trump's nascent presidency briefly lifted. Fox News had its own bombshell to share with its viewers, one that would hit them in the gut and make them feel good all at once.

The story broke through in a way it never had before—a way it never *could* have without the power of Fox News. Many months later a Harvard law professor named Yochai Benkler would study Fox's coverage of Seth Rich and attempt to measure the impact Fox had on amplifying the story. Benkler was originally interested in propaganda in the internet age: how information moved, the networks that spread that information, who the biggest amplifiers were.

Benkler and his researchers didn't set out looking for Fox News; they believed online propaganda was driving the erosion of trust in facts and science in America. They chose several well-known stories to be their case studies—Seth Rich among them—and mapped out a network of misinformation spreaders. It looked almost like a solar system, with large planets surrounded by smaller moons. The larger the dot, the more powerful its influence in spreading propaganda. Fox News was the sun, the biggest of them all. "They are systematically at the rotten core of disinformation in the American political media ecosystem," Benkler said. "More than anything else, and possibly more than everything else put together."

When Fox ran a story on its airwaves, the impact was immediate, Benkler found. "As soon as it goes on TV, it explodes online," he said. Yes, Fox hyped certain stories, but it also created the online attention itself by providing the legitimacy and the exposure to a story like the Seth–WikiLeaks one. "Once Fox News said it, it's no longer a crazy fringe conspiracy," Benkler said. "It's the news." He estimated that, if you combined TV, radio, and online news, 35 to 40 percent of Americans got their news from Fox and believed the network's hosts and correspondents when they said, for instance, that Seth Rich was behind the DNC hack. Even in the internet age, Benkler realized, mass media—cable news and talk radio—still drove the conversation, making them the most powerful force in spreading misinformation. And in the worlds of cable news and talk radio, few could match the influence of Fox's Sean Hannity.

President Trump and Hannity supposedly spoke on the phone nearly every day. Hannity and Trump would talk about what Hannity should cover on his show or what Trump should tweet to his sixty million followers, or else Hannity would simply listen as the president complained. Inside the White House some referred to Hannity as the "shadow chief of staff." But the nickname missed something vital about the nature of Hannity's relationship with Trump and Fox's relationship with Trump's administration. Fox wasn't a mouthpiece or propaganda organ of the White House; it worked the other way around. The president of the United States spent hours every day watching Fox, tweeting about what he'd seen, and demanding that his staff follow up on statements or allegations made by Fox on-air guests that Trump agreed with.

To those who knew him off camera, Hannity had a different reputation. He was "aggressively friendly," as a former Fox host put it. He asked about your kids and how they were doing in school. He engendered loyalty among his staff, handing out generous end-of-the-year bonuses and offering to help in the event of a health scare or personal crisis. "Asshole on the air, but super nice guy" was how the former host described him.

When the two Fox stories about Seth Rich appeared, Hannity tweeted about them dozens of times to his 2.5 million Twitter followers. Hannity's audience even included members of the extended Rich family. One of Joel and Mary's nephews who supported Trump replied to a Hannity tweet about Seth: "First thing I said when my Dad told me [Seth had died] was he knew something and he was murdered. The rest of the family thought I was nuts. See last name." The nephew quickly deleted the tweet, but not fast enough to stop it from being saved and held up as proof: *Look*, it seemed to say, *even Seth Rich's own family members believe it.*

———◆———

Bauman had worked in political communications long enough to know that he and the Riches weren't dealing with a one-day story here. Sitting on his uncle's patio, he tried to devise a plan. If they didn't act quickly, the Seth–WikiLeaks narrative would reach a point where no amount of rapid response and fact-checking would stop the lie from spreading. But before he did anything, he needed to get Joel and Mary on the phone.

Joel picked up at the house in Omaha. He had no inkling just how far the Fox News story had already spread. Bauman asked him to get Mary on the phone too.

"Well, Mary's sleeping," Joel said. "She'll get back to you later."

"Joel. Take the damn phone upstairs now."

Joel walked upstairs and woke Mary.

"The media will wait," she said. "I need sleep."

"Not this time," Bauman said. "We have to have a response *now*."

Bauman didn't sugarcoat his assessment of the mess they found themselves in. Over the past few months, Joel would occasionally type Seth's name in Google and look for any new stories about his son. He might see one or two published in the past twenty-four or forty-eight hours. The latest story he saw in Google went live twenty-three seconds before he logged in, and they kept coming. They had to move fast, Bauman told Joel and Mary. Any new story about Seth that the family didn't swiftly respond to would metastasize. "I'll have a statement written in twenty minutes," he said. "I want you and Mary and Aaron to look at it. You've got ten minutes to give me edits. After you give me edits, that's it. It's final."

He said that Aaron should find Wheeler's contract that banned him from unauthorized media interviews. Bauman would send the contract to a few reporters he trusted, showing how Wheeler had betrayed the family and casting doubt on his credibility. Before he ended the call, Bauman had one last thing to say. In the nine months he'd worked for the Riches, he had never lost his temper with Joel and Mary. They were grieving parents; Bauman had only wanted to shield them from the worst of it all. But in that moment, he needed to level with Joel and Mary.

"I don't know how the fuck I'm going to get all of us out of this one," he said. "But I assure you that I'm running out of rabbits to pull out of hats here."

———◆———

Later that day Mary drove to a hotel on the western edge of Omaha for a job interview. It had taken her some time since Seth was killed to feel like she could work again, but lately she'd felt strong enough to look for a new job. She also wanted to do something that she felt honored Seth's memory, a job that made her feel she was doing something worthwhile.

The company she was interviewing with was a civic-minded outfit that made it easy for individuals and businesses to contact their House member or senator about the issues they cared about. Mary was told that she could make her own schedule so long as she met her quotas. She'd made it to the final round, and someone from the company had flown to Omaha to interview her. The conversation was going well until it took a sudden detour.

"God, have you heard about this Seth?" the rep asked Mary. "Oh, he's all over. It's all over the media. And he's from Omaha."

Mary fell silent for a moment. "Do you know the last name?" she asked.

"Let me think," he said. "No, no, I don't think I do."

"Would it happen to be Rich?"

Mortified, he looked at Mary and said, "Is that your son?"

"Yes, that's my son," she said. "And no, he didn't do it."

The company would extend Mary an offer to work for them, but by the time she received it her health had deteriorated to the point that she couldn't accept the position.

———◆———

Bauman sent the family's response to Fox to every reporter who might be covering the story. "We have seen no facts, we have seen no evidence, we have been approached with no emails, and only learned about this when contacted by the press." The statement also disclosed the terms of Wheeler's contract with the Riches. Bauman reached out to reporters he trusted and briefed them on Wheeler and the holes in Zimmerman's story. And he sent the statement to Zimmerman and asked her to update her story with the family's response refuting it.

The next day he asked her why she hadn't updated her story. Bauman also shared a previously unreported detail with a journalist at NBC News—that a third party, named Ed Butowsky, had paid for Wheeler's services on behalf of the Rich family. Now Butowsky's name began to circulate in the media, with reporters highlighting Butowsky's connection to the Benghazi controversy and to Fox News and Fox Business.

A bigger problem appeared: Hannity announced that he would address Fox's reporting about Seth and WikiLeaks on his primetime show that evening. Rod Wheeler would be his special guest.

17

Panic at the Network

ZIMMERMAN'S STORY HAD landed with such impact that a reporter asked press secretary Sean Spicer for his and the president's reaction at the daily press briefing. Although Spicer had met with Butowsky and Wheeler a month earlier, he said he knew nothing about the case. "I don't—I'm not aware of—generally, I don't get updates on DNC—former DNC staffers. I'm not aware of that." Zimmerman and her editors had to respond. They decided to rewrite the top of her story, incorporating the Rich family's statement high in the piece. But they kept the most explosive allegations in her story, signaling to the world that they stood behind their reporting.

Soon Zimmerman had a bigger problem. A reporter from CNN had interviewed Wheeler about the Fox 5 and Fox News stories, and he had backtracked. He said that he had no evidence to suggest Seth had exchanged emails with anyone at WikiLeaks—a direct contradiction to what Zimmerman quoted him as saying. Wheeler then went further in his repudiation of her story, saying that his only source for any information about Seth and WikiLeaks were the two Fox stories. "I only got that [information] from the reporter at Fox News," he said. In other words, Wheeler had no original information on the central allegations in the story; he'd merely repeated back to Zimmerman what she'd told him in the first place.

For Zimmerman this didn't make any sense. Wheeler *had* texted at least one quote to her on the day before her story ran—she had the text on her phone. As Wheeler's reversal started getting attention, Butowsky frantically tried to reach him. Wheeler didn't answer his cell phone. He tried texting. "Ron," he wrote, spelling Wheeler's name wrong, "speak to no one before you talk to me. Please call." Almost an hour later, he texted Wheeler, "Call me call me call me." A minute after that, he texted again: "Can you FaceTime me."

Zimmerman was also trying to get in contact with Wheeler. "Did you just go on CNN?" she texted him just before four o'clock that afternoon on the East Coast. "My top boss in the Company said you were just on and said there are mistakes in my story." No, Wheeler replied, as a paid Fox contributor he couldn't make on-air appearances on other networks. A CNN media reporter named Oliver Darcy had reached Wheeler by phone. Wheeler told Darcy he hadn't provided the quotes in Zimmerman's story, and Darcy had emailed Fox's PR department for a response.

Despite the mounting questions about what Wheeler did or didn't say, Hannity announced that Wheeler would appear on his show to discuss the alleged Seth–WikiLeaks connection. Zimmerman sent Wheeler a text to calm him down and to get him back on message before his Hannity appearance. "Reread the story we sent to you last night and stick to that script," she texted Wheeler.

———◆———

At just past 10:00 p.m. on May 16, the cameras went live for the latest episode of *Hannity*. The words "MURDER MYSTERY" flashed onscreen. Hannity began his show by teasing "explosive developments" in a "massive breaking news story." Hannity had for months told his audience about the forces lined up to take down President Trump: the "propaganda media," the "never-Trumpers," the "Washington deep state establishment," and all the other fifth columnists. Now, thanks to Fox's own reporting, the biggest crime in American politics since the Watergate break-in was revealed to be an inside job. The press, the intelligence agencies, members of Congress—they had all lied. If in fact a "disgruntled" Democrat had leaked the emails, Hannity explained, it could also suggest that Seth Rich was murdered "under very suspicious circumstances."

Hannity devoted three segments to Seth and WikiLeaks. First he showed footage of an earlier interview he'd done with Julian Assange, in which the WikiLeaks founder reiterated that Russia hadn't given him the stolen DNC emails. Next he interviewed two prominent advisers to President Trump and frequent guests on the show, lawyer Jay Sekulow and political operative Dave Bossie. Was it possible, Hannity asked Sekulow, "that the leaks really came from a DNC staffer and that the media's been wrong for almost a year now?" Sekulow called the timeline of events around Seth's murder and the DNC hack "troubling, to say the least."

And finally, for his third segment, Hannity introduced Wheeler as if the two men were old friends (they weren't), praising Wheeler as "a man of honor and integrity." But anyone hoping Wheeler would set the record straight was in for a letdown. He looked nervous. He rambled. He'd "checked out" the key source in Zimmerman's story, the anonymous federal investigator, and found the person "very credible." But then he said he hadn't seen any emails between Seth and WikiLeaks, didn't know where Seth's computer was, and couldn't say if Seth's murder had any connection to his DNC job. "I don't know as a matter of fact if the emails went out to WikiLeaks or anybody else," he added, "but it sure appears that way."

———————•❘•———————

The news side of Fox News was scrambling to figure out if Malia Zimmerman's story about Seth and WikiLeaks was accurate or a catastrophic blunder. Zimmerman, Butowsky, and Fox News were under growing pressure to defend their story. Wheeler's unconvincing appearance on Hannity's show had only made things worse. As had Wheeler's interviews with CNN and other media outlets in which he repeated the same confusing story about his involvement with Zimmerman and Butowsky. By then Wheeler's credibility was tarnished so much that Fox 5, the local affiliate that ran the first Seth–WikiLeaks story, added an "important clarification" to its interview with Wheeler in light of his comments.

On May 18, Zimmerman received a long email from Joel Rich. The Rich family was calling on Fox News to issue a full retraction of her story. Fox needed to do the "right thing," he wrote, "so we can definitively fight back against the untruthful rumors that continue to haunt our family and Seth's memory." Zimmerman told Joel she forwarded his email to her bosses, and soon it had caught the attention of different departments across Fox News, who wanted answers as to why Zimmerman's blockbuster scoop appeared to be falling apart. Fox's PR department flagged a tweet from the Russian embassy in the UK that "#WikiLeaks informer Seth Rich murdered in US." A Fox PR manager emailed a top editor at FoxNews.com named Refet Kaplan, who managed the entire newsroom for Fox's digital operation. "Do you have any update on whether there will be a clarification/correction to the Seth Rich story?"

An hour later the same PR manager emailed Kaplan again. This time she added Jay Wallace, the head of news programming at Fox, and Irena Briganti, the head of PR. *Newsweek*, *New York* magazine, and CNN had all contacted Fox since the Russian embassy's tweet, she wrote. "We look foolish as we haven't issued any clarifications/corrections to our store [*sic*] despite Wheeler saying we misquoted him to other news outlets," she wrote. She also forwarded Kaplan an NBC story reporting that the Rich family had sent a cease-and-desist order to Wheeler, threatening legal action if he continued to speak out about Seth.

A few hours later, Zimmerman replied to Joel—an email that the higher-ups at Fox had written for her. "We are in the process of reviewing our story in the interest of ensuring fairness and accuracy," it read. "As you know, much of our information came from a private investigator, Rod Wheeler, who we understand was working on behalf of the Rich family." In other words, Rod Wheeler was your problem, not ours.

Zimmerman forwarded Joel's retraction request to Wheeler, saying her bosses wanted a response to Joel's comments. "Please call me asap," she told him. She also sent Joel's email to Butowsky. "Total BS," he wrote back. He told her that he saw the hidden hand of Brad Bauman, the Rich family's spokesman, working in tandem with the DNC to discredit "the great work you and Rod have done." He continued, "I didn't tell you yet but the federal government is involved at this moment, behind the scene[s] and [they] believe your story, Malia."

Eventually, Butowsky, Zimmerman, and Wheeler joined a three-way call, which Wheeler recorded. Wheeler sounded shaken. He read aloud from Zimmerman's email responding to Joel. Zimmerman had told Joel that much of what Fox had reported had come from Wheeler, who of course had been hired by the Rich family—the implication being that any inaccuracies in the story were somehow the fault of the family for hiring Wheeler, not Fox for using him as a source. Wheeler took issue with this description. "That's not accurate, though," he said. "Much of the information did not come from me." Now people were threatening him with lawsuits, he said. "The narrative that's going on around now is 'Rod, Rod, Rod screwed this up,'" he said. "That's the narrative. And that narrative is incorrect as we know." The last thing he wanted was for Fox News to "throw me under the bus because that would be unfair."

Butowsky tried to reassure him that Zimmerman's story was "perfect." People threatened lawsuits all the time, and if Wheeler did get sued, think of the explosive material he could get in discovery. "There's no blame here," Butowsky told him. If anyone deserved blame, it was Brad Bauman. He "is creating all of this." The truth would come out soon enough, Butowsky said. "You're gonna win an award because we're gonna break this thing open real soon. And everyone's gonna see that every word in there is correct."

Wheeler felt aggrieved by the events of the last several days. He had gone on Hannity's show and looked like a fool. Strangers were leaving him angry voicemail messages. He noticed a statement posted to Butowsky's Facebook page titled "Rod Wheeler's response," which claimed he had never violated his contract with the family. But Wheeler had written no such statement. "Who was this response made to?" he asked Ed in an email. "I never approved of this 'response.'" Butowsky called him to apologize and tried to assure him that the blowback they were experiencing "for putting an end to the Russian bullshit" would soon fade. (Butowsky doesn't recall saying this.)

But despite Butowsky's confidence, he and Zimmerman still couldn't come up with the backup needed to satisfy the editors and executives at Fox. On another call with Wheeler, Butowsky outlined a plan to pressure Sy Hersh to give up his supposed FBI source. An old high school friend of Butowsky's who "does a lot of crisis management stuff" would record five seconds of Hersh's voice from Butowsky's original recording. The friend would email the clip to Hersh and say he had three hours to name his source. If Hersh didn't play ball, Butowsky's friend would tell Hersh that "a full recording of everything we have will be at every news agency tonight with your name and phone number on it." But if Hersh complied, he would never hear from Butowsky again. Ultimately, Butowsky never went through with his plan.

Butowsky also sent Zimmerman an audio recording of himself talking to an alleged source at the National Security Agency. Zimmerman, in turn, sent the file to her editor, Greg Wilson. "The NSA guy said my story is accurate," she told Wilson. "He's working to get files from the FBI and from the dark web." Wilson called the recording "very interesting" but said he had "no idea" who's talking to Butowsky. "I only sorta know who Ed is," Wilson wrote. The problem was the Rich family had attacked the story's accuracy, and the only on-the-record source "made a mess of it." He added, "This is not a case of me or anyone going wobbly. The story IS problematic right now."

<hr />

As Fox confronted the possibility that Zimmerman's story was wrong, Sean Hannity became its loudest champion. He continued to tweet about Seth and WikiLeaks:

> Seriously? A 27 year old is murdered and we are told its robbery, yet he had his wallet, phone and watch?

> Julian Assange all but identifies the 27 year old DNC worker as a source and we are to ignore this?

The replies to Hannity's tweets piled up:

> Which one of Seth Rich's parents are conspiring with the 'Deep State'?

> What happened to body police camera, what did he say before he died, what happened to his computer?

> They covered their tracks well.

On his radio show on May 18, the same day Joel asked for a retraction and the family sent its cease-and-desist order to Wheeler, Hannity said Seth's murder "sounds like a hit." He took aim at critics who called such statements conspiracy theories, saying such people "might regret it when more information comes out. I'll take your apology whenever you're willing to give it."

Even as he found himself increasingly isolated at his own network over the Seth–WikiLeaks story, he kept promoting it on his TV show. "I am not backing off asking questions even though there's an effort that nobody talk about Seth Rich," Hannity said. He claimed to "feel sorry" for the Riches, saying that "my thoughts and prayers go out to this family." But in the same breath he returned to the tantalizing possibility that Seth or some other Democratic insider was the source of the stolen emails. "If that turned out to be true that somebody did that," Hannity said on the night of May 19, "wouldn't that completely wipe out the entire Russia lie we've heard for months and months?"

18

Never Say Sorry

As THE EXECUTOR of Seth's estate, it was Aaron's legal responsibility to take possession of Seth's belongings, including his laptop and phone after the police had analyzed them. It was Aaron who shooed away people like Butowsky and Wheeler who wanted access. Not a chance, he had told them. He didn't trust anyone apart from the authorities investigating the murder with access to those devices.

In the middle of the fallout from the Fox story, Aaron noticed strange activity involving Seth's phone number and his Gmail account. He saw various messages that suggested people were trying to reset passwords for Seth's social media accounts. But why were they coming in now?

He opened up his computer and checked the usual sites. A Reddit post caught his eye. *Oh no*, he thought.

Like much of his generation, Seth lived a good deal of his life online. He'd joined Reddit back in high school and over the years posted hundreds of times about his many interests: Newfoundland dogs, University of Nebraska football, American politics, and the newest USA-themed article of clothing he'd purchased for that year's Fourth of July. Each post spoke to a narrow subject, but taken together, they were like a pointillist painting of a life: a photo taken from the plane on the day he moved to Washington in 2012, his complaints about the indignities of commuting by bike in DC, asking other Redditors "if y'all have advice for how dating in a city works differently than from a small city." ("Good luck!" a fellow Redditor replied. "City women are maneaters.")

Seth was savvy enough about politics to know that if he hoped to run for office one day, he couldn't have old Reddit posts resurfacing and disturbing his carefully laid plan. He posted using a pseudonym: MeGrimlock4. But he wasn't terribly hard to find if you knew what his interests were and the broad contours of his biography. Sure enough, a few days after the Fox stories about Seth went viral, a group of Redditors who were "investigating" all things Seth Rich discovered the MeGrimlock4 account and shared it. Aaron wasn't that concerned about this discovery. He wished he'd deleted it before they found it, but to erase it now would only arouse more suspicion. And they didn't have confirmation that the account had belonged to Seth.

Until, that is, the horde of self-anointed Seth Rich sleuths discovered a post of Seth's dated November 15, 2015. "Hey y'all, I don't live in Omaha anymore so not sure the best ways to get this out, but just got word from my folks that their dog got out," he wrote in Reddit's r/Omaha forum. "Please circulate as much as possible." He posted a photo of the dog, Ella. If anyone found Ella, he asked them to contact him or his dad and included their email addresses.

The lost-dog post not only confirmed that MeGrimlock4 was Seth; it also gave the sleuths something tangible to grab on to.

Post after post appeared claiming to have found Seth's accounts on Instagram, Facebook, and Twitter, which set off further investigation into what Seth had said on *those* platforms, whom he'd followed, who had interacted with him. The most innocent exchange was now cast in a sinister light. When someone on Twitter posted about learning that the name for a group of pandas was "an embarrassment," Andrew Therriault, Seth's former colleague, immediately thought it was something Seth would've found humorous. He felt sad that he couldn't share the tweet with Seth. Instead, Therriault retweeted the post and tagged Seth's account, @panda4progress, as a subtle nod to their mutual friends who would recognize the reference. Yet to the Seth Rich obsessives, this tweet became evidence of a cover-up. "WHY is a [*sic*] Seth Rich an embarrassment for getting gunned down in a random robbery incident?" a Redditor posted in r/The_Donald. "THE DNC KNEW SETH WAS THE LEAKER."

What concerned Aaron were the more technologically sophisticated fanatics who now knew Seth's email address and Twitter account; they might be able to use that information to track down Seth's phone number or, worse, break into Seth's devices. Aaron watched as strangers attempted to find their way in. "Hey, this used to be my number. You may have gotten a reset code. Will you send it to me?" one asked.

Given what he did for a living, Aaron knew more than the average person about digital security. He moved quickly to secure Seth's accounts before someone broke in, changing passwords and activating two-step notification. And if Seth's accounts were targets, he had to assume he and his parents were targets too. A friend who worked in security helped Joel and Mary lock down their devices.

For nearly a week, Aaron remained on vigil. He slept so little that Molly worried about his health. Friends pulled shifts so that Aaron could get some rest. New posts on 4chan published phone numbers of Seth and Joel, their email addresses, and long strings of letters and numbers that purported to be their passwords. The mood among the sleuths was jubilant. One wrote,

I TAKE GREAT PLEASURE IN KNOWING THERE IS SOME CUCK IN THE DEEP STATE RIGHT NOW THAT HAD TO GO INTO THEIR BOSS'S OFFICE AND NERVOUSLY SAY . . . SIR, R/THE_DONALD HAS UNCOVERED SOME NEW INFO IN THE SETH RICH CASE. IT'S SIGNIFICANT AND WE CAN'T CONTAIN IT.

———◆———

For Mary Rich the familiar sights of West Omaha, the wide streets and the sprawling shopping centers, the lush parks and the local high school, all dissolved into a tear-streaked blur. Since the Fox story appeared, crippling migraines and crying jags had come upon her without warning at all hours of the day. It was all she could do to stay upright when they gripped her. Sometimes she retreated to the couch or climbed up the stairs and crawled into bed until the moment passed. Now she was alone in her car, a few blocks from the house, with Aaron on the phone, and she could feel the emotion building inside her.

You cannot imagine the loss of a child. That's what she wanted to tell people. It was different than losing a parent, a friend, or even a spouse. Mary had never expected to outlive one of her boys. It was a weight that never lifted, a malign presence that never left her side. And it tortured her to lose her little boy and not know who did it. She'd promised him at his funeral that she would find out. But if they ever found whoever shot Seth, she also wanted to talk to that person. She wanted to tell that person who Seth was and why he cared so much about politics, that he'd wanted to help people, that maybe the policies he'd fought for would've touched the life of that person, who-ever they were.

Mary didn't think her grief could sink any deeper—until Sean Hannity amplified the lies. Mary felt scared beyond anything she could imagine. She studied the cars that rolled down her block, the drivers who pulled up next to her at red lights.

Speaking to Aaron, she could tell from the sound of his voice that he was exhausted. Watching the online chatter about his brother surge to the highest levels he'd ever seen, Aaron imagined the day when his future son or daughter would be old enough to Google his brother's name. Staring at page after page of strange articles and vid-eos, that child would inevitably ask, "Did my uncle do such a terrible thing?"

As they talked, Mary felt so overcome with emotion that she pulled her car to the side of the road. A moment passed in silence.

"This is worse than when we lost Seth," Aaron said. Both of them started to cry. Aaron was right: the Fox story and everything that had come afterward made her feel like Seth had been murdered again, and somehow this felt worse than the original crime. They were torturing her dead son's memory. He couldn't defend himself, and Joel and Mary couldn't defend him either. They had lost Seth's body the first time, but now it felt like they had lost his soul.

Aaron said he had to go. They said their goodbyes. Mary gathered enough strength to finish her drive home. At home in Denver, Aaron got back to monitoring Seth's devices. Not long afterward, he noticed strange activity in Seth's Gmail account.

———•┃•———

As lawyers and editors and executives tried to understand what had happened with Malia Zimmerman's story, the opinion side of Fox News continued to push the story. Reporters who covered Fox knew that Hannity, despite his stature at Fox, often responded to emails sent directly to him. When one reporter emailed Hannity and questioned him about his continued coverage of the Rich story, mentioning his family-man reputation and asking him to imagine what the Riches were going through, Hannity wrote back within minutes. He was just "asking questions," he said. Why couldn't he ask about Seth Rich and WikiLeaks when Democrats and the media were lying about "Trump-Russia collusion"? *That* was the real conspiracy theory, Hannity insisted, and he wouldn't be convinced otherwise.

But he still had no evidence to back up his speculation. Then, on the evening of May 19, almost four days after Zimmerman's story appeared, a tweet got his attention:

> If Congress includes #SethRich case into their Russia probe I'll give written testimony with evidence that Seth Rich was @Wikileaks source.

The account that sent the tweet belonged to a man named Kim Dotcom—born Kim Schmitz—a hacker and internet entrepreneur in his early forties. Physically he was enormous, with pasty skin and a bulbous head, often dressed in a black sweater with a black scarf thrown around his neck. Dotcom was best known as the founder of Megaupload.com, a hugely popular file-sharing platform for downloading movies, music, pornography, games, and just about anything else you could imagine. In 2012, the US Justice Department indicted Dotcom and six others for operating "an international organized criminal enterprise allegedly responsible for massive worldwide online piracy of numerous types of copyrighted works." According to the Justice Department, the proceeds from the operation had totaled more than $175 million. But because Dotcom lived in New Zealand, which had a weak extradition treaty with the US, he had remained at home, where on Twitter he railed against the US government's prosecution of him, the Democrats whom he believed were behind that prosecution, and the virtues of the new president, Donald Trump, who had vowed to rein in the Justice Department.

Hannity was intrigued. "You have that evidence?" he tweeted at Dotcom.

"I'm the evidence!!" Dotcom responded.

Hannity pushed harder: "Can you explain that further?"

What Dotcom said next left nothing to the imagination:

I knew Seth Rich. I know he was the @Wikileaks source. I was involved.

Just when it looked like Fox's story was falling apart, Dotcom's tweet gave it new life. Dotcom called Seth an "American hero" and vowed to "find the political hitmen who murdered him for doing the right thing," tagging Hillary Clinton's Twitter account. Dotcom said he would be meeting with his "legal team" in the coming days. Afterward he planned to issue "a statement about #SethRich." "Please be patient," he said. "This needs to be done properly."

There was one other request Dotcom had. He called on Google to release the contents of three email accounts. One of them was the personal Gmail account Seth had included in the old Reddit post about his parents' lost dog, the same one the Redditors and 4chan sleuths had discovered and tried to break into.

Aaron sensed something was wrong. He had watched someone with a Megaupload account try to plant an email in Seth's Gmail inbox, perhaps to make it look as if Seth had corresponded with Megaupload when he had not. Now Kim Dotcom, the founder of Megaupload, was claiming he'd communicated with Seth and calling on Google to hand over Seth's emails.

Hannity, for his part, was more energized than ever. He called on Congress to investigate Rich's murder. He claimed that "complete panic" had set in at the "highest levels of the Democratic Party"—an assertion that had first appeared in a viral, unsourced, anonymous 4chan post. "Is it possible," he tweeted, "that one of the greatest lies ever told is soon exposed?" Hannity even suggested that someone might kill him for his truth telling. On Twitter Hannity issued a public invitation to Dotcom to appear on his Fox show or his radio show.

———◆———

Mike Gottlieb was reliving Pizzagate all over again. He had encountered the conspiracy theories about Seth during his research for the voter suppression lawsuits he'd filed in 2016. He now followed the blow-by-blow of the Seth Rich–Fox News controversy: the initial Zimmerman story, Hannity's nightly cheerleading, the Reddit threads and 4chan investigators, and now Kim Dotcom's claims.

The more he read about the Riches' situation, the more he felt compelled to help them. He couldn't miss the similarities between their background and his. Like the Riches, he had grown up in the Midwest in a Jewish family. He and Aaron weren't far apart in age, and with a younger brother of his own, Gottlieb could only imagine what Aaron was feeling, the heartbreak and then the confusion and anger and fear of a massive disinformation campaign layered on top of that grief.

Gottlieb couldn't think of clients more deserving of help than Aaron, Joel, and Mary Rich. He detested bullies who used their money and power to push people around, who abused the legal system to silence their critics with threats and lawsuits. One of the reasons he'd become a lawyer was to help people who were taken advantage of or preyed upon. And after his work for James Alefantis and Comet Ping Pong, he had experience in dealing with this particularly modern version of bullying. If anything, based on what he'd seen so far, Fox's Seth Rich debacle was an even more egregious example than Pizzagate.

Once again, another stranger out of the blue was offering to help the Rich family. Except right away they could tell this one was legit. And Joel, Mary, and Aaron desperately needed help.

With the help of Bauman, they had been working tirelessly to shoot down Fox-inspired rumors and correct the record, with mixed success. But they felt helpless to stop Sean Hannity and the rest of the Fox News talking heads. Meanwhile, conservative blogs were pushing a story that Joel and Mary were on the side of the Reddit sleuths and had thanked them in a video for all the work they'd done to expose the truth about Seth's murder. (The video had been created by Aaron and appeared on a GoFundMe page to raise more reward money. Joel and Mary thanked donors to that effort, not the online conspiracy theorists.)

And now, sometime in the next several days, Hannity was planning to interview Kim Dotcom on his daytime radio program, his Fox show, or both. They couldn't know for sure what Dotcom intended to say, but after Aaron caught someone trying to tamper with Seth's email using a Megaupload account, they couldn't rule out anything. The way Bauman saw it, they needed to stop Dotcom from going on Hannity's show. "Otherwise," Bauman would later say, "we were just going to be chasing this thing down forever and ever." All the work they had done—not just in the previous week but in the previous months—to push back on all the lies would fail. Instead, those lies would just metastasize.

Bauman didn't have it in him to open up a whole new front of battle, a battle he wasn't sure the Riches could ever win. As the public face of the family's counteroffensive against Fox, he too had become a target. On Twitter he was called a "hitman," a member of the "modern-day mafia." The DNC had "assigned" him to the Riches to bury the truth about Seth. (Bauman had never worked for the DNC and never gotten paid as a contractor by the group; the decision to help the family was his alone.) His phone pinged with authentication alerts from people apparently trying to access his email account. Strangers called in the middle of the night and told him, "We know what you did," before hanging up. At one point the online vitriol grew so intense that he recorded a video of the nonstop barrage of angry and conspiratorial tweets aimed at him. The tweets cycle past so fast you have to pause the video to read any one of them; let the video play uninterrupted and it looks like a waterfall of hate.

At least Bauman now had help. Mike Gottlieb had offered to help the family free of charge, and everyone in the family was relieved to have the assistance of an experienced lawyer. Bauman and Gottlieb settled on a two-part strategy: Joel and Mary would write an op-ed about the effect of the conspiracy theories on them; Bauman would place it in the biggest news outlet possible. Aaron, meanwhile, would make a direct appeal to Hannity, highlighting Dotcom's lack of credibility and urging Hannity not to put him on the air. Bauman would help Joel and Mary with the op-ed, and Gottlieb would help Aaron with the letter to Hannity.

Joel wanted to issue a challenge to the Hannitys and Dotcoms of the world: *Prove it.* That had been his gut reaction from the start: if someone had evidence of Seth's involvement with the DNC hack or anything to do with WikiLeaks, then show it. And if not, then shut up. But Aaron and Molly argued that if you said that to someone like Dotcom or a conspiracy theorist with enough technical know-how, they were going to falsify the proof and pass it off as real. Instead, Joel and Mary used the op-ed to describe what they had gone through since July 2016: a son murdered and his life and death twisted into a cruel lie. "Every day we wake up to new headlines, new lies, new factual errors, new people approaching us to take advantage of us and Seth's legacy," they wrote. "The amount of pain and anguish this has caused us is unbearable. With every conspiratorial flare-up, we are forced to relive Seth's murder and a small piece of us dies as more of Seth's memory is torn away from us." The *Washington Post* had agreed to publish the op-ed and run it before Dotcom's appearance, tentatively scheduled for the night of Tuesday, May 23.

Aaron's email was addressed to Porter Berry, the longtime executive producer of Hannity's primetime Fox show, but would be copied to a top lawyer at Fox. "Think about how you would feel losing a son or brother," Aaron wrote. "And while dealing with this, you had baseless accusations of your lost family member being part of a vast conspiracy." He went on, "We appeal to your decency to not cause a grieving family more pain and suffering. . . . We urge you not to do the interview." He signed the letter "Seth Rich's family." On the morning of May 23, Aaron read the letter one last time and hit send.

———◆———

Several hours later, Fox retracted Malia Zimmerman's story about Seth and WikiLeaks and removed it from FoxNews.com. In its place, a brief, unsigned statement said the story "was not initially subjected to the high degree of editorial scrutiny we require for all our reporting" and had fallen short of Fox's "standards." The statement ended with a cryptic one-line disclaimer: "We will continue to investigate this story and will provide updates as warranted."

Did Fox plan to continue investigating what had gone wrong with Zimmerman's story—or continue investigating Seth's murder and any connection to the 2016 election? It wasn't clear from Fox's statement, which media critics panned as "woefully inadequate" and "downright cowardly." Still, that Fox had retracted the story sent shock waves through the media business. "Retraction. Wow," one former Fox executive told a reporter. "Roger would brag at meetings how he was proud that Fox never had to print a retraction."

Zimmerman's editor, Greg Wilson, wrote to Butowsky to say that he was "sorry about how this whole thing worked out." Wilson thanked Butowsky for "connecting us with sources and helping us get information," adding that he still believed with "all my heart that our story was correct in substance." But the review of Zimmerman's story and the decision to retract it had been made far above his head and involved Jay Wallace, the network's head of news, and Dianne Brandi, the executive vice president of legal and business affairs.

Hannity now found himself in the untenable situation of trying to defend a story his own network had just retracted. He was also the target of the liberal watchdog group Media Matters for America, which had published a list of Hannity's advertisers to get them to cut ties as long as Hannity promoted unproven theories about Seth Rich. Hannity refused to back down. "All you in the liberal media," he said on his radio show that day, "I am not Fox.com or FoxNews.com. I retracted nothing." He played clips of Assange and Dotcom on the show and vowed that he would not back away from his "moral obligation" to ask questions about Seth Rich.

A few hours after Hannity's radio show, the *Washington Post* published Joel and Mary's op-ed. "We're Seth Rich's parents," the headline read. "Stop politicizing our son's murder." Hannity was unmoved. He shared a clip from his radio show on Twitter with the message, "I stand by everything I said & have said on this topic. More at 10pm tonight."

An audience of millions tuned in for Hannity's show—one of his largest audiences ever. But shortly before he went on the air, Hannity told them, he had spoken with three of his lawyers: there would be no interview with Dotcom.

"Out of respect for the family's wishes, for now, I am not discussing this matter at this time," he said at the opening of the show. However, he did not apologize to the family or retract anything he had said. After the show, Hannity sent Aaron an email. "I care a lot about decency and truth," he wrote. "I also believe I can help you and your family if you want. I will always be available if you would like to talk. Always in my thoughts and prayers, Sean."

Aaron wasn't sure what to do with this. Decency and truth? Thoughts and prayers? If Aaron needed any further reason to doubt Hannity, all he had to do was check Hannity's Twitter feed. Before he went off the air that evening, he sent a message to 2.4 million followers that kept the Rich conspiracy theory alive: "Ok TO BE CLEAR, I am closer to the TRUTH than ever. Not only am I not stopping. I am working harder. Updates when available. Stay tuned!"

19

The Widening Gyre

THE PROFILING PROJECT, the all-volunteer team of George Washington University graduate students led by Burkman and his deputy Kevin Doherty reinvestigating Seth's murder, released its final report in late June 2017. The forty-five-page document read like a sloppy term paper, riddled with typos, formatting errors, and placeholders for citations that never got added.

To no one's surprise, the Profiling Project's report challenged the police's theory of the case. The group posited that the shooting was "likely committed by a hired killer or serial murderer." They provided no evidence for their claim, stating only that the crime scene appeared "very organized" and "sanitized," which indicated "careful planning on the part of the offender." The authors acknowledged that they had no access to any police records and had obtained just a single photo of the crime scene but never confirmed its authenticity. A different section of the report contradicted the claim that a hitman was responsible, saying it was *unlikely* that Seth's murder was the work of a professional because he didn't die at the crime scene.

At a press conference to accompany the report's release, Burkman misidentified the hospital that had treated Seth after the shooting. Doherty, the Profiling Project's chief investigator, backpedaled from the report's language, saying it was "a possibility" that a "proficient killer" was to blame. The evidence for that, he said, was "the absence of clues" at the crime scene. "We'd love to talk to Julian Assange," Burkman said in response to a question about the WikiLeaks founder. "If he has any information relevant to this murder, bring it to the Profiling Project. We'll reach out to him right here and now." Burkman said the report was just the start for the Profiling Project. Nor was he finished with his search for who had killed Seth. "I will spend whatever necessary," Burkman said. "We will not stop."

Behind the scenes, though, Burkman's relationship with Doherty had become strained. Burkman had sued DC's mayor and its attorney general, demanding access to surveillance footage, the ballistics report, and the autopsy from the Rich homicide case. The suit claimed that MPD had "essentially terminated their efforts in late October 2016" to solve the crime and therefore releasing the requested information "would not and could not harm MPD's efforts in any way." This, of course, was completely false. To make matters worse, the suit—which listed the Profiling Project as the plaintiff—contained numerous typos and errors.

Doherty emailed Burkman a week after the suit was filed to say that most of the Profiling Project's team of grad students and researchers had quit. They had "caught a lot of flack" after the critical news stories about the lawsuit and didn't want to be associated with the project any longer. Burkman and his PR rep, Glenn Selig, continued to push for more coverage of the Profiling Project's efforts even if the students were no longer involved. *Inside Edition*, for instance, wanted to film a segment about the project's work. "This is the most important thing yet," Burkman wrote. "Will put PP in a new dimension."

Doherty had other plans. In early June, he registered the name Profiling Project LLC with the state of Virginia. Three days after the release of the project's Seth Rich report, Doherty told Burkman and Selig that ownership of the Profiling Project belonged to him. He asked the two men to disavow any connection to the organization. "Thank you and good luck," he wrote. Burkman's response was indignant. "We gave you the opportunity of a lifetime," he responded.

"Yesterday, we offered you a chance to appear on *Inside Edition*—and this is our repayment?" The email demanded that Doherty "cease and desist" from claiming any affiliation with the Profiling Project. If Doherty continued to lay claim to the organization, "you will be exposing yourself to massive civil and potentially criminal liability."

Burkman's message ended on a defiant note: "I trust fully that this will be the end of this matter and the end of our relationship."

———◆———

A Facebook page started by a group of conspiracy theorists promoted candlelight vigils for Seth on the first anniversary of the murder in New York City, Chicago, Los Angeles, San Francisco, Austin, St. Louis, Miami, Louisville, Detroit, San Diego, and Cleveland.

A group of demonstrators gathered in a small park on Capitol Hill on the anniversary and marched to DNC headquarters. From a distance they looked like a ragtag group of patriotic revelers who had showed up for a Fourth of July party nearly a week too late. An older woman with a kind face dressed in capris and New Balance sneakers carried a handwritten sign: "I AM SETH RICH," it read. A scowling, stubbled fellow in a USA-themed plastic top hat carried a sign of his own: "ARREST JOHN PODESTA." Yet another sign asked, "WHERE ARE THE BODY CAMS?" The TV reporters moved through the crowd, recording this bizarre scene and engaging in the occasional interview. "We are not racists. We are not conspiracy theorists," one attendee insisted. "We are coincidence theorists."

When the demonstrators arrived at the headquarters, they lined up on the opposite side of the street, holding their signs aloft and trying to get the attention of any DNC employees. One man chanted "Pizzagate! Pizzagate!" A sizable chunk of the crowd held a phone in one hand or had one clipped into a selfie stick, taking photos or broadcasting live on Facebook or Periscope. Jack Posobiec, a conservative influencer who had played a critical role amplifying Pizzagate in its earliest days, moved silently through the crowd, livestreaming the proceedings to an audience of nearly thirty-seven thousand people. "These are people who are asking for answers," he said later, "not only for themselves but justice for the Rich family."

A woman addressed the crowd with a megaphone. "We'd like to honor Seth Rich," she said. This was a young man who had sacrificed his life for freedom, she told the crowd. "He was investigating voter fraud. We know this from several of the tweets, Reddit. I know some of you think that's fake news," she continued, "but it's just alternative news now. We all have cameras and phones. We are all part of the news now, and this justice movement."

She asked for a moment of silence. People bowed their heads and held up signs:

"#JUSTICEFORSETH"

"Let's See: Police Report Body Cam Footage Ballistic Report"

"#whokilledseth"

Joel and Mary tried to carve out some peace for themselves on the anniversary. It was hard to do with the vigils and the tweets. They had issued a statement through Bauman that took aim at the "partisan" operatives seeking to exploit their tragedy. Roger Stone, the ex–Trump aide and Republican operative, took aim at them.

> Does anyone else thinks it's odd that Seth Rich's parents have no interest in finding out who killed their son? #payoff?

It was beyond cruel, the suggestion they'd gotten paid to hide the truth of their son's death. Even mild-mannered Joel felt rage rising up inside of him. But there was nothing they could do about it, and so they stayed close to home on the anniversary.

They visited Seth's gravestone. At Joel and Mary's request, the cemetery did not include the location of Seth's grave on the search tool on its website. They couldn't control whether any deranged individuals tried to visit it, but they could at least make it a little bit harder to find. They visited Seth's grave often in the year after his death. Small American flags encircled the headstone, fluttering in the wind. One time they found a bottle of Bell's Two Hearted half buried in the ground—Seth's friends had drunk a beer in his honor and left one for him.

Joel and Mary's grief had steered them in different directions. Joel's mind worked more like Aaron's; he was rational, analytical, calculated. To process the events of the last year, it helped Joel to organize his feelings into four categories. The first was the experience of losing a child—no matter what the cause, it brought trauma, bone-deep grief, powerlessness. The second was the absence of any resolution or closure, the fact that Seth's murder remained unsolved. The third was all the conspiracy theories that swirled around Seth's life and death, a scenario so absurd and macabre that if you tried to make a movie out of it, people would deem it too unbelievable to be true.

And the fourth category was the hopeful one, the coping mechanism that gave Joel "something to grab on to." His instinct had always been to keep Seth's name alive however possible. At first he believed speaking out and giving interviews to the media was the best way to do that, but the past year had shown him how naïve that belief was. Talking about Seth created more trouble than it resolved.

And so he threw himself into finding ways to protect and preserve Seth's memory. He helped create scholarship funds named for Seth at their synagogue, Beth El, and at his alma mater, Creighton University. The Nebraska Society of DC started its own fund named for Seth to support an intern each summer. Joel organized a memorial concert and invited Donna Brazile, the former DNC chairwoman and well-known political strategist, to fly in and speak at the event, which would raise money for the synagogue scholarship fund to help kids attend Seth's summer camp. When people asked him how he was doing, these were the things he wanted to discuss, the scholarships and memorials, all the ways he tried to keep Seth alive.

Mary's grief consumed her. When she saw a tweet or a story pushing the conspiracy theories about Seth, she took a screenshot and saved the image on her cell phone. This had become like a reflex for her: see something crazy, screenshot it. Especially the violent stuff. She became an archivist of her own pain, filling up her phone with copies of the hideous lies told about her family. She took so many screenshots that Joel had to buy her more storage.

She preserved it all because she wanted proof. A tweet or a blog post could vanish in an instant, disappeared without warning, and she wanted hard evidence she could show to anyone who couldn't understand or doubted her when she described what her family had gone through. If that ever happened, she could pull out her phone, open the screenshots, and say, "There, you want to tell me that I didn't get hate messages, that we weren't part of an attack?" she would later say. "Because we've been attacked, it is torture, and anyone that reads all the shit that I've got, they would sit there and say, 'Yeah, I'm in fear for my life. I'm in fear for my family's life. And I'd be [looking] backwards most of the time.'"

Joel would come to understand that Mary's desire to hold on to these screenshots was a symptom of a deeper crisis. Both he and Mary had battled depression and anxiety in recent months, withdrawing from their social lives, wracked with fear and paranoia about the next twist in the conspiracy theories about Seth as well as their own personal safety. A therapist would later conclude that Joel and Mary showed symptoms consistent with post-traumatic stress disorder or obsessive-compulsive disorder. The stress had also aggravated a neurological condition that Mary had dealt with for years, leaving her bedridden with crippling migraines and unable to take any job that required the usual nine-to-five work shift.

Mary appreciated the scholarships and the memorials, and she loved to hear from old friends of Seth's, swapping stories about the mischief her son had gotten into. What she wanted most, though, was justice. Someone needed to pay for what had happened to her son. She couldn't hide her frustration at the DC police's inability to solve the case or even announce a suspect. She complained that if only the cops had taken the case more seriously from the outset, if they had brought out more gun-sniffing dogs or drawn a wider search radius in the hours after the attack, they might've caught the shooter and this whole nightmare with Fox News would have never happened.

Instead, Seth's name and memory would never be the same. No amount of fact-checks, corrections, or retractions could undo what Fox and Hannity, Butowsky, Zimmerman, and Wheeler had done. For Andrew Therriault, Seth's former colleague at GQR who had helped get him the job at the DNC, not a day went by in the year after the murder that he didn't think about Seth. "Normally, when somebody dies, they're gone," he would later say. "They're dead. The world starts to move on. This was the exact opposite." Therriault had confronted proponents of the conspiracy theories about Seth on social media, which only led to trolls accusing *him* of conspiring with Seth and covering up the truth. "It was like picking at a scab that never healed and gets infected and becomes far worse than the original wound ever was."

Seth's family and friends also lived with the uncertainty that at any moment another iteration of the conspiracy theory might appear, a new variant that would send the internet into a frenzy once more. Two weeks after the anniversary, a group of former US intelligence officers and analysts released a report titled "Was the 'Russian Hack' an Inside Job?" The document contended that the DNC hack had in fact been the work of an employee or a contractor who had physical access to the DNC's computers. The evidence for this claim, the report said, was in the leaked emails themselves, specifically in their metadata. An analysis of this data seemed to suggest that the speeds at which the emails had been downloaded off the DNC's server ruled out the possibility of a remote hack and could only mean that the documents had been copied onto a USB thumb drive. In other words, the hack was really a leak, and these former intel officials supposedly had the data to back it up.

The organization that had compiled the report was called the Veteran Intelligence Professionals for Sanity, VIPS for short. The group's members included some of the most revered intelligence whistleblowers of the twenty-first century, including William Binney and Thomas Drake, both former NSA employees who had warned about the American government's secret plans to engage in mass surveillance of its own citizens. Other VIPS members had worked for the CIA, the State Department, and branches of the military. Going back to 2003, VIPS was known for its condemnations of the CIA's use of torture and its aggression toward Iran and was seen as a thoughtful critic of the nation's increasingly powerful intelligence agencies.

"Was the 'Russian Hack' an Inside Job?" was VIPS's fiftieth memo, and its controversial assertions—which rested almost entirely on the word of an "independent analyst" who used to work for IBM and an anonymous source called "The Forensicator"—had driven a wedge between the members of VIPS. Thomas Drake, the NSA whistleblower and one of the best-known members of VIPS, believed the analysis was so shoddy he refused to sign it. The analysis was premised on the notion that it was impossible to extract all those files and transfer them at such high speeds across the world, so they must've been downloaded from inside the DNC. Drake ran his own experiment, running a file transfer between his home in Maryland and eastern Europe, and found he could easily re-create the transfer speeds used by the Russians. The memo was bogus, Drake declared, "a conspiracy theory draped in very thin gossamer robes, which when pulled aside basically revealed nothing."

The Seth Rich conspiracy theorists seized on the memo as evidence they were right all along. They especially pointed to the fact that Bill Binney, the legendary NSA whistleblower, had signed the report, giving it his full endorsement, along with a dozen other VIPS members. The memo earned coverage in right- and left-wing media, prompting a long story in the *Nation*, the 120-year-old liberal magazine. The *Nation* article provoked a strong backlash, with many accusing the magazine, whose editorials had long taken a sympathetic stance toward Vladimir Putin's Russia, of once again minimizing Russia's aggressions.

The VIPS memo led to an invitation for Binney to appear on Tucker Carlson's Fox News show, where he repeated his belief that the DNC hack could only have come from an insider. "Many people are emotionally tied to this agenda, to tie the Russians to President Trump," Binney said. VIPS, on the other hand, was nonpartisan and "tries to look at . . . the facts." Binney's appearance on Fox took many of his friends and allies in the whistleblowing community by surprise; after all, this was the same network that had guests on its programs who had called for the execution of another NSA whistleblower, Edward Snowden. But if Binney's old allies were shocked by his remarks on Carlson's show, President Trump watched Binney's appearance and came away intrigued. He wanted to know more.

———— ◦◦ ————

On August 1, 2017, Rod Wheeler filed a lawsuit in a federal court in New York against Fox News; its parent company, Fox Corporation; Ed Butowsky; and Malia Zimmerman. From a legal standpoint, the thrust of the suit was a strange one: Wheeler claimed that Butowsky and Zimmerman had somehow defamed him by fabricating the quotes attributed to him that appeared in Zimmerman's now-retracted story about Seth and WikiLeaks. He also accused Fox of racial discrimination, alleging he wasn't hired full time because he was Black.

Wheeler's lawyer had stuffed the complaint full of raw evidence—text messages, emails, voicemails, excerpts from phone calls. The texts Butowsky sent about how President Trump had read a draft of Zimmerman's story and "wants the article out immediately," Butowsky and Wheeler's meeting at the White House with Sean Spicer, Butowsky's role in recruiting Wheeler and helping guide Zimmerman's investigation—it was all in Wheeler's complaint. A reporter at NPR, David Folkenflik, broke the story of Wheeler's lawsuit on the day it was filed, writing that Fox and Butowsky had allegedly "worked in concert under the watchful eye of the White House to concoct a story about the death of a young Democratic National Committee aide" to distract from the revelations of Russian interference in the 2016 election.

As Joel, Mary, and Aaron read Wheeler's complaint, they encountered one revelation after another. They realized Butowsky, Zimmerman, and Wheeler had worked together for months to produce a story that smeared Seth. And they had done it behind the family's back. With the benefit of hindsight, Aaron had sometimes wondered if there was more going on with Wheeler, Butowsky, and Zimmerman than he knew; he imagined them connected by gray dotted lines, suspicions that he had no proof to back up. Now he and his parents had their proof. There was a word for what Wheeler, Butowsky, and Zimmerman had done: conspiracy.

They read the follow-up stories David Folkenflik at NPR published about Fox and Butowsky, and their shock soon gave way to rage. For the first time, they began to think about what options they had to repair some of the damage caused by Butowsky, Zimmerman, and Fox. It haunted them that people they'd trusted had used them, played them for fools. Sean Hannity and Fox News had transformed their family's tragedy into a political cudgel, turning any parent's worst nightmare into a way to score points for the Republican Party and help out the president. And even though Fox had retracted Malia Zimmerman's story, no one at Fox ever gave them a clear accounting of what went wrong and why. No one had ever apologized.

And no matter how hard they tried, Joel and Mary couldn't put an end to the lies. Their voices weren't loud enough to break through the noise and spread what they knew to be true. "Whatever we did," Joel would later say, "we got drowned out."

They felt like they had no other choice but to bring a lawsuit. "If this is what it takes to try to prevent people from pushing lies, this is what we want to try to do," Joel remembers thinking. "We knew we had the truth on our side."

They asked Mike Gottlieb if he was interested, but Boies Schiller, Gottlieb's firm, represented a separate division of News Corporation, which meant he had a conflict and couldn't bring a suit of any kind that involved Fox News. Gottlieb had someone else in mind. He put Joel and Mary in touch with an old college friend who worked for a small Chicago-based law firm called Massey Gail. The firm showed interest in Joel and Mary's situation. But theirs was not a clear-cut defamation case. Joel and Mary had not been targeted themselves. Nor could they seek relief on Seth's behalf: it was long-established US law that when someone dies, their claim dies with them. So what options did Joel and Mary have?

———◆———

The old truck sped along the George Washington Parkway as Bill Binney sat in the passenger's seat and wondered what he'd gotten himself into. It was late fall and the leaves blazed yellow and green and auburn on the half-bare trees that lined the old two-lane road. Binney's driver pulled off at one of the last exits before crossing the Potomac River into Washington, DC. Up ahead stood a thicket of warning signs and, beyond that, a heavily fortified gate. Binney gave his name to the security officer on duty, and the gate opened onto one of the most secure government facilities in America. Binney felt the tension rise inside of him as the car neared its destination, the headquarters of the Central Intelligence Agency.

The secretive world of spy craft and intelligence was, on one level, familiar terrain for Binney. For two decades he had worked for a different arm of the US national security apparatus, the National Security Agency. He was regarded as one of the agency's most brilliant employees. In the late 1990s, he and his team at the NSA's Signals Intelligence Automation Research Center were asked to devise a solution to a modern problem: How could the US government sift through the ever-increasing amount of data to root out criminals without infringing on the Fourth Amendment rights of American citizens? Binney and his colleagues created an algorithm, code-named Thin Thread, to do just that, but in the aftermath of the September 11 terrorist attacks, Binney saw that his creation would now be used for the warrantless surveillance of Americans. Outraged, he quit the agency and blew the whistle on what he saw as the government's unconstitutional abuses. To civil libertarians, Binney, a self-described conservative and a registered Republican, was a hero and a truth-teller in the tradition of Daniel Ellsberg and Edward Snowden. To the government that had once entrusted him with its secrets, Binney was an enemy of the state, persona non grata.

And so almost two decades later, when his wife got a call at their house in suburban Maryland from someone who said she worked for the CIA, Binney was skeptical. Was this a prank? A setup? A friend of Binney's suggested he call the person back and ask for some sort of proof, confirmation that the person was legit. He did so and was told the caller worked as the special assistant to Mike Pompeo, the CIA director. Director Pompeo wanted to meet with Binney at his earliest convenience. How soon could he come in?

Binney never imagined he would ever again set foot inside a classified facility. He worried he might be interrogated or arrested if he did. Not that he posed much of a threat: he was seventy-four years old and in poor health. He'd had both legs amputated at the knee and used crutches or a wheelchair to get around. He sat in his wheelchair as his business partner and driver for the day, Chris Parker, pushed him through the front entrance at CIA headquarters a few weeks later. Waved through the security screening, Binney was met in the lobby by Pompeo's assistant and escorted to a private elevator used by the director. The elevator climbed to the building's seventh floor and deposited him outside of the CIA director's office. As he waited to go inside, Binney still had no answer to the question that most nagged at him: Why was he here?

Pompeo emerged and welcomed Binney into his office. (Parker was asked to wait outside.) The CIA director's office was a massive wood-paneled room with sweeping views of the forests that surrounded Langley, the informal name for CIA headquarters. A tattered American flag that had once flown at the World Trade Center in New York City was hung in a frame behind Pompeo's desk. Pompeo and Binney took seats around a long conference table. Two CIA analysts invited by Pompeo also joined the meeting.

Pompeo got to the point. "The president has directed me to see you," he said to Binney.

Trump had watched Binney's appearance on Tucker Carlson's show where Binney discussed the VIPS memo and the inside-job theory. At Trump's request, Pompeo wanted Binney to explain why he believed the CIA's analysts were wrong about the most damaging foreign interference operation carried out on American soil. He wanted to know why Binney believed that attack was the work of a DNC insider, possibly even Seth Rich.

Binney laid out his theory for Pompeo and the two analysts. The conversation lasted a little over an hour. At the end Pompeo asked Binney if he'd be willing to talk to the FBI and NSA about his theory. Binney said he would so long as that wouldn't mean violating anyone's constitutional rights. The way Binney saw it, he had just handed the

Trump administration a motherlode of information. Pompeo would be a hero to the president and his followers if he were the one to show, once and for all, that Russia didn't hack the DNC. But as far as Binney could tell, Pompeo didn't do anything with the information. Binney never heard from the CIA again.

———————◦|◦———————

Deb Sines had followed the controversy around Fox's Seth Rich story with a mix of disgust and annoyance. She wanted to put her fist through the TV as she watched Hannity turn Seth's death into a conservative cause célèbre. She also understood that the blowback from Fox's coverage would only make her job more difficult. This was hardly the first time that one of her homicide cases had garnered major media coverage and attracted its share of cranks, attention-seekers, and conspiracy theorists. But never before had one of her decedents—she rarely used the word "victim"—ended up in the white-hot center of the political news cycle like Seth had after the Fox blow-up, and certainly not in the "fucked-up" way, as Sines put it, that had happened when Fox published Zimmerman's story and then retracted it a week later.

Sines knew that this would be one of the most difficult cases of her career. The lack of evidence and eyewitnesses, the time that had elapsed since the crime occurred—all of it worked against her. Forget the conspiracy theories and this was still one of the top-three toughest cases she'd prosecuted. And the longer she spent on the case, the more she felt the online noise and the fantastical speculation about Seth and the 2016 election was infringing on her ability to run a homicide investigation.

Even before the Fox blow-up, she had started to feel paranoid about the case. For one, she felt a tension with the Rich family. She wanted to tell Mary and Joel about the progress in her investigation, but when she heard the Riches divulge sensitive information about the case in media interviews and press conferences, Sines knew she had to exercise caution about what information she shared with the family because she didn't know who they were going to share that information with. Otherwise she risked polluting her investigation when the media published information that only the killer would know, like the number of gunshots or the type of weapon used. "We didn't trust anybody," she would later recall.

But from the moment Sines had taken the investigation, the internet was overflowing with speculation, conspiracy theories, and partisan fever dreams about Seth. As a prosecutor running an investigation, she couldn't ignore these theories about her decedent when she discovered them on Reddit, Facebook, or Twitter. She felt she had to disclose them to the grand jury hearing evidence in the investigation, which meant she had to vet those theories so that she could show they were false. Sines soon found herself running down rabbit holes as much as she was doing real-life investigating. When she read somewhere that Seth had allegedly received payment for giving the stolen DNC emails to WikiLeaks, she checked his bank records for any unexplained income or suspicious expenditures. She saw the same deposits every two weeks. He paid his student loans. He liked to buy funny socks. He lived within his means. There was nothing in his finances to confirm the theory. "You're delving into somebody else's life looking for anything aberrant—and it's not there," she'd later say. "It's very frustrating, because what you want to do is catch the real killers."

In the fallout from the Fox story, Sines struggled to keep track of the new offshoots and variants of the Rich theories. In one case, she read online that there was a lawyer in her office, the US attorney's office for Washington, DC, who was undermining her case. His name was Steven Wasserman. He was the brother of Congresswoman Debbie Wasserman Schultz, the DNC chairwoman at the time of the Russia hack. The allegation was that Steve Wasserman, who worked in the narcotics division, had "deep-sixed" her case, as Sines put it. The rumor seemed to have started on Twitter. An account named "Deplorable FOR TRUMP" shared a photo of Wasserman's LinkedIn profile and tagged the account for Rep. Wasserman Schultz:

#ItWouldBeAShameIf ppl found out that @DWSTweets brother is Asst. US Dist. Atty in DC. Player in burying #SethRich case!?

Gateway Pundit, the far-right blog that routinely published unverified stories sourced to social media posts taken from Twitter or Reddit, ran with the headline "Debbie Wasserman Schultz's Brother Steven Wasserman Accused of Burying Seth Rich Case." To make this claim, the post relied on Deplorable FOR TRUMP's tweet and a Facebook photo showing Debbie Wasserman Schultz, her kids, and her brother. "Love you, Steven!" she wrote.

Sines knew Wasserman from when he worked in the Homicide Section. His office had been next to hers. But he had moved to a different section a few years earlier focused on organized crime, narcotics, and racketeering cases. She had to follow orders and confirm that the accusation against Wasserman was bogus. She had to investigate one of her own colleagues.

Sines started with Wasserman's boss.

"Are you guys doing some secret-squirrel shit on my case and not telling me?" she asked.

"No," was the reply.

"Have you authorized Wasserman to look at my case?"

"No."

She asked Wasserman's boss for permission to speak with him directly.

"What's he done?"

"I don't think he's done anything," Sine said, "but I have to specifically ask him."

She apologized to Wasserman for having to ask about whether he'd touched her case. He assured her he hadn't. He didn't even know where she kept the case file. Sines wrote a memo for her case file about the Wasserman theories, and by that time she'd encountered another name in her online searches that she needed to vet.

Dr. Jack Sava was the director of the top trauma surgery team at the hospital where Seth was taken. Sava had performed emergency surgery on Steve Scalise, the Republican congressman from Louisiana who was shot and critically wounded during a practice session for the annual congressional baseball game in June 2017. Online sleuths searched through the WikiLeaks archive of DNC records and found

Sava and his wife listed in a spreadsheet of Democratic donors who had attended an event in Martha's Vineyard in 2015. Sava's wife, Lisa Kountoupes, had worked in the Clinton administration and had gone on to launch her own lobbying firm. A DC tabloid had featured her on its "Top Lobbyists 2016: Hired Guns" list. Sava and Kountoupes were active in philanthropic circles and something of a power couple in Washington. The real bombshell for the sleuths was when they found a political fundraising invitation for a Democratic candidate for US Senate that listed Kountoupes and John Podesta as the cohosts.

To conspiracy theorists, the few connections between Sava and the Clintons—the 2015 donor event on Martha's Vineyard, his wife's name on the fundraising invitation—were more than enough evidence of a smoking gun. On Reddit and Twitter, the sleuths, who already believed it suspicious that Seth had died at the hospital after being found responsive at the scene of the crime, said Sava had "facilitated" Seth's murder or outright killed Seth himself. When Sava gave updates on Congressman Scalise's condition after he had been shot, Sava's name started trending on social media due to all the Rich conspiracy theorists sharing false information about him.

DR. SAVA THE SAME DOCTOR INVOLVED IN THE #SETHRICH-COVERUP NOW ATTENDING TO @SteveScalise PLEASE HELP HIM @realDonaldTrump #Scalise

Odd, when #SethRich was rolled in to see Dr. Sava he was in imminent danger of living. https://t.co/SxZuocOxCW

Sines had to run down this rumor too. She talked to the doctors at the hospital where Seth was treated and asked them who had operated on Seth and who hadn't. A different surgeon had operated on Seth, she learned. Sava wasn't even in the room.

And there were times when it felt like the conspiracy theories had reached such a critical mass that they had found their way into the minds of possible witnesses. Once, the police had questioned an inmate about an unrelated case and slipped in a question about Seth's murder on the off chance he knew something. The man replied that yes, he had heard something.

"The government did it," the inmate said. "The government killed that guy."

Precious time slipped by as Sines chased one rumor after another, crossing names off her list, pursuing leads that led nowhere. She felt no closer to finding Seth's killer.

Then, a few months later in 2017, she received an alarming message from the woman who was the closest thing to a witness in the Rich case. This was the woman who told police that she had taken her old, incontinent dog out to relieve itself when she saw two Black men sprinting away from the intersection where Seth had been shot. The woman said that she'd been contacted by strangers who said they were private investigators from an organization she'd never heard of. They had tried to call her, left notes at her home, and visited her at work. Somehow they knew she was a witness—the only witness—in the Rich case.

ACT III
The Dead Have No Defense

20

Q Clearance

ON A BLINDINGLY hot day in the summer of 2018, a hulking black car rolled to a stop in the middle of the Mike O'Callaghan–Pat Tillman Memorial Bridge. Suspended nearly nine hundred feet above the Colorado River, the bridge spans the Arizona-Nevada border and carries traffic between two of the West's biggest cities, Phoenix and Las Vegas. From the northbound side, visitors enjoyed a breathtaking view of the Hoover Dam, a marvel of human engineering and one of the country's most critical pieces of infrastructure. The vehicle, which looked like a retrofitted Brink's security truck, lined up at a right angle across the bridge's southbound lanes, stopping cars in both directions and sending state and federal police scrambling to the scene.

Seated behind the wheel of the truck was a thirty-year-old man with a crew cut and puffy beard. Over his T-shirt he wore a tan Kevlar vest. His name was Matthew Wright. A former marine, Wright had struggled to keep a job upon his return to civilian life. For months he'd slept in a makeshift bedroom in the back of his truck, which he parked outside his mother's home in a suburb of Las Vegas. A German shepherd sat in the passenger seat. Within minutes of stopping on the O'Callaghan–Tillman bridge, law enforcement had surrounded him. At which point Wright pulled out his phone and began to record a message to Donald Trump.

Wright was distraught. He felt betrayed. The president, *his* president, had vowed to arrest an evil cabal that ruled the country. Deadlines had passed and no arrests had been made. The government was sitting on an explosive report that would expose the criminals, but Trump had not yet released it. "We elected you to do a duty," Wright said. "You said you were going to lock certain people up when you were elected. You have yet to do that," he said, adding, "Uphold your oath."

The standoff between Wright and state and federal authorities went on for close to an hour. Someone in a nearby car stranded on the bridge claimed to see a rifle stick out one of several portholes on Wright's vehicle, a claim Wright's lawyer would later dispute. At one point Wright held up a sign in the driver's-side window. Scrawled in red ink were the words "RELEASE THE OIG REPORT." Finally, at around one o'clock in the afternoon, Wright started up his truck and drove into Arizona. He rumbled over spike strips, shredding his tires. When he reached a police barricade, he steered the truck off the interstate and onto a dirt road. His vehicle limped along for another few miles before he surrendered to the police.

Police booked Wright into the nearest county jail. They searched his van and discovered a small arsenal inside—an AR-15 assault-style rifle, another rifle, two handguns, nine hundred rounds of ammunition, and a device for firing "flash bang" projectiles. They also found another sign in addition to the "OIG report" one. This one read, "WHAT HAPPENED IN LAS VEGAS?" in an apparent reference to the mass shooting there in October 2017. Wright had not harmed anyone or fired a shot, but, given where he'd staged his protest and what police found inside the van, authorities charged him with multiple offenses, including terrorist acts and unlawful flight from law enforcement.

Held inside the Mohave County jail, Wright asked for paper and a pencil. He proceeded to write several letters. His handwriting was neat, his grammar almost flawless. The letters did not appear to be the product of a broken or twisted mind. "I am a humble God-fearing American patriot despite what the media may portray me as," he wrote in his first letter, which he addressed to "whom it may concern." He was not a seditionist or an enemy of the government, he explained. "I love my country and ALL of its people," he wrote, and added that the few people in his life who "truly know me would say the same."

But in the country that Matthew Wright loved there existed evil among a "select few in power," and he wanted them brought to justice. In his second letter, this one addressed to the "Honorable Mr. Donald Trump, President of the United States of America," he apologized for his behavior. He had undergone a "Great Awakening," he explained. He offered to help the president rid the nation of the corrupt cabal who wanted to silence the people who had elected Trump as their leader. "If there is anything I can do for yourself, your family or this great nation, please do not hesitate to contact me," he wrote.

Wright ended his two jailhouse letters with the same sign-off. At that time, in the summer of 2018, the phrase he used was best known, if it was known at all, as a line from a mediocre '90s disaster movie starring Jeff Bridges titled *White Squall*. "Where we go one," Wright ended his letter, "we go all."

———————— ✦ ————————

An inspector general's report, vague suspicions about the Las Vegas shooting, mass arrests by the president of the United States—to the untrained ear, none of it made any sense. What was Wright talking about? And why would he risk years in prison to bring attention to this assortment of seemingly unrelated subjects?

For a small but growing online community burrowed deep into the internet, Wright's message made all the sense in the world. These people had come to believe that Democratic politicians, Hollywood celebrities, and wealthy liberals ran a secret criminal cult of Satan-worshipping pedophiles that trafficked young children and extracted those children's adrenal glands for a life-prolonging chemical called adrenochrome. The members of this syndicate included the Clinton family, liberal financier and philanthropist George Soros, Representatives Nancy Pelosi and Adam Schiff, actor Tom Hanks, and talk show hosts Oprah Winfrey and Ellen DeGeneres. One hero in this story was John F. Kennedy Jr., the son of the former president. As the theory went, JFK Jr. had not died in a plane crash in 1999 but had been living in hiding until the day he would come forward to help take down the Satanist cabal.

The man who would lead that crackdown was none other than Donald Trump. Away from the public eye, Trump was locked in battle to expose the cabal and bring it to justice. A long-awaited report by the Justice Department's Office of the Inspector General would reveal the many crimes committed by the Clintons and their accomplices. Trump would then approve mass arrests, sweeping up hundreds of people and toppling a criminal enterprise that had operated for far too long. Believers like Matthew Wright referred to this day of reckoning as "the Storm."

In the beginning, that's what outsiders trying to parse this new conspiracy theory called it: the Storm. In truth it was more than a single theory. It folded in elements of numerous other panics—the reference to Democratic pedophiles and sex trafficking evoked Pizzagate, a panic of more recent vintage, but the notion of a shadowy, all-powerful cabal of elites took inspiration from earlier fears of a New World Order, or the Trilateral Commission, or the Bilderbergs, or the anti-Semitic tropes fixated on the wealthy Jewish financiers of the late nineteenth century who helped build modern America. It was a conspiracy against an entire nation. The conspiracy theory that united these people, people like Matthew Wright, was, on its face, absurd.

Trump was the hero of this new mythology, but there was another person who played a pivotal role. An insider who left hints and clues about Trump's behind-the-scenes machinations, updates on the secret war against the criminal cabal. No one knew if this supposed insider was a man or a woman, a single person or a collective, what government agency they might work for or where they got their information. They referred to this anonymous source by a single letter: Q.

———◆———

Q's first drop had appeared the previous fall, on a late-October afternoon in 2017:

HRC extradition already in motion effective yesterday with several countries in case of cross border run. Passport approved to be flagged effective 10/30 @ 12:01am. Expect massive riots organized in defiance and others fleeing the US to occur. US M's will conduct the operation while NG activated. Proof check: Locate a NG member and ask if activated for duty 10/30 across most major cities.

The cryptic message appeared on 4chan, a more extreme version of Reddit. 4chan's founders and moderators took an absolutist view toward free speech: no amount of racism, homophobia, misogyny, violent fantasies, or harassment could get someone kicked off the site. Everyone posted anonymously, which only gave its participants even more license to be racist, misogynistic, or threatening. 4chan was best known for its "politically incorrect" forum, known to its users simply as /pol/. They spun wild conspiracy theories about the Clintons and the Democratic Party. They often coated their paranoid venting with irony, as if to suggest they meant none of it. *It was all a joke; lighten up, man.* But of course it wasn't a joke, not when it meant publishing Joel and Aaron Rich's phone number or the addresses of employees at Comet Ping Pong. Both of which had already happened on 4chan.

On its face the post was hard to decipher. Why was Hillary Clinton being extradited? By whom and to where? Who would be rioting and fleeing the country? Maybe in the mind of the most hardcore adherent of the Clinton hit list, Hillary was finally facing justice for all those people she and Bill had knocked off over the years. But wouldn't the police just arrest her, or the Justice Department indict her? What did the National Guard have to do with any of it?

Still, something about the post caught people's attention. Maybe it was the way it used shorthand—"NG" for National Guard, "US M's" for US military personnel—as if the author were fluent in the technical jargon of the military but too busy or too important to spell everything out. Maybe it was the certainty with which Q relayed these cryptic details. Or maybe it was how Q dared the 4channers to validate its ominous prediction: "Proof check: Locate a NG member and ask if activated for duty 10/30 across most major cities."

Years later linguists and historians and anthropologists would study and scrutinize Q's first post as if it were an ancient text or a secret code. But at the time, the 4channers responded to it with a shrug. "If that was the case it would be leaked already," one replied. And it wasn't as if this post was the first self-identified anonymous government insider, better known as an "anon," to step forward and share "intel" on 4chan. There had been FBIAnon, a "high-level analyst and strategist," who claimed to have information about a federal investigation into the Clinton Foundation. There was CIAAnon, who shared alleged dirt from inside Langley. And there was WH Insider Anon, who, well, you get the point. This latest anon chose to go by Q, a reference to Q clearance, one of the highest classification levels in the US government. And so what some had referred to as the Storm became QAnon.

The prophecies of Q didn't start to reach a wider audience until a few days later, thanks to a little-known YouTuber named Tracy Diaz. In her thirties, Diaz lived in South Carolina with her husband and child. She had first gotten interested in politics when she followed libertarian Ron Paul's presidential campaigns in 2008 and 2012, and she had hosted several fringe talk shows for an obscure media company named Liberty Movement Radio. She got her news from the Drudge Report, Alex Jones's Infowars, and videos on YouTube. But the growth of YouTube also meant Diaz could record videos from her living room and post them on YouTube, and if they drew a big enough audience, YouTube would run ads before the videos and give the creator a cut of the revenue. Growing up, she had been nicknamed Beanz by her friends, and so when she launched her own YouTube channel, she chose the name Tracy Beanz.

On the crowdfunding platform Patreon, Diaz described herself as an "independent journalist and activist" who was "fighting to get the truth out to the masses" and "researching and exposing what is really going on." In substance, what she was doing wasn't all that different from Milton William Cooper a generation before her. The difference was her easy access to tools that would allow her to reach a much larger audience and make serious money in the process. YouTube and Periscope were the megaphone. Reddit and 4chan provided an inexhaustible supply of topics to fill all those hours of recording time. And when viewers liked her content, Patreon made it easy for them to make one-off donations or pay for subscriptions. With a few clicks, Diaz had created her own media company.

She started posting several videos a week in the fall of 2016, videos about Hillary Clinton's supposed failing health, purported evidence of election fraud, and the latest revelations in the WikiLeaks DNC email dump. "Lordy, lordy, hello, folks," began one video. "There is another dump today and I am going through it and boy is it full—I mean, full—of stuff." Her videos, which usually depicted Diaz's voice narrating an email or a news article on her computer screen, rarely received more than a few thousand views. Like other fringe "researchers," Diaz lurched from one viral subject to the next, WikiLeaks to Pizzagate to the murder of Seth Rich.

On the morning of November 3, 2017, Diaz posted a new video to her YouTube page titled "/POL/ - Q Clearance Anon - Is it #happening?" "As many of you know, I do not typically do videos like this," she started off. "However, due to the very specific and kind of eerie nature of what's been going on over at /pol/, I've decided that it's important for me to cover this *just in case*," here she laughed, "this stuff turns out to be legit.

"Because honestly," she added, "it kind of seems legit."

Diaz spent the next thirty-five minutes explaining what Q clearance was and parsing every word of Q's first drop and several that had followed. The impression these posts left was that they were written by someone with access to government secrets who was trying to guide his followers to the truth:

> Why did Adm R (NSA) meet Trump private w/o auth?
> Does POTUS know where bodies are buried?
> Does POTUS have the goods on most bad actors?
> Was TRUMP asked to run for president?
> Why?
> By who?

Any day now, Q predicted, Trump would execute his plan to take down the cabal:

> On POTUS' order, a state of temporary military control will be actioned and special ops carried out. False leaks have been made to retain several within the confines of the United States to prevent extradition and special operator necessity. Rest assured, the safety and well-being of every man, woman, and child of this country is being exhausted in full. However, the atmosphere within the country will unfortunately be divided as so many have fallen for the corrupt and evil narrative that has long been broadcast.

Q's messages told the story of a Manichaean struggle between a brave president taking on a corrupt "deep state." Q talked about the "calm before the storm," the "storm" signifying the day Trump brought a cabal of criminals to justice. As it happened, a few weeks before Q's first drop, Trump had met with a group of military leaders at the White House. During a photo opportunity afterward, Trump stood alongside the generals and their wives and remarked, "You guys know what this represents? Maybe it's the calm before the storm." Was there a connection between Q's posts and Trump's comment? Had Trump hinted at something to come? Trump's "storm" comment only solidified the belief by Q's growing audience that whoever Q was, they knew what they were talking about and should be taken seriously.

Tracy Diaz certainly did. She pored over Q's messages, searching for "breadcrumbs" that would lead the way to a deeper understanding about what was really going on in her country and sharing her findings in videos that were, in her words, "helping people to wake up." Her first Q-themed video drew several thousand viewers. She posted several more, and with each video her audience swelled, reaching tens and then hundreds of thousands of viewers on YouTube.

That there was a natural audience for QAnon-related commentary came as little surprise. After all, QAnon conspiracies sounded a lot like Pizzagate, which meant it had a built-in audience to tap into. What made QAnon different, and what gave it more potency, was how it folded in elements of other conspiracy theories while also making itself more resistant to criticism, like a newer, stronger strain of virus. Pizzagate dealt in specifics: *these* politicians run a sex-trafficking operation out of the basement of *this* Washington pizza joint involving *these* children. The specifics made it that much easier to debunk the theory. QAnon was vague and gnomic, the predictions about mass arrests and classified reports all happening behind closed doors and in classified environments. Disproving them was almost impossible, which made them that much more tantalizing to those who wanted to believe.

But Tracy Diaz's early success wasn't owed entirely to organic interest. According to internal data later released by Twitter, fake accounts backed by the Russian government boosted Diaz's tweets promoting her early QAnon videos. And it wasn't only Diaz: in November and December 2017, Russian-backed accounts shared QAnon hashtags upwards of seventeen thousand times, more than any other hashtag. Russia amplified QAnon in its infancy for the same reasons it had created phony Twitter accounts and inflammatory Facebook groups during the 2016 presidential race: in QAnon, the Russian government saw an opportunity to pump up a narrative that would spread confusion and distrust among the American people. Russian accounts had promoted Diaz's tweets about domestic issues before Q appeared, but by the time she had championed QAnon, as many as forty different Russian accounts were sharing her content for months. On a few occasions Diaz even exchanged messages with her Russian followers. After one sent her a tip, she tweeted back, "There are so many connections— that's a good one I hadn't seen yet :)."

---◆---

It didn't seem to deter Diaz or anyone else obsessed with QAnon that Q's predictions never came true. In several early drops, Q had said that John Podesta, Hillary Clinton's former campaign chairman, would be indicted on November 3, 2017. Three days later, Q said, the authorities would sweep up Huma Abedin, Hillary Clinton's trusted aide-de-camp. Of course nothing happened to either Podesta or Abedin. Yet Q explained away these false prophecies by hinting at ever-larger forces at work. They had to "trust the plan," as Q put it. And to those who grew doubtful of such prophecies, Q reminded them that for justice to be done, they needed to stick together. Every so often Q would include "WWG1WGA": where we go one, we go all, a rallying cry and mantra, seven words that would, in time, signify a movement and a quasi religion that attracted Americans by the millions.

Tracy Diaz had discovered QAnon in its infancy and helped it reach a larger audience. Still, even she was surprised at how quickly QAnon found new followers in the final months of 2017 and the early months of 2018. What started as a few inscrutable posts had turned into hundreds of drops a month, first on 4chan and later 8chan, a rival message board. As Q's output grew, followers spent hours analyzing Q's drops in YouTube videos and Facebook groups and on Q-focused podcasts with names like *Patriot Soapbox*. They refused to be called "conspiracy theorists"; they were "conspiracy researchers," seekers of the truth.

In late January 2018, Diaz put out a request to her forty-six thousand Twitter followers:

I need several VERY DEDICATED patriots with experience in event planning/organizing. I don't want to have to say this, but you will have to be thoroughly vetted.

Several weeks later she uploaded a video to her YouTube channel titled "Operation Justice: We The People - A March for Transparency." It opened with a montage of images and news headlines all tied to popular far-right conspiracy theories: Fast and Furious, Benghazi, Seth Rich. A brief clip played of Diaz appearing on a fringe online show called the *Hagmann Report*. "We should be doing something to make our voices heard," Diaz says. The video called on anyone who wanted to show their "discontent with our justice and the corruption" to descend on Washington for "an organized display of peaceful protest."

On April 7, a crowd of roughly one hundred people gathered in Washington, DC. "We want justice," they chanted outside the White House. "We love Nunes," they yelled, a reference to Congressman Devin Nunes of California, the ardent defender of President Trump who led the intelligence committee and trafficked in his own conspiracy theories. Diaz, who by then had become a celebrity among the Q faithful, spoke at the rally. The crowd marched to the Department of Justice to demand the release of the secret Office of the Inspector

General report that would reveal Hillary Clinton's many crimes. The march wasn't billed as an explicitly QAnon-themed event, but the signs carried by many in the crowd left little doubt about why they had come to Washington. "Pedogate is real," one read. Another said, "I see Q people!"

A few months later, Matthew Wright parked his van on the Mike O'Callaghan–Pat Tillman Memorial Bridge and demanded the release of the same explosive OIG report that Diaz and her fellow marchers had called for. (There is no evidence any such report ever existed.) Prosecutors charged Wright with a raft of crimes including terrorist acts and unlawful flight from law enforcement. He later pleaded guilty to the terrorism and unlawful flight charges, and a judge sentenced him to eight years in prison. Wright's family never spoke about the case.

The QAnon faithful had their own explanation for what occurred. Wright was an enemy agent. His actions on the bridge that day were a false flag operation intended to give their movement a bad name. They weren't going to be fooled so easily.

21

Never Call Him Brother

IT STARTED WITH a single tweet: "Our Teams are digging into the brother of Seth Rich, Aaron Rich. He has Top Security Clearance, and the IT know how to make you go hmmm."

The message appeared on July 14, 2017, four days after the first anniversary of Seth's murder. Up until that moment, Aaron had not been mentioned by the conspiracy theorists obsessed with his brother, so it made him uncomfortable to be singled out by name. He tried to ignore it, a stray remark by some blogger on the internet. A few weeks later—on the same day Rod Wheeler sued Fox, Ed Butowsky, and Malia Zimmerman—Big League Politics, a far-right site, published a story about Aaron. It said he worked for a major defense contractor that provided cybersecurity services to the US government, which was true. It said that Aaron held a security clearance for his job, which was also true. Aaron rarely talked about what he did for a living, in part because a lot of it *was* classified, which made the Big League Politics story that much more unnerving. How had this fringe website learned these private details about his life?

On his semiregular searches for Seth's name on social media, Aaron started to see his own name appear with greater frequency. When he retraced these comments, they often led back to the same source, a man named Matt Couch.

198

By all indications, Couch was a diehard Trump supporter. His Twitter handle, @RealMattCouch, paid homage to Trump's, and his bio included the hashtags "#Trump #MAGA #USA #NRA." Judging from his picture, Couch looked to be in his late thirties or early forties, a self-described "Christ follower" with three kids and a pretty wife. He was heavyset and pale-skinned with a flick of gelled hair, and he liked to wear aviator sunglasses.

In his bio Couch called himself a "Conservative Truth Slinger" and "Investigative Journalist" who hosted a website called the America First Media Group, another nod to the president. Couch was a prolific Twitter user, sending dozens of tweets a day, and he also broadcasted live on Periscope, the free livestreaming app. He posted videos sitting inside his car or from an oversized leather chair in what looked like a home office. "Happy Tuesday, everyone. Matt Couch here with America First Media Group," he said as a country music song played in the background. As he waited for more people to join the livestream, Couch took a swig from a bottle of Powerade Zero and said, "Lots and lots of information to talk about."

A lot of what Couch wanted to talk about was Seth and Aaron Rich. Couch endorsed the conspiracists' primary assertion that Seth, not Russia, had leaked the DNC emails to embarrass the Clintons. But Couch was the progenitor of a new twist in that story: Seth had stolen all those DNC emails with the help of his older brother, Aaron. It was Couch who sent the tweet about "digging into" Aaron's background, the one that mentioned Aaron by name. Throughout the summer and fall of 2017, Couch churned out video after video and tweet after tweet accusing Aaron of not just one but multiple crimes—hacking into the DNC's computer network, stealing emails and other property, and obstructing the official investigation into Seth's murder. "We've been trying to say for some time that Aaron and Seth leaked together," Couch said on an August 15, 2017, livestream on Periscope. "There is no Russia story. Russia is dead. Guccifer 2.0 was fake. The leak was an inside job. We have proven that."

Couch claimed that Aaron had gotten paid by WikiLeaks for supplying the stolen emails and called on the DC police or the FBI to open an investigation into Aaron and search his bank records for evidence. "The money trail will tell everything in this investigation," he said. He accused the entire Rich family—Joel, Mary, and Aaron—of perpetrating a cover-up. "They know about the money," Couch said. "They know about the leaks. They know Aaron and Seth did the leaks together. They know all of this information."

"I don't have any remorse for the family," he said in a different Periscope. His tone was indignant. "Because the family, the Seth Rich family has had every opportunity in the world to come forward. They are involved. They are 100 percent involved in this cover-up."

One night in September, Couch made his most extreme accusation yet. He claimed that Aaron had known ahead of time that Seth was going to be killed and did nothing to stop it. "Aaron Rich definitely knew the hit was coming," Couch declared. Aaron had warned Seth's ex-girlfriend to get out of Washington the weekend of Seth's murder, but he had not warned his own brother, Couch insisted. This was not idle speculation, Couch said. This was information given to him by his "sources." "It's heart-wrenching," he said, "but everything I've just told you is 100 percent factual and true."

With each video and tweet, Couch's audience numbers seemed to inch upward. As with Tracy Diaz and her QAnon videos, the more extreme Couch's assertions were, the more people tuned in online and the larger the potential monetary rewards grew. Couch's followers responded to his videos and tweets with their own demands ("Waterboard Aaron Rich! All the truths will be found") and their own claims ("Aaron, not Seth, is the IT guy. Aaron got Seth into those files or he decrypted them. He has a role in what Seth did or Aaron did it himself").

More than a year after Seth's murder, the conspiracy theories were expanding, not receding. And the conspiracy theorists were coming for Aaron.

———◦┼◦———

Couch lived in northwest Arkansas, a corner of the state best known as the birthplace of Walmart. The retail behemoth built its massive headquarters in neighboring Bentonville and drew thousands of suppliers and subsidiaries to open offices in the area. Rogers, where Couch had grown up, was a company town, and Couch's father had worked in the logistics business. After getting a degree in business at the University of Arkansas, Couch worked in sales for several big shipping companies.

But Couch had bigger aspirations. For years he ran a mixed martial arts company, promoting and hosting fights all over the state. He launched his own marketing company, helped his wife sell Christmas goods, sold sports collectibles. Part of this hustling surely arose from a need to make money: by the time he turned forty, he had married, divorced, and remarried. He had a wife and two kids at home to support, while paying several hundred dollars a month in child support to his first wife, who lived in Missouri. Yet Couch's early business ventures never panned out. In 2014, he declared bankruptcy, telling a judge that he and his second wife had more than $100,000 in debts and liabilities, which included back taxes and unpaid child support. As for their assets, apart from two cars, a house, and their wedding bands, they had $1,000 in a bank account and $10 in cash on hand.

Seated behind a microphone, however, Couch thrived. He liked to joke that he had a face for radio, but he certainly had the lung capacity required to fill hour after hour of airtime with commentary and banter, which was harder to do than many people realized. A sports junkie who hung photos of wrestler Hulk Hogan on his wall, he booked gigs cohosting shows about University of Arkansas sports on a regional ESPN sports radio channel and on satellite radio. He spun off one of those shows and made it into a podcast, *In the Zone*, which he cohosted with an old friend named Josh Flippo.

But by the time Donald Trump took office in early 2017, Couch had sensed an opportunity. He identified as a conservative and did little to hide his disdain for Barack Obama and the Democratic Party, but politics hadn't figured much into his day-to-day life. Now, as a crop of online influencers, pseudojournalists, and livestreamers built huge audiences (and the financial windfall that came with those followings) on the back of Trump's rise to political stardom, Couch told his friend Flippo he wanted to shift his focus to political commentary full time.

Flippo said he was crazy. "I said, 'I don't dispute that I'm crazy,'" Couch would later say.

He changed his Twitter handle to @RealMattCouch—an homage to @RealDonaldTrump—and started tweeting at a prolific clip. He chose for the background of his Twitter profile an illustration of Trump standing in front of an explosion, money raining down, as a bald eagle flew by firing a gun. His early commentary mostly consisted of retweeting the president, parroting Trump's bombastic statements, and fueling incendiary claims.

> When is the last time you saw an American President tell another Nation it's time to pay up! Love President Trump! @POTUS

> President Trump has 30 years on me, and he runs circles around everyone. Amazing his spirit!

> Ivanka Trump is brilliant. She's helped her Father and Brothers build a 10B Empire. I'm fine with her new role Snowflakes, get over it!

In the beginning a few thousand accounts followed him. But by virtue of how often he tweeted and his willingness to weigh in on any story that was trending on Twitter or dominating the conversation in right-wing media, Couch's audience shot upward. He applauded the new president every chance he got and defended Trump against his critics. He dismissed the evidence of Russian interference in the 2016 election and instead said it was Democrats who had conspired with Russia, once tweeting that there were "rumors swirling" about Clinton adviser John Podesta taking $35 million from the Kremlin—a complete fiction. The more extreme Couch's claims became, the more his online following exploded, surpassing ten thousand and then twenty thousand within a span of months.

But it was the Seth Rich story more than any other that propelled Couch to a new level of influence in conservative circles. Couch had first become interested in Seth's murder after Julian Assange's interview on Dutch TV. When Fox News reported in May 2017 that Seth Rich had been WikiLeaks' source, Couch finally saw the evidence that his hero, President Trump, had been innocent all along, and the

Russian interference story was nothing more than a ploy by the left to take down the president. Couch refused to back down after Fox retracted the story, stringing together dozens of tweets laying out his questions, suspicions, and theories.

> 35) Seth Rich had almost $2,000 Cash, A Rolex (This wasn't a normal watch), Gold Chain, Credit Cards, and Cell Phone on him. Nothing taken.

> 75) Washington D.C. Metro Police Chief Cathy Lanier resigns 30 days after Rich's murder. Gets 7 Figure job as Head of NFL Security.

Little of this was true. Seth wasn't carrying two grand in cash or wearing a Rolex when he was killed. Nor was there any evidence that his murder had anything to do with former DC police chief Cathy Lanier's decision to take another job. That didn't matter to Couch, apparently. Thousands of people shared and liked his Seth Rich–related content. He quickly became a go-to voice in the pro-Trump online community for all things related to Seth Rich. Ever the entrepreneur, Couch rebranded himself as an investigator and enlisted a group of what he said were former PIs and cops to launch the America First Media Team. He asked his followers to donate money so that he and his new team of sleuths could travel to Washington, DC, and mount their own investigation.

> I'm in w/ [money] & [pray] that God leads the way to #JusticeForSethRich, keep pushing this daily Matt.

> Oh I am SO donating!! If all of us give a few dollars to this investigation it will help immensely. We should all do it . . . for Seth Rich

Once he arrived in DC, Couch posted Periscope videos at a rapid clip. He reported live from the "vigil" for Seth outside DNC headquarters. He zoomed in to show the vigil rally up the street, then turned the camera back to face him. In his telling, Couch drew a clear line between this crowd and himself. These people weren't doing anything to help Seth Rich; they were making matters worse. "To me, this is what this is not about," he said. "This is politicizing his murder."

A few days earlier, Couch had left his home in Arkansas and traveled to Washington with his team of investigators. They had visited different locations around the capital. The bar, Lou's, where Seth had gone the night before his death. The intersection in Seth's old neighborhood where the shooting happened. Typically, Couch would either open the Periscope app and start a livestream on location, or he would spend all day in the field and update his followers with a fifteen- or thirty-minute "scope" at his hotel that night.

Now he stood outside DNC headquarters, watching the demonstrators up the street with a sense of disgust. These were nutjobs, paranoiacs, fringe types. They weren't *investigators* like him and his team. They weren't part of the solution; they were part of the problem.

"We're investigating, and we're uncovering almost more than anyone else has," he said, gazing into his phone. "And when all of this is said and done, we will release it to Metro and the FBI, whoever else we need to." Couch believed the Rich murder was "a politicized hit," and in the same breath he ripped the conspiracy theorists and the mainstream media for "politicizing" it. They may have done their own research, but they weren't investigators, not like Couch and his team. "My team came here to solve a murder," he said. "I did not come here to start a political agenda. Yes, it's probably a political hit. But I'm doing exactly what the family asked."

Couch spent several days in Washington, traveling with what he called his "security detail." By day he retraced what he believed to be the path Seth walked home on the last night of his life, tweeting photos of the neighborhood where Seth's favorite bar was and of the convenience store across the street from where the shooting took place. In the evenings he livestreamed on Periscope about the newest "bombshells" he and his team had uncovered. In one hour-long video, he divulged what he had learned so far, claiming to know which ambulance had transported Seth to the hospital and the name of the surgeon who had operated on him. When one of his viewers asked him who had "ordered the hit" on Seth, Couch replied, "I don't know at this point, but I've got some theories."

When he got back to Arkansas, Couch turned his attention to Seth's friends and his ex-girlfriend. He mentioned them by name in tweets and Periscopes and questioned whether they were telling the truth about the circumstances of Seth's murder. His fixation on Seth's ex became so intense that Twitter suspended him for twelve hours— the equivalent of a warning shot. Couch's obsession with Seth Rich got to the point that he even referred to Seth as his "brother."

Couch was no different from the thousands of other keyboard warriors defending their beloved president from the "corrupt" Democrats and the "lying" mainstream media. He was a part of the noise. A nobody. Still, he remained attuned to whatever the latest obsession was in conservative media circles. In the summer and fall of 2017, that obsession was the death of Seth Rich and the fallout from Fox's discredited story about Rich and WikiLeaks. Couch didn't buy the official narrative of a robbery gone wrong. Didn't buy that Fox had truly backed away from its reporting about Rich. Didn't buy pretty much anything else he'd read in the media about the circumstances of Rich's murder. He saw something far more nefarious at work.

He also saw an opportunity. He filed paperwork to create a new company named America First Media Group and listed himself and three others as founding members. Their motto: "We investigate." Couch kept "conservative truth slinger" in his online bio but now added the title of "investigative journalist." Whenever Couch had tweeted about Seth Rich before, he'd gotten a spike in shares and replies. Seth would be one of their first investigations.

He fired off tweet after tweet, dozens and hundreds and thousands of them, related to Rich and what he sometimes called the #SethRichCoverUp.

Where are the Body Cams and Audio that Four of the Six responding Officers were wearing that responded to Seth Rich??? #SethRich

Where is the Caliber of Weapon from D.C. Police in the murder of Seth Rich??? #SethRich

Now why would Julian Assange, the Founder of Wikileaks, reach out about Murdered DNC New Voter Registration Director Seth Rich? #SethRich

The more Couch talked about Seth Rich, the more his profile grew. His Twitter following doubled and then quadrupled, hitting forty thousand and then fifty thousand. He opened an account on Fundly, a crowdfunding site, and asked for donations to fund "the Investigations of the unsolved murder of DNC Staffer Seth Rich," the page said. As he put it in a tweet, "We're your voice for Truth in American Politics & Investigations." By the end of August, eighty-two donors had given more than $6,000. It was short of his $25,000 goal but enough to cover flights and hotels.

He talked about his "investigation" into Rich's murder with certainty and swagger, as if he were the only one in search of the truth, a sane man in a world gone mad. He talked a lot about how solid his "sources" were, and how the information he shared with followers was "ironclad," and how he never put out any new "intel" without "vetting it." People who tuned in to his Periscope livestreams—his "'scopes," as he called them—could comment in real time, and Couch seemed to take pleasure in calling out the doubters and haters, the people who still believed Rich had been murdered in a botched robbery.

> If that's what your belief is, we're never going to convince you because you believe in unicorns and things of that nature, leprechauns. If you want to look at facts, then you need to stay in this chat and you'll understand what's going on. Either you trust us or you don't. We have no reason to lie to you.

To underscore his commitment to the Rich case, Couch told his viewers that he'd started spending almost every waking hour working on it. He'd lost his job. He'd sacrificed time with his wife and three kids. "I'm all-in at this point," he said.

———◦|◦———

There was a line in one of Couch's early Periscopes that Aaron kept snagging on. "We have tried to keep Aaron Rich out of this narrative because the family asked us to keep, you know, out of it," Couch had said. Because "the family asked us"? Aaron wasn't aware of anyone in his family who had communicated with Couch. Why in God's name would they? Yet in the same way that Couch's tweets about Aaron's security clearance or his employer gave him pause, so did the mention of Aaron's family. Couch was getting information from *someone*.

Aaron had suspected that Ed Butowsky might have something to do with this latest mutation in the conspiracy theories about Seth. After all, Butowsky had never gone away after the Fox retraction. Butowsky had texted Aaron back in July to say that a story about him would soon appear, and indeed the far-right website called BigLeague-Politics.com disclosed the name of his employer and accused him of blocking the investigation into Seth's murder. Butowsky had also sent Joel Rich a series of angry emails explaining his involvement with the family and accusing the Riches of possibly misleading *him*. "I had no agenda at all except being a nice person," Butowsky wrote in one email. "I want to be able to go back on Varney and [C]ompany on Fox Business and discuss GDP numbers." He added, "I could easily turn it around on you and your agenda but I don't. Many have wondered if you set me up but I don't think so." In other words, in Butowsky's version of events, *he* was the victim. "I haven't said a hurtful nor harmful thing about you," Butowsky wrote in another email to Joel. "You on the other hand could care zero for my wife and children and what happened to a man who simply thought he was privately helping a man (you) and your family. You can assign any agenda you want to me but I never had one. You are going to be very busy this high holiday."

On August 15, Couch opened Periscope and started a new livestream. He had planned to update his viewers, of which more than fifteen thousand were tuning in, about the latest news in his Seth Rich investigation when a special guest made an appearance. "Hi," a user named "EdButowsky" said in the comment section along the right-hand side of the screen.

"Good to see Ed Butowsky in the chat with us," Couch said. "Great to have you, my friend."

About forty minutes into the livestream, Butowsky commented again. "Aaron Rich needs to come and admit money is in his account," he wrote. Couch echoed Butowsky's claim and then went one step further: "Ed and I have had a couple of phone calls, where we had a couple of great talks, and Ed just put it out there—Aaron Rich accepted money. Aaron Rich had money from WikiLeaks go into his personal account. Think about that."

"Correct," Butowsky said in the comments. "Parents confirmed."

Couch went out of his way to play up Butowsky's role in providing him the information behind his claims. "If you guys wondered who America First Media was talking to . . . Ed Butowsky's here right now, folks," he said. "Yeah, he's one of my sources, America."

There was more to Butowsky's connection to Couch than anyone in the Rich family knew when Butowsky confirmed that he was helping Couch. In late September 2017, Butowsky hosted a group of people at his house outside of Dallas. Butowsky allegedly referred to the group he'd summoned to his home as his "private militia." (He denied saying this.) Among the guests were Matt Couch, Josh Flippo, another member of the America First Media team, as well as Malia Zimmerman. Butowsky had also invited a Los Angeles–based composer named Thomas Schoenberger, an early and influential proponent of QAnon, and Manuel Chavez, a YouTuber and computer expert who went by the name Defango.

The focus of the conversation was the fallout from Zimmerman's retracted Seth Rich story and what to do next. According to testimony given by Schoenberger, Butowsky blamed Rupert Murdoch's sons for Fox's decision to retract Zimmerman's story. As far as Butowsky was concerned, Fox News was now part of the cover-up.

———— ✦ ————

It was the headline that made Deb Sines sit up straight in her chair: "America First Media Group Identifies Police Witness in Seth Rich Murder Case." Sines had recognized Matt Couch's byline on the story; Aaron had told her about Couch's harassment of him. But as she continued to read, she saw another name. There in the second paragraph was the name of her witness, the dog-walker. Couch wrote that he'd learned about a witness to the Rich murder and had tried to contact her, calling her and then visiting her home in DC, and when she didn't respond to him or his team, he said, it was "appropriate to take the next step"—namely, dox her.

Until that moment, the witness's identity wasn't public. That was by intent. Sines knew how dangerous it could be for a murder witness whose identity was revealed. She thought back to her prosecution of DC serial murderer Azariah Israel, who specifically targeted people in his neighborhood who had cooperated with the police and US attorney's office. Now her only witness in the Rich murder had been outed, the woman's name revealed to the world, which sent the speculation into overdrive.

Matt Couch's blog post on The DC Patriot, one of his websites, further stoked that conjecture by claiming that the witness had worked in the intelligence community and was possibly a "plant." Couch claimed that the witness had worked for Leidos, a government contractor that "the CIA uses to hire people." What the post didn't say was that Leidos held contracts with dozens of other agencies, from the Social Security Administration to the Department of Health and Human Services. Couch said the witness had "worked for the CIA for a decade," which there was no publicly available evidence to support. The post went on to say that this onetime intelligence agent now worked as a veterinary technician, but even that run-of-the-mill job carried a sinister undertone according to Matt Couch. From there, Couch suggested the witness had a role in the death of a man named Shawn Lucas. A process server, Lucas had starred in a viral 2016 video in which he delivered a lawsuit to the DNC accusing the committee of fraud in its treatment of Bernie Sanders. Three weeks later, Lucas was found dead in his apartment from an accidental overdose of fentanyl, muscle relaxants, and kratom, according to Washington's chief medical examiner. Like Seth, Lucas became the source of conspiracy theories about the DNC, and now Couch suggested that the witness in the Rich murder case had something to do with Lucas's overdose. Working as a vet tech, Couch wrote, meant the witness "has access to such goodies as fentanyl." He added, "Now we know what you're thinking, why are we telling you all of this about her Vet Tech job? Well, you should probably look into how Shawn Lucas was found dead at his home three weeks after the murder of Seth Rich. That will explain a lot there."

Sines called the witness after she read Couch's post. "You didn't tell me you were a fucking spy," Sines said jokingly. The witness burst out laughing. "Sorry, I forgot to tell you," she replied. But Sines could tell her witness was frightened and in a vulnerable position. Sines hadn't told anyone about the witness. Neither had the detective working on the case. Yet this guy Matt Couch had too much specific information—down to the correct spelling of her fairly uncommon name—to have made an educated or lucky guess. Apart from the police, the witness had told one neighbor what she'd seen and no one else. Sines doubted the conspiracy theorists had gotten the information from the woman's neighbor—that seemed implausible. That left one explanation: the name had come from someone on the inside.

22

The Worst Best Option

EIGHTEEN MONTHS AFTER Seth's murder, the conspiracy theories, rather than receding, were only expanding. Once again, Aaron found himself seated at his computer, staring at the words of a letter he never wanted to write: "Dear Mr. Couch, I do not know you, and you do not know me or my parents. Unfortunately, you never had the chance to meet my brother Seth. If you had, I know you wouldn't be spreading lies about me, my parents, and my brother on all of your various social media accounts."

The conspiracy theories fed by Couch had slowly engulfed Aaron's life. He received death threats. The photo of him and Seth at Aaron's wedding was turned into a conspiracy meme. He shut down his social media accounts. Worst of all, Aaron felt like there was nothing he could do to stop Couch or any of the others from saying horrible and false things about him, his brother, and his family. Aaron had seen enough to know that he couldn't go on Twitter and try to correct the record—that would only embolden the trolls.

At least now he had an advocate in his corner. Mike Gottlieb had helped the family through the worst of the Fox News controversy earlier in the year. If Aaron decided he wanted to—or needed to—file a lawsuit against Couch and Butowsky, Gottlieb said he'd take the case.

At the end of 2017 and in early 2018, Aaron sent letters to Couch and Butowsky. He called their allegations "completely false" and demanded they stop telling lies about him and his family. Think about your experience as a husband and a father, Aaron wrote to Couch. Imagine if someone had accused *you* of knowing about your own brother's impending murder and doing nothing to stop it. "If you were a man of decency," Aaron wrote, "you would consider the harm you have caused me and my family, and apologize. But, of course, you've already decided that decency and honesty take a back seat to advancing your personal and political agendas."

Aaron noticed that Couch had referred to Seth as a "brother." It infuriated him. "Lastly, don't ever call Seth your brother," he wrote. "He has only one brother, and it certainly isn't you."

Couch never responded to Aaron. Instead he read the letter during a livestream in January 2018. "I'm not changing who I am for you, not now, not ever," Couch said defiantly. "Our investigation rolls on! We are closer to the truth than we have ever been." He asked for donations from his viewers now that he had a "direct line of communication with Aaron Rich."

In early March 2018, the *Washington Times*, the conservative daily newspaper based in DC, published an op-ed by a retired navy admiral named James Lyons with the headline "More Cover-up Questions." Lyons wrote that it was "well known in the intelligence circles that Seth Rich and his brother, Aaron Rich, downloaded the DNC emails and were paid for that information." Lyons asked why law enforcement hadn't interviewed Aaron. The only source named in the op-ed was Butowsky, who had served alongside Lyons on the Citizens' Commission on Benghazi. On a Periscope livestream a few days later, Couch directed his viewers to the op-ed. It had been "put out to help vindicate our team," he explained.

The op-ed was the first time the conspiracy theories about Aaron had broken through to what qualified as a mainstream news organization. The lies and smears about him showed no sign of stopping, and he lived every day on edge, bracing for whatever the next story or video about him might say. He couldn't go on much longer like this. Yet

Aaron didn't want the attention a lawsuit would bring. He never wanted to go on *Good Morning America* or see his name in the news. He wanted to be left alone to spend time with his family, work at his job, and grieve in private. Suing Couch, Butowsky, and the *Washington Times* would change all that.

Aaron had a strong case. Couch and Butowsky had made many unequivocal claims about him helping Seth steal the DNC emails, getting paid by WikiLeaks, and obstructing justice in the search for Seth's killer. But Aaron also understood that a defamation suit was a wrenching experience. To prove the falsity of those facts, you had to open up your life to your tormentors. He knew that the people he sued would be able to subpoena his bank records, his emails, and anything else they asked for. They would get the chance to question him under oath and force him to answer page after page of questions about his work, his family, and his private life. Aaron had to decide if he was prepared to go ahead with this.

———— ◆ ————

As Aaron weighed what to do, Gottlieb and a colleague at the firm, a thirty-seven-year-old associate named Meryl Governski, gathered all the evidence they could find that might prove useful in a lawsuit. They'd hired a digital forensics firm to gather and preserve every available tweet, blog post, livestream video, and meme created by Couch and Butowsky. Before becoming a lawyer, Governski had gotten a master's at Northwestern's journalism school and worked at a TV station in western Virginia. She didn't miss the dismal pay, or the long hours, or the dead-of-night phone calls from her producer. That was why she decided to go to law school: she could hold on to the same values she prized—getting the facts right, telling the truth, taking on injustice—and get paid better and maybe even see results.

When she heard that Gottlieb was the lead counsel in James Alefantis's action against Alex Jones and Infowars, she asked if she could work with him if he had another case like it. For several months, Governski went through and organized the potential evidence, the sound of Couch's voice constantly playing in her ear. To be fair, Couch and Butowsky hadn't made it *that* difficult for her. The two had done little to hide that they were collaborating as they talked about Aaron. Governski and Gottlieb would eventually amass several gigabytes' worth of evidence, and that didn't even touch on what the two men might have said to each other in private.

Still, Gottlieb knew that Aaron's case wouldn't be as straightforward as a defamation claim brought against a TV network, say, or a newspaper. The case law, for starters, had yet to catch up to the digital age. The opinions that Gottlieb had dug up were full of references to landline telephones, physical mail, and fax machines. Technology changed as quickly as the law moved slowly.

The biggest question that loomed over Aaron's potential case was what degree of protection the law provided for Butowsky or Couch. For an established media organization like a major newspaper or magazine, the First Amendment served as the bedrock protection for what they published, but a few landmark Supreme Court rulings created additional layers of protection. The opinion doctrine held that a publisher could be sued only for false statements of fact, not for hypotheticals or speculation. If Couch and Butowsky had raised leading questions about Seth's murder—*Isn't it suspicious that he worked at the DNC and was killed right before the leak? What if he was the WikiLeaks source?*—the opinion doctrine would shield them from a defamation suit. But Couch and Butowsky had gone further. As Couch put it in a livestream, "We know for a fact that Aaron Rich and Seth Rich were involved and did the leaks together."

The other question was whether a court provided Couch with the same level of protection afforded established media organizations. If anyone could start a blog or a YouTube channel and call themselves a journalist, did that entitle them to the same protections as a news company? As Governski put it, "When you have an organization like Infowars where the business is hyping conspiracy theories, what kinds of protections do they have? At what point do courts look at Infowars and sites like it and say we're not going to give you the same benefit of the doubt that the *Wall Street Journal* or the *New York Times* get?"

If a court chose to treat Couch and Butowsky as journalists and afford them the same protections, Aaron's case would be that much harder to prove. In Gottlieb's view these questions only underscored how difficult it was for a private person like Aaron who'd been the victim of a conspiracy theory to go to court and clear his name. That was why Gottlieb had decided to take on the case in the first place. "I wanted to help people who are the victims of this and give them the institutional backing and power of a national litigation firm, and hold people accountable," Gottlieb would later say. "We want a public trial to clear our client's name. But if some of these people run away as soon as they're facing the prospect of a real lawsuit and settle with our clients, that's fine too."

———— ✦ ————

One morning in the winter of 2018, Mark Mueller, the neighbor who'd heard the gunshots that killed Seth a year and a half earlier, received a phone call from a woman who said she was investigating Seth's murder. Mueller had given a few short interviews to news outlets right after it occurred, and these had led to kooks and conspiracists calling and emailing him. When he searched his name online, he discovered memes that compared him to the serial killer in the show *Dexter*, as if he had had something to do with Seth's murder.

Mueller asked the woman to prove her identity. "The only way I can really prove it is if you come down to the office," she told him. Sure, he said. A few hours later he arrived at 555 Fourth Street, which he identified right away as a government building. Waiting for him in the lobby was assistant US attorney Deborah Sines.

They got into an elevator to go to her office. Sines was wearing one of her trademark outfits—a turquoise blazer, black slacks, and matching turquoise Converse sneakers. "Is it OK for you to wear high-top Converse shoes to the office as long as they match your business suit?" Mueller asked. "I'd like to see them fucking try to tell me what shoes to wear," she replied. Mueller thought to himself, *Oh, I like her.*

Sines's office had faded photographs on the walls, police manuals strewn on the floor, and a closet full of shoes. To Mueller it looked straight out of the 1980s cop show *Cagney & Lacey*. They talked for several hours about Seth, and about the neighborhood, and about her investigation. At one point she asked him, "Mark, what do you think is going on here?"

"You mean, the overall what's going on here?"

"Yes," she said. "What do you think is going on here? What's the big picture?"

Mueller had his own ideas, he'd grasped bits and pieces of it, but said he'd rather have Sines tell him than take a guess. "Mark, it's about the presidency of the United States," she told him. It was about Trump defending his legitimacy and the Republican Party trying to distract from the facts of Russia's interference in the 2016 election. That was it, she said.

Then she asked him if he would testify in front of the grand jury hearing evidence in the homicide case. Yes, Mueller immediately responded. He didn't have anything to hide.

He and Sines took another elevator down several floors. In the hallway outside the jury room, she said she needed to speak with the jurors for a few minutes. She would come get him when she was ready. A door opened out of a different jury room and two people sat next to him in the hallway. He turned to one of them, a woman he didn't know, and asked, "Is this a grand jury? Like I'm going to testify in a grand jury?" She grabbed his leg and said, "Sweetheart, if you don't know where you are, you better figure it out fast and don't go in there without a lawyer unless you're very sure."

He took a deep breath. He knew the truth, and he knew what he'd seen that morning in July. He needed to go into the room confident, because if the jurors looked at him and saw fear, they might not believe a word he had to say.

Sines came and brought him into a small, auditorium-style room. He gave a brief statement and took questions from Sines and then the jurors themselves, most concerning what he'd heard and seen on the night of the murder and the crime in the neighborhood at that time. One juror, a woman, raised her hand. "Wait, wait, wait, wait. I need to ask something. I don't buy this," she said. "You said you were woken up at 4:19 in the morning by your cat wanting to go outside. Cats don't do that—dogs do that—so I don't buy what you're saying at all."

Mueller couldn't help but laugh. He heard somebody else in the jury laugh too. He asked the juror, "Have you ever owned a cat?" She hadn't. Now two more jurors started laughing, while others chimed in to say that, yes, their cats woke them up at night too. Mueller's grand-jury testimony had devolved into a debate between cat and dog owners. By that point Sines had gotten what she needed. She thanked Mueller for his time and sent him home.

Around the same time, Sines received a tip about a member of Couch's America First Media Group investigators. Sines had been following Couch ever since he outed the name of her only witness in a blog post on The DC Patriot. Couch's fixation on Aaron also gave her concerns, given that Aaron had cooperated extensively with her homicide investigation, which included appearing before the grand jury convened in the case. She'd known for months that someone had divulged the identity of her witness to Couch, but she didn't know who it was or how it happened.

The tip directed Sines's attention to a member of Couch's team. Some who worked with Couch used their real names, such as Couch's friend Josh Flippo and a DC-area private investigator named Bill Pierce. Others went by pseudonyms or their social media usernames. There was one team member whose Twitter account was @ThinBlueLR, a nod to the "thin blue line" slogan used by police officers and their supporters as a statement of solidarity. The bio for @ThinBlueLR showed a photo of a middle-aged man in running gear and described him as a "Reagan Conservative," "Blue Collar," and an "LEO," shorthand for law enforcement officer. This person had also appeared on several podcasts with Couch, during which Couch took pains to not use the man's actual name, instead referring to him as "Blue." Despite using a pseudonym, Couch dropped some hints about Blue's identity, like that he was a law enforcement officer who worked in the "swamp."

The tipster who contacted Sines had combed through Blue's Twitter account. Blue tweeted at a prolific clip. Judging by his posts, Blue loved President Trump and Fox News's Tucker Carlson. He had raged against "third-world savages" coming into the United States and Democratic mayors "who continue to demonize the police" and "favor the criminals." He posted full-throated attacks on the city he patrolled ("a criminal cesspool") and its mayor, Muriel Bowser ("the head felon"). But what caught the tipster's attention was what he wrote about the Seth Rich case. He said Seth was the source of the WikiLeaks emails and accused Mayor Bowser and Cathy Lanier, the DC police chief at the time of Seth's murder, of engaging in a "cover-up" and telling the detectives to "stand down":

> Does anyone have a clip of @MayorBowser attending or speaking at a press conference after #SethRich was gunned down in her city in cold blood? I don't recall . . . Maybe it's because she was instructed by the DNC to sweep it under the rug? Bowser spoke today at a murder presser.

Blue had also tweeted about a "witness":

> What MPDC never told the public is that a witness was interviewed the night of the #SethRich murder. She gave a description of 2 suspects . . . Their clothing and race. They were seen fleeing the area. A BOLO [Be On the Lookout] was never voiced over the radio nor posted on the police Twitter feed.

But it was an appearance by Blue on an episode of Matt Couch's podcast that offered the best clue as to his identity. Blue, Couch, and Couch's friend Josh Flippo talked for more than an hour and a half, and Blue was more vitriolic than usual. When the subject of that year's midterm elections came up, Blue was adamant that Republicans had to show up and vote en masse if they wanted to defend Trump and beat back the Democratic Party. "We can't have low turnout," he said. "These fucking basement-dwellers and losers and never-do-wells, they're all gonna come out and vote. All these resistance morons, they're gonna be out there voting."

As Couch saw it, the Democrats would do anything necessary, legal or illegal, to take control of Congress and regain power. "They'll cheat, they'll lie, they'll steal," Couch said.

"They will kill people!" Blue interjected. "They killed Seth Rich. They've killed a lot of other people." He went on, "They will fucking assassinate people." Democrats, Blue said, will stuff a ballot box and steal an election "right in front of you and say, 'What are you going to do about it?' They will do that fucked-up shit in every Democrat-run city."

More than an hour into the podcast, Flippo, Couch's friend and cohost, slipped up and used an actual name—Doug—when he referred to Blue. Later, Couch mentioned another detail: that Blue was once named officer of the year. It didn't take the tipster long to piece together a convincing theory of who Blue really was. His name was Douglas Berlin, the tipster wrote. He worked as a cop for the DC Metropolitan Police Department.

———————◆———————

Berlin was unlike most rookie cops who signed up with the DC police. For one, he was approaching his fiftieth birthday, which made him ten or fifteen years older than some of his academy class. He had already made a career running a chain of successful Gold's Gyms in the greater Washington area. As a cop he would make in a year what he had earned in a single month in the gym business. He was also a fitness fanatic who competed in ultra-marathons. Tall, square-jawed, and muscle-bound, he won the physical skills award in his MPD officer training program despite being one of the oldest members of his academy class.

He started in 2014 as a lowly beat cop in the Shaw neighborhood, south of Bloomingdale and LeDroit Park. He patrolled his small pocket of DC on foot and sometimes logged as many as eighteen miles a day. He responded to active shootings, secured crime scenes for detectives, and once chased down a badly injured dog that had escaped from a burning house, which led to an award from the local Humane Society chapter. The neighbors came to recognize him when he visited the local recreation center; most nights he ate dinner with the same homeless man in the café at the Giant grocery store in Berlin's precinct. He was respected enough within the department that his superiors felt comfortable sending him to local community meetings that were typically attended by higher-ranking police officials. In December 2015, he was named officer of the year for his police service area.

The following summer, when Berlin first heard about Seth Rich's murder, something didn't sit right with him. He was aware of hundreds of robberies, and victims rarely got killed in the process. The department's armed-mugging-gone-wrong theory—it didn't make any sense to him. He thought the whole thing sounded suspicious. The day after the murder, he talked with a detective that he knew in a different district. "You know what happened, don't you," the cop asked Berlin. "Yeah," Berlin replied, "the DNC whacked him."

He wasn't joking. Berlin, who identified as a conservative and harbored a deep disgust for Democratic politicians such as Barack Obama and the Clintons, couldn't believe that Seth's murder was related to a robbery. He believed it had to be a political hit ordered by Democratic Party leaders or someone powerful in politics. He had no role in the investigation into the shooting, which had taken place outside of his service area and in an entirely different police district. But by the summer of 2017, he could no longer suppress his suspicions about Seth's killing and the police's handling of the case. He believed that the DC police chief, the DC mayor, and Democratic elites had conspired to block the investigation and bury the truth about how Seth had died. He wanted to do everything he could to uncover the truth about Seth's case. He chose to air his theories through his Twitter account, @ThinBlueLR.

> This is either the most inept, disorganized, half-assed, bungled, clueless & futile murder investigation, or it's a huge coverup. #SethRich

> #SethRich was a hero. He died b/c he wanted to expose the corruption in the DNC. Regardless of your politics, he's a hero.

> This one is bigger than Watergate. You have Hillary, DNC, Podesta, Bowser, Lanier, MPDC, possibly FBI, crony DC Dems, Brazile . . . #SethRich

Berlin noticed one Twitter account in particular that had taken up the cause of Seth Rich with zeal: @RealMattCouch. Couch seemed to be the loudest voice on the conservative side challenging the police's theory of the case and questioning whether there had been foul play or a cover-up by Democratic officials. One day, Berlin sent Couch a direct message on Twitter. "I said, 'Listen, I think something's fucked up with this thing,'" Berlin would later explain. "I just felt like the department didn't want to solve the case."

The two men discussed the case over the phone. Berlin shared his doubts about the official narrative and put forward his own theories about why Seth had been killed. When Couch traveled to Washington around the first anniversary of the murder, he met Berlin for the first time and they discussed the case. Berlin eventually agreed to help Couch's America First Media Group team, so long as he remained anonymous.

But Berlin had more to offer Couch than his own half-baked theories about the murder. As a cop, Berlin had access to private case data available only to MPD employees. One day, as he was sitting in a patrol car that belonged to a friend on the force, Berlin pulled up the internal file for the Rich murder. The report laid out the basic facts of the case; it also included a page that listed witnesses and their statements to the police. There, Berlin read that a neighbor who was out walking her dog had told the responding officers that she'd seen two Black men running away from the crime scene. Berlin tweeted about the existence of this witness and what she told police. Then he went one step further and gave the witness's name to Couch.

———◆———

Sines retraced the series of clues in the tipster's email to her about Berlin. She compared the photo of Berlin in his Twitter account with a photo taken at the ceremony where Berlin received the award for rescuing the dog. It looked like the same guy. She watched a short interview he'd given with a local news station at the ceremony, and the voice sounded similar to Blue's voice on the podcast. She found a tweet confirming that Berlin had won an officer-of-the-year award. There was one other place to check: the electronic database used by the US attorney's office and the DC police. Sure enough, an MPD IT employee found an access entry by a beat cop who worked in the Third District. The cop had nothing to do with her investigation.

Sines had no choice but to report Berlin to the police department. He'd accessed the internal file for a homicide he had no role in and leaked a witness's identity to a conspiracy-theorist blogger. He had also made many incendiary and downright offensive statements on Twitter. He railed against "savages from BLM who murder cops," described DC as a "criminal cesspool" and its mayor as "the head felon," and claimed that the "crimes Obama committed that we know about are enough to have had him hanged if convicted not too long ago." If it ever came out that Berlin, a working DC cop, had made those statements, any prosecutor who wanted to use him in a trial would have to disclose to the defense lawyers that Berlin had made these statements. There was no way a prosecutor could put him on the stand now.

Sines called the Internal Affairs department at MPD and told them what she'd found. Soon afterward when Berlin arrived for work, Internal Affairs said it was revoking his police powers and wouldn't say why. Berlin had worked with a lieutenant who was now in Internal Affairs. When he asked her why he was being punished, she said it was based on social media comments. Berlin's union representative said he'd likely face a thirty-day suspension and told him to go along with it until the controversy blew over. But Berlin refused to do it. He handed over his gun and his badge and resigned. "I loved that job. It was my passion," he would later say. "But I couldn't allow this department to tell me that I can't talk about something that's bothering me." He added, "It's the First Amendment. I'll say whatever the hell I want to say."

———◆———

On the morning of March 13, 2018, a new case hit the docket in the Southern District of New York. "Joel and Mary Rich, grieving parents of a murdered child, seek justice for having become collateral damage in a political war to which they are innocent bystanders," read the complaint's opening lines. The Massey Gail lawyers had partnered with another firm, Susman Godfrey, which specialized in litigating high-profile cases. The complaint named Fox News, Ed Butowsky, and Malia Zimmerman. The first count alleged intentional infliction of emotional distress and argued that the actions of Butowsky, Zimmerman, and Fox were "so outrageous in character and so extreme in degree as to go beyond all possible bounds of decency and are atrocious and utterly intolerable in a civilized community."

Mary and Joel's legal team had chosen to build the case around a personal injury tort in New York State law called "intentional infliction of emotional distress," or IIED. If victims could prove that the aggressor had engaged in behavior so outrageous or repugnant that it caused the victims severe emotional or physical harm, the victims could claim intentional infliction of emotional distress and seek damages. IIED was extremely hard to prove because the victims had to show not only that the behavior had caused them harm but also that the aggressor had acted intentionally or recklessly. Joel and Mary would have to convince a judge that a massive media organization, Fox News, had acted so recklessly that it had emotionally tormented the Riches with little or no regard for their well-being.

For the second time in two years, Joel and Mary sat before a camera crew from *Good Morning America* and told their story. Sitting in their living room, Mary struggled to get the words out as she described the effect of watching Fox stain her dead son's name and reputation. "We lost his body this first time, and the second time we lost his soul," she said. "We want our son's life and his soul restored. And I want our life back, so we can move forward again."

When the interview ended, the segment cut back to host George Stephanopoulos and the network's chief legal analyst, Dan Abrams, who was skeptical of the intentional infliction of emotional distress strategy. "You effectively have to be able to say, 'They did this to hurt us. That's *why* they did this,'" he explained, which was a "very tough standard to overcome." The challenge for the Riches, he said, was whether they could convince a judge that their intentional infliction claim had enough merit to proceed to a trial. "Because if they can get in front of a jury, you could find a sympathetic jury. But the first thing they have to do is get a judge to say, 'I'm going to let this move forward.'"

Two weeks after his parents filed their case, Aaron sued Butowsky, Couch, and the *Washington Times* in federal court for the District of Columbia. The conspiracy theories revolved around events that took place in DC, and Couch had traveled there to advance his lies—it only made sense to bring the case there. "Our constitutional system leaves wide room for debate on issues of public concern," the suit read, "but individuals like Defendants poison that deliberate space when they flood it with fabricated information about private figures like Aaron." In a sixty-page complaint, he alleged defamation, invasion of privacy, civil conspiracy, and also intentional infliction of emotional distress. The suit demanded a jury trial.

23

Rendezvous

JACK BURKMAN NEEDED a new act. The staged reenactment of Seth's final hours had gotten panned in the press. So, too, had the TV ad he paid for and appeared in calling on Special Counsel Mueller to investigate Rich's murder, complete with Russian subtitles. A judge had dismissed his lawsuit seeking the ballistics report and autopsy in the Rich homicide case. A second lawsuit, this time on behalf of a Bernie Sanders supporter, Gary Frazier, alleged fraud and negligence by the DNC for stealing the party nomination from Sanders and "exposing" Frazier's personal and financial information during the 2016 hack. Burkman said he filed the suit primarily to gain access to the DNC's servers, which according to the suit would "shed light" on Seth Rich's "possible role in the dissemination of DNC information." He announced the suit standing next to Frazier at a press conference outside the DNC's headquarters, but the case went nowhere in the court, and he quietly dropped it a few months later.

In February 2018, Burkman fell back on one of his go-to ploys: a reward offer. Washington was consumed with speculation about Special Counsel Robert Mueller's ongoing investigation into Russian interference in the 2016 presidential election. The partisan campaign to distract from or discredit Mueller's work led by the president and his advisers continued when leading Republican congressman Devin

Nunes released a memo accusing high-ranking officials at the FBI and Justice Department of political bias. In a rare move, the FBI preemptively disputed what became known as the Nunes memo for what the bureau called "material omissions of fact." Trump, in turn, hailed the memo, saying it "totally vindicates" him.

Burkman sensed an opportunity. He sent out a press release to every reporter he could think of. He was offering a $25,000 reward to anyone who came forward with evidence of FBI wrongdoing. Once again, Burkman was putting up reward money. Once again, he was casting himself as the reasonable one, a neutral arbiter who only wanted to get the facts. "The American people are between a rock and a hard place," he said in his announcement. "Whether it's the White House or FBI, someone isn't telling the truth and it puts everyone in danger. If there's a member of the FBI who wants to settle this, I'm ready to help."

Soon afterward a man contacted him. He said he was a high-ranking FBI official who had confidential information about Andrew McCabe, the acting director of the FBI. McCabe had overseen the bureau's investigation into whether Hillary Clinton mishandled classified information as secretary of state by using a private email server. Suspicions that McCabe had leaked sensitive details of the Clinton probe to a reporter prompted an internal review. In McCabe's first meeting with the president, Trump had asked him whom he voted for in 2016; McCabe replied that he had voted in the Republican primary but hadn't cast a ballot in the general election. McCabe had worked for James Comey, whom Trump had fired, and soon Trump came to despise McCabe too, viewing him as a member of the "deep state" and a friend of the Clintons. (McCabe's wife had run for elected office as a Democrat and received donations from a longtime Clinton fundraiser, but McCabe himself had no ties to the Clinton family.)

Burkman and his source agreed on an exchange: once Burkman wired several thousand dollars, the source would leave a sampling of internal FBI documents in the parking garage at the Key Bridge Marriott. Following instructions, Burkman arrived at the garage and looked for a traffic cone. A lobbyist wearing designer loafers and toting a small yappy dog roamed a dingy parking garage for a secret drop point: it was *All the President's Men* directed by the Coen brothers. Burkman located the traffic cone, lifted it up, and found printed-out emails underneath. He took the documents home and showed them to his then-partner. They contained details about the US Foreign Intelligence Surveillance Court, the judicial body that oversees American intelligence agencies and approves or denies warrants for foreign wiretapping requests. Susan questioned the authenticity of the documents. Burkman believed they were authentic. "I thought I had the story of the decade," he would later say.

He and the FBI source arranged for a second drop at the garage and then a third, which would be the biggest leak yet: the full inspector general's report on whether McCabe had leaked classified information or committed other wrongdoing during the FBI's investigation into Hillary Clinton's use of a private email server. The report had taken on a mythical status among the president's supporters, who believed it would vindicate Trump and validate his suspicions about the FBI's bias and the "deep state" forces arrayed against him. But the Justice Department still hadn't released it, which meant Burkman could potentially have it before anyone else. He wired another payment, then he and the source agreed on a date for the next drop.

———— ◆ ————

On the evening of March 13, the same day Mary and Joel's lawyers filed their lawsuit, Burkman left his home in Arlington and walked to the Marriott. His dog, Jack Jr., tugged at his leash as they neared their destination. Burkman's informant had emailed him earlier that day with instructions for how to retrieve the newest batch of documents. He told Burkman to wait until after 5:00 p.m. and then walk to the second floor of the hotel's parking garage. "You will see a trash can and a yellow cone," the informant wrote. "The file is taped inside the yellow cone." When he arrived at the hotel, Burkman bought a cup of coffee and drank it in the lobby. He tried flirting with one of the hotel's female employees, handing her an envelope with his phone number written on it, but she threw it away and walked off. His previous rendezvous had caught the attention of the employees, who noticed him wandering the parking garage and looking under traffic cones. They watched as Burkman nursed his coffee until it was close to 5:30 p.m. Then he stood up and walked toward the back of the hotel, past the ballroom, through the sliding glass doors, and into the garage.

When he reached the garage's second floor, he looked for the traffic cone. He saw only one, closer to neon green than yellow. Burkman scooped Jack Jr. up into his arms and knelt down to lift up the cone. He saw an envelope stuck to the inside of the cone with black tape. Right then, he felt a searing pain in his buttocks, like small, hot rocks pelting him from behind.

Burkman grabbed the cone and ran toward the exit gate of the parking garage. He felt more hot rocks hitting him from behind. "Help!" he yelled. His screams were loud enough that guests in the hotel heard him and ran to their windows. One guest saw him sprinting toward the exit clutching the cone and Jack Jr.'s leash and collar, but there was no sign of the dog. He exited the garage and was running away from the hotel when a black Lincoln Navigator raced up alongside him and swerved into him, knocking him to the ground. Burkman staggered to his feet and continued to ask for help until an employee found him and dialed 911. It wasn't until Burkman arrived at the hospital that he learned he'd been shot.

While a local police officer interviewed Burkman from his hospital bed, Arlington County detectives descended on the Marriott. They scoured the garage for clues as to the shooter's identity, requested the hotel's security footage, and located witnesses. (They also found Jack Jr. hiding under a car across the street.) The employee who had called the ambulance for Burkman told the authorities that, hours before the attack, he had noticed a black SUV parked in an unusual way on the garage's upper level. The vehicle had a Florida license plate. The employee couldn't remember much about the driver's appearance, but he had noticed the driver dumping items into a trash bin. The police rummaged through the contents of the bin and retrieved a trove of evidence: unused ammunition for a .22 rifle, oil filters that can be repurposed into silencers, receipts from a nearby toll road, and a balled-up piece of black tape that matched the type on the inside of the cone.

They also recovered an Amazon Prime shipping box and a ripped-up ID card. The Amazon package was addressed to a "Kevin Doh." The ID card listed the name and address of a man named Kevin Doherty, Burkman's former investigator.

Within a matter of days, the police had compiled enough evidence to arrest Doherty. He had purchased several guns at nearby sporting-goods stores in the days before the shooting. Surveillance footage showed him renting a black Lincoln Navigator from Washington's Reagan airport on the morning of the attack. Inside Doherty's house the authorities found the rifle that had been used to shoot Burkman. His computer contained phony emails Doherty had sent to Burkman pretending to be an FBI whistleblower. The bureau said the emails that the so-called informant had given to Burkman were fake. The FBI badge that the informant had shown Burkman to prove his bona fides was available for sale in an online store for movie props. And the $15,000 Burkman paid? The money was in an account controlled by Doherty.

Burkman told the police that he believed Doherty had attacked him because of their dispute over control of the Profiling Project. The Arlington County police also interviewed people who knew Doherty, including his girlfriend at the time. But no one could explain why he concocted such an elaborate plot to carry out a violent attack on Burkman. The police tried to ask Doherty himself why he had done it, but after the lead detective on the case advised him of his constitutional rights, Doherty requested his attorney and the interview was over.

Prosecutors would later charge Doherty with two counts of malicious wounding, a crime that carried a heavier penalty in Virginia than attempted homicide. Doherty pled guilty to the first malicious-wounding charge in exchange for prosecutors dropping the second one. A judge sentenced him to nine years in prison.

———◆———

"When you get two bullets in you, the world changes," Burkman said to the small group of reporters. It was about six weeks after the attack. With his arm cradled in a sling, Burkman was replaying what the police had told him—that Doherty had shot him with a low-powered rifle akin to a .22. "I mean, if you want to kill somebody, my god, you could use just an M1 rifle or a Glock," he said. "It's weird. None of it makes any sense. That's why we're launching this, because I gotta figure out what's this tied to. Who's behind him? Is anybody behind him? What's going on here?" As ever, Burkman saw a conspiracy at work, and he intended to unravel it.

Burkman had rented out a ballroom in the Holiday Inn across the street from the Marriott to announce that he had hired a new investigator, a retired special agent from the Naval Criminal Investigative Service, to lead the rebranded Profiling Investigative Center. The attack, he said, had "reenergized" his interest in the Rich case. "Today is the rebirth," he said. "Today is our renaissance." Afterward, as Burkman stood around talking with the reporters, he replayed what he'd believed might be his final moments alive. "I passed out in the ambulance," he said, "and the last thought I had was, *I'm the next Seth. I'm the new Seth.* That's the last thought I had."

———◆———

On Friday, March 9, 2018, Sines walked out of DC Superior Court at the end of a weeklong trial. While leading the Rich homicide investigation, she also had juggled several other high-profile cases. One was a pair of murders committed by a DC teenager named Maurice Bellamy. The first victim was an off-duty Secret Service officer whom Bellamy had gunned down during an attempted robbery. The second was a fifteen-year-old boy who was waiting to catch a Metro train with his mother and younger sisters on Easter weekend. Bellamy claimed the boy had looked at him the wrong way, so he shot the boy dead in front of his family.

At trial Bellamy's mother blamed her son's crimes on DC's struggling public education system. His lawyers sought leniency from the jury given that Bellamy was seventeen at the time of both murders. Sines argued that the jury should treat Bellamy as an adult. "This wasn't an accident," she told the jurors. "This wasn't self-defense. This was on purpose. Under our laws, if you kill someone when you are seventeen, you are held responsible, just as if you are a man." The jury returned a guilty verdict on two counts of first-degree murder, one count of armed robbery, and a weapons offense.

Sines would normally go out for drinks with her colleagues after a big court victory. Instead she went home, climbed into bed, and stayed there for two straight days. The Bellamy trial had been challenging, but the exhaustion she felt ran deeper than that. "That's when I knew I'd been doing this too long," she would later say.

Sines had worked in the Triple Nickel long enough to know that her office had a problem with prosecutors who stuck around for too long. As they got older, they started making mistakes, but the US attorney's office wouldn't force them out. Sines didn't want to be one of those old prosecutors who humiliated herself and her department. "I didn't want to go out like that," she'd later say. She told her superiors that she would retire at the end of April.

The timing made sense to her. The Bellamy trial had gone smoothly, and she knew she wouldn't get a better sendoff than that. She planned to sell her row house in DC and move to Florida, and she had already found a place down there that she liked. The biggest regret she felt was that she would be leaving the department without closing the Rich case. She called Aaron and Mary to tell them about her decision. "I'm too tired to keep doing this," she told Aaron. She said she had extracted a promise from her bosses that Seth's case would be assigned to a good lawyer.

She also made sure to share with the special counsel's investigation run by Robert Mueller everything she'd learned in the eighteen months she'd spent investigating Seth's murder. On March 15, she welcomed an FBI agent and a federal prosecutor into her office to talk about Seth Rich. She explained that she had examined the contents of Seth's computer and cell phone. She'd pored over his bank records. She'd interviewed his bosses, coworkers, friends. She found nothing to suggest he played any part at all in the stealing and leaking of DNC emails during the 2016 campaign.

Sines couldn't say for certain what Mueller's staffers did with the information she provided them. But given the experience and caliber of the people with whom she met, she was confident that Mueller was fully investigating the Rich conspiracy theories about the DNC hack, WikiLeaks, and the election. "There is no question in my mind," Sines would later say.

The case had led her down one conspiratorial dead end after another, and she had documented the many theories and rumors she found in a series of memos she added to the case file. But debunking them had brought her no closer to finding the killer. Still, she stood by her theory, shared by the DC police, that Seth had been murdered while being robbed. At the end of April, she boxed up her Chuck Taylors, Nietzsche plaque, and framed "Killers Fear This Woman" story and left the US Attorney's Office for the District of Columbia for the last time.

Extreme and Outrageous

MARY LOVED TV legal procedurals. As she arrived at the federal court-house in downtown Manhattan, she felt like she was living in one. She and Joel had flown to New York to attend a critical hearing in their case against Fox. When they got to the courthouse, their lawyers took them inside through a private side door to avoid the press camped out front. As they walked through the courthouse, their lawyers shielded them from the reporters and photographers and surrounded them as they rode an elevator up to Courtroom 11A. With its dark wood walls, high ceilings, and US seal affixed to the wall above the judge's bench, the space lived up to what Mary had imagined after a lifetime of watching courtroom dramas. Joel and Mary sat down in the first row of the gallery behind the table reserved for the plaintiff's attorneys. Eli Kay-Oliphant, a member of their legal team, sat one row behind the Riches to act as a buffer and to answer any questions they had. Mary joked that Eli was her and Joel's "babysitter."

"All rise for the Honorable George B. Daniels," the clerk announced.

A slim, balding man dressed in robes and a necktie entered the courtroom. Judge Daniels was sixty-four years old and one of the few Black judges in the Southern District of New York, where he had served for almost two decades. Born in the South Carolina Lowcoun-try, the son of a minister and a teacher, Daniels moved to Brooklyn with his mother at a young age; many years later a hint of Bedford-Stuyvesant could still be heard in his voice. He attended Yale and the University of California's Boalt Law School. After returning to New York, he worked as a defense attorney, a federal prosecutor, and an adviser to the city's first Black mayor, David Dinkins, before President Bill Clinton appointed him to the bench in 2000.

Given the Southern District's jurisdiction over all of Manhattan, Daniels heard many high-profile cases that covered a remarkable breadth of legal issues: a landmark wrongful death suit brought by the relatives of September 11 victims against the Islamic Republic of Iran, a decade-long terrorism case involving the Palestinian Authority and the Palestine Liberation Organization, a scandalous price-fixing suit involving the owner of the Sotheby's auction house, and several financial crimes cases that implicated Wall Street giants.

Daniels had been assigned Rod Wheeler's lawsuit against Fox filed the fall before, which meant he would bring a depth of knowledge to Joel and Mary's case. Still, the lawyers for the Riches considered Daniels a tough draw. He moved at a notoriously slow pace: at one point in the early 2000s, he had more pending motions in civil cases before him than any other federal judge in the country. The *New York Times* dubbed him the "unchallenged king of delayed decisions." He could be impatient in the courtroom and idiosyncratic in his rulings. Over time Daniels had come to believe that right and wrong were empty concepts in a court of law. "There are instead answers that work and answers that do not," he once said. "The only time both sides go away happy," he liked to say, "is when I perform a wedding."

Representing the Riches were five lawyers from two firms, Massey Gail and Susman Godfrey. Fox had retained a team of respected First Amendment lawyers with the firm Williams and Connolly, who sat alongside Zimmerman's and Butowsky's lawyers. Daniels asked who wanted to speak first, and with that the hearing began, on June 20, 2018.

Fox's defense opened with an aggressive strategy. Its lead counsel, Joseph Terry, said Joel and Mary's lawsuit was a ruse. It was a defamation claim in disguise, he said, a ploy by the Riches to seek damages on behalf of their dead son. In order to do so, the Riches had sought to "shoehorn" their allegations into a claim for intentional infliction of emotional distress. If the court disagreed with this interpretation, Terry went on, nothing the Riches had put in their complaint "comes close" to meeting the exceedingly high bar for intentional infliction: conduct "so outrageous in character, and so extreme in degree, as to go beyond all possible bounds of decency, and to be regarded as atrocious, and utterly intolerable in a civilized society." If anything, Terry said, the lawsuit was "an attack on the institutions of Fox News or the political point of view they ascribe to."

Fox had every reason to try and get the case tossed in its earliest stages. If Judge Daniels ruled against the network, the case would proceed to the discovery stage. The Riches' lawyers could demand reams of internal documents related to Fox's inner workings; they could force people like Sean Hannity and Malia Zimmerman to sit for depositions. But if Daniels agreed with Fox, the network wouldn't have to provide a single piece of paper to the other side.

Daniels let Terry make his case, interjecting with the occasional question or clarification. The judge was more skeptical, and at times hostile, to the arguments made by Leonard Gail of Massey Gail, one of the firms representing Joel and Mary. Daniels asked Gail if he could point to specific actions by Fox, Butowsky, and Zimmerman that rose to the level of "outrageous" and "extreme." Gail said the judge needed to look at the case holistically, a months-long campaign of cruelty and deceit that added up to intentional infliction of emotional distress. "Your Honor, with all due respect, if you slice up each thing that was done and identified in isolation, there is always going to be an argument that any one thing in isolation doesn't constitute outrageous conduct."

"I understand that," Daniels replied. "Also, as I always say to the lawyers, there is another basic theory—that zero times ten is still zero." A visibly irritated Daniels kept interrupting Gail, and at one point the judge told Gail to describe for him "what is the bad thing that you are suing them for." Not a promising sign.

Daniels eventually called a recess for lunch. The hearing had lasted for nearly two and a half hours, and they weren't close to done. Eli, Mary's favorite of the legal team, had told her they expected to be done by lunch, in time to catch flights out of New York that afternoon. Now it looked like everyone was going to miss their flights. As Joel and Mary stretched their legs, an older lawyer on Fox's team approached them. He said he wanted to give his condolences for the loss of their son. He didn't mention the case and said he was speaking in a personal capacity, not on behalf of his client. Mary despised Fox and everything it stood for. Still, she appreciated the gesture. *That's what anybody should've done*, she thought.

The break would at least give the Riches' legal team a chance to regroup. A different lawyer, Arun Subramanian, took over after the break. While Daniels remained skeptical, he seemed to respond better to Subramanian than he had to Gail. The lawyers for each side took questions from the judge for another few hours before the hearing ended. Daniels vowed to issue a decision "as early as possible."

———◆———

Aaron's luck wasn't much better when it came to the judge assigned to his case, *Rich v. Butowsky*. DC district court judge Richard J. Leon had a reputation for moving slowly like Judge Daniels did in New York. He was presiding over several other major cases at the time. He was also an active participant in the Federalist Society, the most influential, powerful, and well-funded conservative judicial organization in the country and a pipeline for Republican judicial nominees. But Gottlieb believed that if he and his team won a favorable ruling from Leon, it would be that much harder to dismiss the decision as the work of a liberal activist judge.

Gottlieb also received early indications that the defendants would prove more complicated than he'd expected. Matt Couch had decided to represent himself pro se, which would only complicate things if and when the case moved into discovery. Ed Butowsky left long, rambling voicemail messages for Gottlieb—something no respectable defense attorney would allow their client to do. Butowsky's first defense attorney withdrew from the case after a few months, leaving Butowsky without a lawyer. At one point Butowsky asked the court for permission for a solo practitioner named Ty Clevenger, a former journalist and cop who had gone to Stanford Law, to represent him. Butowsky had contacted Clevenger after reading a post on Clevenger's blog, Lawflog (tagline: "Because some people just need a good flogging"), in which he cast doubt on the robbery-gone-wrong theory for Seth's murder. Clevenger's motion to appear in Butowsky's case, which listed his address as a post office box in Brooklyn, mentioned that he had resigned from the District of Columbia Bar after the court had fined and suspended him.

At first Aaron's lawyers did not object to Clevenger being granted permission to appear in the case. But then Clevenger sent an email to Aaron's entire legal team attaching an affidavit he'd written, which he asked Aaron to sign. The letter purported to eliminate source privilege on behalf of Seth and waived Aaron's right to bring a legal claim against WikiLeaks, Julian Assange, and Kim Dotcom for anything they had said about the Rich brothers. Clevenger didn't represent WikiLeaks, Assange, or Dotcom, and it was unclear any of them wanted what Clevenger had asked for. Yet if Aaron refused to sign it, Clevenger wrote in a follow-up email, "I think the media (and the public) will find that very interesting."

Gottlieb read the document in disbelief. It was an invitation for Assange and Dotcom to defame Aaron and Seth, which then asked Aaron to promise not to take legal action if they did. Gottlieb told Clevenger that no lawyer would ever allow their client to sign such a document. It also looked to Gottlieb like an obvious publicity stunt. Not long after, Clevenger attacked Gottlieb and Governski on his blog, calling them "creeps" and "oily shysters" who appeared to be "well-versed in the dark art of spinning a story." Clevenger went on to speculate that perhaps a third party was "bankrolling" both of the Rich family's lawsuits as a way to "muddy the waters" about the DNC hack and to obscure that Seth Rich had leaked the emails. "Some of my friends have warned me to stay away from the Seth Rich case because it's too fringe, and because it will damage my credibility," Clevenger added. "I think that's what Michael Gottlieb and his ilk are trying to achieve."

Gottlieb and Governski filed a motion to block Clevenger's attempt to join the case. In their motion they revealed that Clevenger had failed to disclose in his application to appear on behalf of Butowsky how many times he had been sanctioned by various courts. In DC, three district court judges had sanctioned him for repeated misconduct. The DC appellate court had also sanctioned him and ordered him to be publicly censured. And the district court's governance committee had recommended his disbarment. Clevenger ultimately resigned from the DC Bar.

It's uncommon for one side's attorneys to oppose the other side's request to admit a lawyer, and courts generally grant such requests. Shortly after Aaron's lawyers filed their opposition motion, a judge in a different case released a scathing decision rejecting Clevenger's motion to appear in a case in the Southern District of New York. The judge noted that Clevenger had "amassed a cavalcade of disciplinary issues in various courts, all of which display a lack of respect for the judicial process." Clevenger's recent behavior related to that case "forecasts trouble ahead, and Clevenger certainly has a history of trouble behind," the judge added. The New York judge denied Clevenger's motion. The next day Clevenger withdrew his application to appear in Aaron's case before Judge Leon could rule on it.

Meanwhile new evidence further undercut the Seth Rich conspiracy theories. On July 13, a grand jury convened by Special Counsel Robert Mueller returned an indictment against twelve Russian intelligence officers. The indictment laid out in detail, for the first time, how the Russian government had hacked the DNC, the Democratic Congressional Campaign Committee, and former Clinton campaign chairman John Podesta. Units 26165 and 74455 of the GRU, Russia's military intelligence agency, employed a combination of sophisticated malware tools and more rudimentary bait-and-switch techniques to obtain passwords and gain access to personal email accounts and Democratic Party servers. The Russian officers first disseminated the stolen material through two online personas, DCLeaks and Guccifer 2.0, then worked with an intermediary identified as "Organization 1," which was unmistakably WikiLeaks. In announcing the indictment, the Justice Department said there was "no allegation in the indictment that any American was a knowing participant in the alleged unlawful activity or knew they were communicating with Russian intelligence officers."

Gottlieb called it a "very satisfying vindication for our client and for us." Yet the conspiracy theorists read the same indictment and either found it implausible or convinced themselves that just because the indictment *didn't* mention the Riches didn't mean they *weren't* involved. They continued to hold up the flawed analysis put forward by Bill Binney and the Veteran Intelligence Professionals for Sanity that said the DNC hack was really an inside job.

———◆———

On August 2, Judge Daniels in New York issued two opinions in the Fox News–related lawsuits before him. The first was Rod Wheeler's case, the second was Joel and Mary's.

Daniels rejected Wheeler's claim that Fox, Butowsky, and Zimmerman had defamed him by publishing made-up quotes attributed to him. A defamation claim must, first and foremost, show that the statement in question was wrong. Wheeler's suit had failed to meet that basic threshold, Daniels wrote. After all, when it came to those supposedly damaging quotes that Wheeler was now complaining about, he had said nearly identical things to other news outlets, and he wasn't suing over *those* comments. Daniels further pointed out that before Wheeler had sued Fox and Ed Butowsky, he had willingly participated with those same parties in what Daniels called a "collective effort" to publish a "sensational claim regarding Seth Rich's murder." Wheeler "cannot now seek to avoid the consequences of his own complicity and coordinated assistance in perpetuating a politically motivated story not having any basis in fact." But he also denied Butowsky's request to be awarded attorneys' fees. From the outside, it appeared Daniels wanted nothing more to do with Wheeler's case, writing in his decision that "the situation in which all parties now find themselves hardly engenders sympathy."

While Daniels voiced some sympathy for Joel and Mary Rich, he ruled against them and dismissed every count in their complaint. Fox's arguments had prevailed: Joel and Mary's allegations against Fox News were simply defamation claims styled as something else. There was a standard, he wrote, for what qualified as a "deliberate and malicious campaign of harassment or intimidation"—described by one court as "an unrelenting campaign of day in, day out harassment" or harassment "accompanied by physical threats." What the Riches had put in their complaint fell well short of that standard, Daniels said.

When Bauman spoke to Joel and Mary after the decision, they sounded gutted. People had exploited their trust, had published conspiracies about Seth, and there was nothing wrong with that from a legal standpoint? How was that possible? Were there no protections against smearing the name of the deceased? But Joel and Mary were also resolute. They would exhaust every legal avenue at their disposal to appeal Daniels's ruling. As they saw it, the case was not finished.

———— ◆ ————

As for Ed Butowsky, he felt vindicated. More than that, he was angry— angry at the Riches and Rod Wheeler for suing him, angry at the lawyers who had filed the suits and the news outlets that believed them, angry at everyone who had wronged him since Malia Zimmerman's Fox News story had been published.

A few days after Daniels's decision, Butowsky gave an interview to the financial trade publication *Investment News*. He said he "didn't see anything wrong" with Zimmerman's Fox News story. The fallout from the story and the ensuing lawsuits, he said, prompted clients to leave his firm and led to the loss of a third of his business, and much of the blame lay with unscrupulous lawyers who had made him out to be some kind of Trump-supporting villain. "Lawyers can put anything they want in a lawsuit; there's so much flexibility, it's hideous," he said. "For a year I've been known as the guy who is Trump's backer, and as someone who loves Trump and made up stories to divert attention from what really happened." He went on, "Anybody who did anything negative to me as a result of the lawsuit will pay. I'm going to sue the hell out of a lot of firms. I want to see these people choke on their nerves and go through the same crap I had to go through."

25

A Sign in the Crowd

A CROWD OF tens of thousands of people packed into an arena in Tampa, Florida. The crowd roared when President Trump made his entrance as Lee Greenwood's "God Bless the USA" poured from the speakers. *And I'm proud . . . to be . . . an American!* The president had traveled to Tampa in late July to endorse one of his most loyal understudies: a Republican House lawmaker named Ron DeSantis who was running for governor. The scene was typical of the rallies that were a fixture of the Trump years—the bright red Make America Great Again hats, the playlist trapped in the amber of late 1980s pop tunes, the tent-revivalist-as-stand-up style of Trump's remarks. DeSantis got a few minutes to speak; Trump spent an hour holding forth on whatever entered his mind. With every punchline his fans cheered, hoisting their signs skyward, "Promises Made, Promises Kept," "Buy American, Hire American."

The rally also marked the national-TV debut of a different slogan. One man wore a T-shirt with a giant Q on it. One sign read, "We Are Q." Another appeared next to it. Written in shaky block letters, it included the hashtags #QAnon and #WWG1WGA. Above those hashtags was another message: "His name was Seth Rich."

Before that rally QAnon had been strictly a social media phenomenon, a product of online communities and influencers on the fringes.

Now, for the first time, QAnon had begun to spread, bleeding into greater view and entering the public consciousness. "We're no longer talking about an exposure of a million people," one online disinformation expert said at the time. "If a rally is broadcast on a major news network, we're talking tens of millions of people are now exposed to this whole concept of 'Q.'"

It was also one of the first inklings that QAnon believers helped make up the Republican Party's base. A month later a self-described "conspiracy analyst" for Alex Jones's Infowars named Michael LeBron tweeted a photo of himself and his wife standing next to a grinning President Trump in the Oval Office and added several QAnon hashtags. LeBron, whose online persona was "Lionel Lebron," was an early and influential promoter of QAnon. In a video he later posted, LeBron said he had received a "special guided tour" of the White House. While he said he didn't bring up QAnon in his photo op with the president, "I think we all know he knows about it." (White House press secretary Sarah Sanders downplayed LeBron's tweets, saying he had merely been part of a "large group [that] came through the White House for a brief tour and a photo.")

By the fall of 2018, it was highly unlikely that Trump didn't know what QAnon was. Alex Jones and Infowars had released more than a dozen posts about QAnon with titles like "High Level Intelligence Source Confirms QAnon Is REAL." The actors James Woods and Roseanne Barr, both Trump supporters with a history of amplifying fringe theories, tweeted about QAnon to a combined audience of more than a million followers. Some of the same far-right influencers who promoted Pizzagate now shared QAnon content.

QAnon signs and shirts kept appearing at Republican campaign rallies. Q—whoever he or she or they were—posted nearly one thousand drops that summer and fall. The posts drew on the language of forbears like Milton William Cooper and the leaders of the John Birch Society, urging followers to be "sheep no more" and lead a "grand awakening" that would vanquish the criminal cabal of Democrats and Hollywood elites. The substance of Q's posts also became much more of a megaphone for pro-Trump Republican candidates. Q urged as many people as possible to vote in the upcoming election, predicting a "red

October" that would see huge Republican gains. Q also warned about election fraud by the Democrats, who were supposedly destroying legal ballots or recruiting noncitizens to vote.

In December 2018, six months after Matthew Wright's standoff near Hoover Dam, police arrested a man from California who had bomb-making materials in his car. They alleged that he was part of a plot to blow up a holiday display from a satanic group at the Illinois state capitol in Springfield, Illinois. According to an FBI intelligence bulletin that was later released, the man, who was not identified, told a law enforcement officer that he wanted to "make Americans aware of Pizzagate and the New World Order." A few months later, a twenty-four-year-old named Anthony Comello drove to the Staten Island home of Francesco "Franky Boy" Cali, a leader of the Gambino mafia family, according to prosecutors. Comello attempted to serve a citizen's arrest on Cali, and when Cali refused, Comello shot him to death.

When Comello appeared in court for his arraignment a week later, he raised his left palm. Scrawled in blue ink was a giant "Q" and the slogans "MAGA Forever" and "Patriots in Charge." Comello's lawyer would later inform the court that his client had posted thousands of times online, sometimes under the handle "RealAmericasVoice," sharing conspiratorial memes and messages about the "Clinton Crime Family" and election fraud. According to his lawyer, Comello believed Cali, in his position as a mafia leader, was a part of the "deep state" and that when he tried to arrest the mobster, he believed he had "the president's full support."

Weeks before the 2018 midterms, a Nevada woman tweeted a You-Tube video with the title "Q – We Are the Plan." The video, posted by an account named "Storm Is Upon Us," talks about a "vast transgenerational criminal mafia" that controls the world "through a system of threats, blackmail, and bribery. . . . You may know them as the deep state, or cabal." The members of this cabal were "a dark and deeply sinister death cult with a strong reliance on symbolism and numerology with levels of cruelty unimaginable to all right-thinking people."

This rhetoric, while disturbing, was standard fare for QAnon content. The striking part was the person who shared it. Joyce Bentley was a candidate for Congress. As far as anyone could tell, she was the first

QAnon-promoting candidate to appear on the fall ballot. She stood no chance of winning Nevada's heavily Democratic First District. But rather than shun Bentley for her outlandish views, the Nevada Republican Party and a state affiliate of the National Rifle Association both endorsed her.

———•|•———

Butowsky had embarked on a legal blitz. In a span of months, he would file six lawsuits against nearly fifty defendants, accusing all of them of defamation. In all of these suits Ty Clevenger represented him. He sued NPR, its CEO, several of its top editors, and its media reporter David Folkenflik, who had published several stories about Butowsky and Seth. His financial firm sued the Charles Schwab Corporation, alleging that Schwab had hurt his reputation and business when it severed ties after news stories and litigation revealed Butowsky's role in Fox's Seth Rich reporting. He filed a racketeering case against Douglas Wigdor, the New York City lawyer who had filed Rod Wheeler's lawsuit against Fox.

The suits kept the Seth Rich conspiracy theory alive. In his suit against Aaron, Butowsky claimed in one filing that he was "aware of evidence suggesting that the Plaintiff helped his brother leak emails from the DNC to WikiLeaks." He did not say what that evidence was. In the case against Douglas Wigdor, Butowsky alleged that Fox had retracted its story about Seth and WikiLeaks not because it was inaccurate but because Rupert Murdoch's daughter-in-law, Kathryn, had made the call to remove the story: "At Kathryn Murdoch's request, and for no other reason, Fox pulled Zimmerman's article." In the NPR suit, Butowsky repeated the allegation that Aaron, in tandem with the DNC, was "blocking the investigation" into Seth's murder. Rebutting these statements wasn't as simple as sending a correction request to a reporter: it required motions in court and possibly oral arguments, a process that could take months.

Now Butowsky had come up with a more convincing narrative. He had never wanted to get involved with the Rich family, he said.

However, he had a politically connected *liberal* friend, Ellen Ratner, who in 2016 had paid a visit to Julian Assange, who, Butowsky claimed, told her Seth was the source for the DNC leak. Even though Ratner denied this ever happened, Butowsky maintained that Ratner asked him to relay this information to Seth Rich's family. Butowsky hesitated. Finally, after months of agonizing, he agreed to do it. "This was just me doing this to help a family find out who murdered their son," he would later tell an interviewer.

In Butowsky's telling, during one of his conversations with the Riches, Joel confided in him something startling: "We know what our boys did." To Butowsky's ears, Joel had just confirmed Seth and Aaron's involvement in the DNC leak. The work with Zimmerman and Wheeler and Fox News—he was just trying to correct the record about Trump, Russia, and the election.

Even though Butowsky had first contacted Joel back in late 2016, even though he had proposed hiring Rod Wheeler, and even though he had helped Malia Zimmerman craft her story—in spite of all of this, Butowsky believed he was the victim. *His* reputation lay in tatters for trying to help a grieving family get answers.

This was the story Butowsky told anyone who would listen. The problem was that his account didn't match anyone else's. According to Ellen Ratner, Assange never used Seth Rich's name during her meeting with him. As for Joel Rich, he couldn't remember saying "we know what our boys did." He might have spoken those words, but in no way was he implying that his sons had anything to do with the DNC leak. "Maybe I was responding to some suggestion about Seth and Aaron stealing the emails: 'We've heard that before, but we know what our boys would've done,'" he said. "It wasn't 'We knew what they did.'"

———◆———

After Judge Daniels dismissed their case, Mary and Joel decided to appeal to the Second Circuit, which scheduled oral arguments for early February 2019. The hearing was held in a large reading room on the campus of the University of Connecticut's Law School in Hartford.

Mary was feeling ill, so Joel flew to Connecticut alone to attend the hearing. Three judges would hear arguments in several cases over the course of the day. Law students packed into the room in the morning, but *Rich v. Fox News* was the last case on the schedule, and the courtroom was almost empty by the time the case came before the judges.

Joel recognized the Fox lawyers from the hearing. He also noticed a man with white hair and a deep tan walk into the room using a crutch. It took Joel a moment to realize that he had never seen Ed Butowsky in person. He knew that Butowsky had suffered hip problems for years—he had been recovering from an operation on his hip when Joel and Mary sent him a marbled cheesecake back in early 2017.

Judge Guido Calabresi, a soft-spoken man in his eighties who had been on the bench for more than two decades, led the questioning. The case, he said, was a "very unusual" one.

The crux of the case, he seemed to say, was the same question Fox had hammered on before Judge Daniels: Were the Riches' claims really defamation in disguise, or did they stand on their own as allegations of intentional infliction of emotional distress? Judge Calabresi reminded the lawyers that the decision before the Second Circuit was not whether the Riches' argument had merit but whether their case should proceed to the discovery phase. "It isn't even a question of whether they have now enough evidence, but whether they have pleaded enough that is plausible, so that a jury would be allowed to find insufficient evidence of it," Calabresi said. "Am I right or am I wrong?"

26

Defendant

WHEN I HEARD that Deb Sines had retired from the US attorney's office, I decided to write her a letter. Sources of mine who knew her said it was unlikely she'd respond. She could be a prickly character and might not want to speak about an investigation that remained ongoing. I had to try. I tracked down an address for her near Daytona Beach. I wrote that I wanted to speak with her about Seth's murder and her work on the case. I mentioned that Seth and I ran in similar circles and that I had obsessed over his death and everything that came afterward, both as a journalist and as a peer of Seth's. This was more than just another story for me. Now that she was retired, I thought she might be open to an interview. I put my letter in the mail and waited.

A few days later, she emailed me. She was reluctant to talk, but she appreciated the letter. She liked that I had written it by hand. We traded emails for a few weeks until she agreed to a phone call. After a series of calls, she invited me to pay her a visit.

On a cloudy spring day in 2019, I arrived at a taupe-colored house a few miles from the ocean. "Well, you found me," Sines said as I got out of my rental car. "Aren't you so smart."

She stood inside the front doorway. There was a bright-blue Jeep Wrangler parked in the garage, the kind with removable doors and a soft-top roof. The Bermuda grass in the front yard looked like a putting green. In the backyard there was a pool and some newly planted lemon and orange trees. It was hard to imagine a setting more diametrically opposite from the streets of DC. Sines waved me inside and introduced me to her new dog, a cute mutt named Bruno. She was pretty much as I had imagined her: acerbic, funny, a natural-born raconteur. She was shorter than I had expected, which may have been a product of all my reading about her impressive presence in the courtroom. She invited me to join her on the back patio near the pool. She lit a Marlboro Gold and asked if I wanted a shot of Jack Daniels. It was just past noon on a weekday. I downed the shot, and we started talking about Seth.

Sines walked me through the eighteen months she spent on the case. How it got assigned to her, piecing together Seth's meandering walk home from the bar, watching the body-camera footage, and of course chasing down all the conspiracy theories about Seth that had infected her homicide investigation. She occasionally digressed into stories about other cases she'd handled, cases she'd closed, such as Azariah Israel, and ones she hadn't, such as Chandra Levy. "There are still cases that keep me up at night," she told me. "This is one of them."

Everything she'd seen in her investigation, she went on, led her to believe that Seth had been targeted by his assailants as he walked home from the bar. Not because he worked for the DNC but because he was out late, talking on the phone, drunk. "When you're by yourself at 4:00 a.m., and you're that drunk, you can't protect yourself," she said. "Any idiot can see there's a good target right there." Sines suspected the murder had been the work of a couple of teens. They'd tried to rob Seth, he'd fought back, and so they shot him and fled. Crimes of that nature had happened in DC before and they would continue to happen in the future. These were amateurs, she told me. "I use the term 'amateurs' because a seasoned armed robber knows how to control a scene. That's not what this was at all."

There was no vast conspiracy, she said, no hit team or Russian assassin. "It's just the mean streets of DC," she told me. And if it was in fact the work of amateurs, Sines believed the case could still be solved. "Someone will tell," she said, "because young boys—they don't know how to keep their mouth shut." Maybe a witness who had gotten into trouble in a different case would give up information in exchange for a lesser sentence. It happened all the time.

I could tell Sines still beat herself up for not solving the Rich case. It haunted her. "While I have no intention of ever going back," she said, "I would go back for that one."

———— ◆ ————

On March 12, 2019, Gottlieb was in a meeting when he noticed his administrative assistant trying to contact him. He had recently left Boies Schiller and joined the Washington office of Willkie Farr Gallagher, a firm founded in the 1800s, and had brought Aaron's case with him. His assistant said there was a visitor waiting for him in the lobby who had documents that Gottlieb needed to come pick up.

Gottlieb already knew why the courier was looking for him. Ed Butowsky had just filed a defamation lawsuit against him in a federal court in Texas. Not just him. There were twenty-two different defendants named in the complaint: major media organizations such as the *New York Times* and the parent company of CNN, which had run stories about Butowsky; reporters and hosts for those outlets, including Anderson Cooper; the DNC; Brad Bauman; every lawyer who was representing Joel, Mary, and Aaron Rich; and the law firms that employed them. Gottlieb's name appeared first, and so the case was titled *Butowsky v. Gottlieb et al.*

The complaint alleged that he and the other defendants were "unscrupulous political activists" who had perpetrated a "smear campaign" about Butowsky by saying he had promoted a debunked theory about Seth Rich and WikiLeaks in order to deflect scrutiny from the president. According to the complaint, Butowsky's claim that Seth had leaked the DNC emails was "accurate," and the real lie was that there had been any "collusion" between President Trump and Russia. The complaint said the "lies" told about Butowsky had led to death threats, lost business, and the necessity of hiring a bodyguard for his son after someone posted a countdown clock for when his son returned to college, which Butowsky and his family took as a clear threat. "Now it's time for the Defendants to answer for the lies that they spread and the harm that they caused," the complaint said.

Suing a lawyer for defamation after they'd already sued you for the same claim was an unorthodox strategy, to say the least. The parts of the complaint related to Gottlieb focused on an interview he'd given to CNN's Anderson Cooper on the day he filed Aaron's suit. Butowsky claimed Gottlieb had defamed him when he said that "all of this, all of it, is made up," referring to Butowsky's allegations about Seth and Aaron. Gottlieb believed that, under what's known as the absolute litigation privilege, a lawyer could not be sued for describing in public the allegations a client had made in court.

After he'd read the complaint several more times and scanned the names of all twenty-two defendants, Gottlieb couldn't escape the conclusion that this was designed to harass the Rich family's lawyers. He had thought Clevenger might take actions like filing suit against Gottlieb for malicious prosecution once Aaron's case was finished; he had hinted at it. But with a federal lawsuit like Butowsky's, even if a judge found the allegations to be meritless, it could take a year or more to get rid of the case.

Aaron's legal team had secured some victories. After months of negotiations, the *Washington Times* retracted the op-ed that asserted it was "well known in the intelligence circles that Seth Rich and his brother, Aaron Rich, downloaded the DNC emails and were paid by WikiLeaks for that information." In a statement, the *Times* acknowledged the column made claims that "we now believe to be false" and apologized to the Rich family. Separately, Judge Leon ruled that Matt Couch was not entitled to receive reporter's privilege, which would have allowed Couch to shield certain source information and communications sought by Aaron's lawyers. For the purposes of the case, Couch was not a journalist, Leon said, and would not receive the same protections as a reporter at the *Wall Street Journal* or the *Washington Post*.

Aaron's team had also extracted an apology and retraction from Jerome Corsi, a conspiracy theorist who had published an article on Infowars that parroted the *Washington Times* column. Later that day

Corsi appeared on Anderson Cooper's prime-time show and conceded he'd been wrong about Aaron Rich. But he then went on to say he believed the theory that Seth had stolen the DNC emails and provided them to WikiLeaks. When Cooper pointed out that Corsi had been a vocal proponent of the Obama birth certificate conspiracy theory—he'd written an entire book about it, *Where's the Birth Certificate?*—Corsi's lawyer cut in. "The birth certificate," he said, "there's been forensic analysis on that. He never said that Obama was born in another country, but the birth certificate appears to be fraudulent."

Corsi's appearance left Gottlieb fuming. He could spend months fighting for retractions and apologies from people who'd spread lies about Aaron, but that wasn't the same as beating back the conspiracy theories themselves, as Corsi's interview had shown. "It's still a win for Aaron," Gottlieb said. "But it feels like less of a win to me."

At least Aaron's case was moving ahead. A few weeks later, Judge Leon denied Butowsky and Couch's motions to dismiss the case. The case would proceed to discovery and likely a jury trial. Another boon to the Rich family's cases was the release of Special Counsel Mueller's final report. The document laid out, in great detail, how hackers with Russia's GRU military intelligence service stole the DNC files and transferred many of them to WikiLeaks. Between the indictment of the twelve GRU officers and the full report, Mueller and his investigators referenced at least twenty-nine different sources to support their conclusion that Russian hackers had hacked into the DNC and stolen private emails and party data. It also debunked any connection between Seth and WikiLeaks. Assange's comments on Dutch TV and other news networks were "apparently designed to obscure the source of the materials that WikiLeaks was releasing," the report said. In other words, Mueller concluded, WikiLeaks had used Seth's murder to sow confusion about the true source of the stolen DNC emails.

Few things about the case proceeded like a normal court case should. Butowsky and Couch missed one deadline after another to produce documents and responses to written questions known as interrogatories. Butowsky hired and parted ways with multiple attorneys, causing further delays in the litigation. Couch, who was representing himself, neglected for months to answer Aaron's original complaint, putting him at risk of Judge Leon unilaterally deciding the case in Aaron's favor. As Couch and Butowsky dragged the case out, they continued to claim that Seth and Aaron had leaked the DNC documents. Despite telling the court that he had "removed any and all content referencing Aaron Rich," Couch talked about Aaron in his livestreams and on Twitter, repeating Butowsky's story about Joel "confirming" that he "knew what his sons did." Butowsky gave a series of interviews to obscure podcasts and shows, continuing to assert that Ellen Ratner was the reason he'd "got involved" with the Rich family, that Malia Zimmerman's story was "completely correct," and that—here was a new wrinkle—former FBI deputy director Andrew McCabe knew that Seth had leaked the DNC emails. How Butowsky knew this he did not say, and there was no available evidence to support that claim.

As he waited for the case to progress, Gottlieb began looking for experts who could testify on Aaron's behalf. Gottlieb flew to the United Kingdom to meet with a British computer scientist named Duncan Campbell, who was a friend of Binney's and who had written an article pointing out the flaws in the VIPS theory that the DNC hack had to be an inside job. When Campbell shared his conclusions with Binney, Binney agreed that his inside-job theory had been overstated. Campbell offered to provide expert testimony about why the VIPS memo claiming an inside job was nonsense. Gottlieb also sought out Thomas Drake, the NSA whistleblower who had refused to sign off on the VIPS document. He also agreed to assist with Aaron's case.

Gottlieb also asked Judge Leon if he would take the extraordinary step of asking the British judicial system to force Julian Assange to sit for a deposition. Police had removed him from the Ecuadorian embassy and taken him to prison, where he awaited possible extradition to the United States for criminal charges. Assange's American lawyer had refused to act on a subpoena. With Assange in prison and WikiLeaks having no known physical address, Gottlieb also sent subpoenas to WikiLeaks' Twitter and email accounts; those went unanswered or bounced back. Gottlieb asked Leon to issue a "letter rogatory," a formal request from the judiciary of one country to the judiciary of another seeking assistance. Leon would be asking the British courts to allow Assange to respond under oath to a "limited set of questions" about Seth and Aaron Rich. Leon agreed to issue the letter.

Gottlieb and Governski made another request of Judge Leon. They asked the judge to block the suit filed by Butowsky against them and the other Rich family lawyers through what's known as an anti-suit injunction. Butowsky's suit was "little more than a vehicle" to challenge Aaron's claims in the DC case, Gottlieb argued. He asked the judge, in other words, to put a hold on an ongoing case in a different judicial district halfway across the country—a decision no judge made lightly. But if Butowsky's Texas suit proceeded, it would set a terrible precedent, making every defendant in a defamation case think they could sue their accuser's lawyers in a different court and get away with it. If that happened, chaos would ensue.

———◆———

On September 13, 2019, Mary got a call from Eli Kay-Oliphant, one of their lawyers. The Second Circuit Court of Appeals had ruled on their appeal.

Writing for the majority, Judge Guido Calabresi wrote that the Riches had mounted a compelling enough argument that the case deserved to proceed to the fact-finding stage: "We have no trouble concluding that—taking their allegations as true—the Riches plausibly alleged what amounted to a campaign of emotional torture." Now the case would return to the Southern District of New York. Mary felt so elated that she said she was going to send Calabresi a box of Omaha Steaks. Joel had to remind her that wasn't something you could do.

———◆———

There was still an unresolved question that remained at the center of both Aaron's and Joel and Mary's lawsuits, a festering unknown that nagged at the family's lawyers. Malia Zimmerman's 2017 story for FoxNews.com about Seth and WikiLeaks—the inciting event that perhaps did more than any other article, tweet, or Reddit post to amplify the conspiracy theory about Seth to the masses—had relied on two sources. One was Rod Wheeler, the Rich family's former PI, who went on to recant his quotes, embarrass himself on national TV, and shred his credibility. The second source in Zimmerman's story was the more important one: an anonymous "federal investigator" who had supposedly read an FBI report about the contents of Seth's computer compiled soon after the murder. Zimmerman cited the investigator claiming that Seth had contacted WikiLeaks via an intermediary and had "transferred" tens of thousands of emails and attachments to the group. "I have seen and read the emails between Seth Rich and Wikileaks," the investigator was quoted as saying.

The investigator had been vital to Zimmerman's story and, at least in theory, would be important to her and Fox News's defense in Joel and Mary's litigation in New York. The identity of the investigator and the veracity of their claims could also factor in Ed Butowsky and Matt Couch's defense in Aaron's case in Washington. But as both Rich lawsuits advanced through the courts, the mystery surrounding the "federal investigator" only grew.

Wheeler handed over thousands of pages of documents, text messages, and other records in Aaron's case. One piece of evidence that came from Wheeler was a voicemail message Butowsky had left for him on the day after Fox issued its retraction of Zimmerman's story. Butowsky said that he believed Fox had removed Zimmerman's story about Seth and WikiLeaks in part because CNN had "misquoted" Wheeler in its own coverage of Fox's reporting. But the other reason for Fox's decision, Butowsky went on, was that "Malia did not actually speak to someone. She heard." In other words, Butowsky appeared to suggest that Zimmerman had not herself spoken with the primary source in her story before publication. If that were true, it would be nothing short of a major breach of journalistic protocol.

Another email unearthed in court showed Zimmerman sending her editor, Greg Wilson, a recording of "an NSA source" speaking with Butowsky and defending Zimmerman's story. Wilson replied that the audio was "very interesting" but her story was still "flawed" and "problematic" given that Wheeler had backtracked on his quotes and the Rich family had challenged the story's central premise. Perhaps the NSA source would figure into Zimmerman's and Butowsky's defense? In an email to Aaron's legal team, a lawyer for Butowsky said it was his understanding that neither he nor Butowsky knew the name or identity of the "high-level NSA source" referenced in some of Butowsky's filings in Aaron's case. Meanwhile a reporter for Yahoo News gleaned details about Fox's internal investigation into what went wrong with Zimmerman's retracted story. When Fox issued its retraction of Zimmerman's story, it had said in a statement that it would "continue to investigate this story and will provide updates as warranted." According to Yahoo's reporting, "frustrated" executives at Fox "were unable to determine the identity" of the federal investigator. "The Fox editors came to have doubts," the story said, citing a source familiar with Fox's probe, "that the person was in fact who he claimed to be or whether the person actually existed."

Perhaps even more damning was what *did not* appear in the Rich cases. In the thousands of pages of public filings submitted in court, Fox, Zimmerman, and Butowsky did not put forward a name or identifiable detail for the federal investigator, nor did they offer a shred of evidence that the alleged FBI report about Seth's computer actually existed other than what they had heard second- or thirdhand. These disclosures about the sourcing—or lack thereof—for Zimmerman's story raised more questions about how the article came to be and how Fox operated. Had anyone at Fox News asked Zimmerman to identify the source? Did one of the biggest media outlets in America run a potentially explosive story without any real vetting?

There was another possibility for who the source might be. An anonymous Twitter user surfaced in the chaotic days after Zimmerman's story was published and claimed to have given documents about Seth and WikiLeaks to Zimmerman and several others. This person used the Twitter account @Whysprtech. The @Whysprtech account posted online what it claimed was a redacted FBI report about Seth, but the document was quickly revealed to be a poorly concocted forgery. Was @Whysprtech connected to the federal investigator?

Gottlieb intended to find out. Fox was not a party in Aaron's case, and Judge Leon limited the number of depositions allowed by each side to no more than ten. When Gottlieb submitted the list of people he intended to question under oath, he included Zimmerman.

At first it seemed that Fox would allow Zimmerman to testify in Aaron's case. She would not discuss the reporting of her article, which was protected by reporter's privilege, but she could discuss the aftermath. Under oath, Zimmerman could potentially speak to what came of that internal investigation and whether the federal investigator, if that person existed, had ever been identified within Fox. Fox seemed open to allowing Zimmerman to testify when it looked like Joel and Mary's case in New York was going nowhere considering Judge Daniels's dismissal. But after the Second Circuit issued its reversal, Fox's lawyers changed tack. It was possible that evidence in Aaron's case, in which Fox was not a defendant, could be later subpoenaed in Joel and Mary's, in which Fox was the lead defendant. After Judge Leon issued a ruling that Gottlieb could take Zimmerman's deposition on a narrow set of topics related to post-publication events around her story, Fox scrambled to convince Leon to reconsider his decision. Press freedom groups took Fox's side and said it would set a terrible precedent if Zimmerman were ordered to testify even about post-publication matters. In the end, Leon changed his mind and ruled against Aaron, saying Zimmerman would not have to testify.

Gottlieb concluded that pursuing Fox wouldn't get him any closer to solving the mystery about the federal investigator's allegation that Seth was WikiLeaks' source. There was one other approach he had in mind. For more than a year, he had tried to get a meeting with Julian Assange's personal lawyer. Her name was Jennifer Robinson, and she was a barrister at the well-known firm Doughty Street Chambers in London, the same firm where Amal Clooney, the human-rights lawyer and wife to actor George Clooney, worked. Gottlieb and his team had convinced Judge Leon to sign off on a letter asking the British courts to help depose Assange in Aaron's case. But with Assange being held in the notorious Belmarsh prison as he awaited possible extradition to the US, taking the deposition would prove extremely difficult. Gottlieb instead wanted to ask Jennifer Robinson if Assange would agree to a more informal interview. Aaron would waive any source privilege on behalf of himself and Seth, and Assange, a believer in radical transparency, could say whatever it was he wanted to say about Seth Rich.

Assange had said little in public about Seth since the 2016 election. A British judge in April 2019 had sentenced him to fifty weeks in prison for jumping bail. Police dragged Assange out of the Ecuadorian embassy and locked him up in Belmarsh prison, where he waged a desperate legal battle to fight the American government's attempts to extradite him and prosecute him for alleged crimes related to past leaks of classified materials. Before his imprisonment, however, an interviewer had asked Assange about Seth Rich and whether he recognized his role in stoking the rumors about Seth and causing pain for the Rich family. Assange was evasive, defensive, and cryptic in response. "I would never name a source," he told the interviewer, *New Yorker* writer Raffi Khatchadourian. When Khatchadourian suggested that Assange had mentioned Seth to divert attention from Russia's role in stealing the DNC emails, Assange said it was Khatchadourian who was the conspiracy theorist. "My actions are more than appropriate," he said. "The issue is how to prevent them from being distorted."

Gottlieb thought that if he could convince Robinson, Assange's lawyer, to have her client answer a few questions, it would go a long way toward putting to rest the festering theories about both Seth and Aaron. Robinson agreed to meet with Gottlieb in late 2019, only to cancel after Gottlieb had already arrived in the United Kingdom. They rescheduled the meeting for February 2020. As early news reports about a troubling flu-like virus in China appeared, Gottlieb touched down in a cold, soggy London. The next day he and a colleague from his firm's London office took a black taxi to the offices of Doughty Street Chambers.

Seated across from Robinson in her office, Gottlieb made his plea. He did his best to describe the torment and heartache experienced by the Rich family—the compounding levels of pain they felt not only from the death of a loved one but as they watched that tragedy weaponized into a viral conspiracy theory and a politically convenient lie.

Even if Assange didn't grasp his own role in creating this chaos, he was in a unique position to mitigate it. All it would require of him was to answer a few simple questions. If he believed so passionately in transparency, here was an opportunity to issue a clarification that could provide a semblance of solace and resolution for a grieving family.

In Gottlieb's recollection of the conversation, Robinson said it was terrible what the family had endured and she sympathized with their plight. Her access to Assange was limited, however, and he had more important matters to deal with than this. Julian's fighting for his life, Robinson said, and this just isn't something that we're able to devote any energy to. Gottlieb asked if another representative of WikiLeaks might answer questions about Seth and Aaron. Robinson said her client was Assange, not WikiLeaks, and it wasn't her role to speak for the organization.

Gottlieb left the conversation feeling torn. Robinson had recognized that what happened to the Riches was awful. What's more, nothing she had said gave the impression that there was any evidence to back up Assange's intimation about Seth being his source. Yet presented with an opportunity for her client to correct the record, she had effectively thrown up her hands and said there was nothing she could do. Even when it was abundantly clear from the reams of evidence in the special counsel's report and other government investigations that Assange and WikiLeaks had not received the DNC emails from Seth, Assange seemingly couldn't bring himself to say so. More than two years into Aaron's litigation, Gottlieb's capacity to be shocked and surprised had dimmed. Still, he felt taken aback by the unwillingness of Assange and others to simply admit to what they had unleashed, when all it would take was one or two sentences.

He and the other lawyers in the Rich cases would have to proceed without fully resolving the question about the "federal investigator" and the WikiLeaks connection. Aaron's team took it as an encouraging sign that Judge Leon had signed off on a scheduling order for the case, which meant Aaron had his trial date: June 8, 2020.

27

Birth of a Lie

LATE WINTER, 2020. Las Vegas. Kayleigh McEnany, the chief spokeswoman for the president's reelection campaign, walked among a crowd of supporters with a microphone in her hand and a cameraman behind her. She stopped to talk with a man who, two days earlier, had become a minor celebrity in the pro-Trump community. At a rally in Arizona, the man, whose name was Jason Frank, had helped carry a wheelchair-bound World War II veteran to his seat, receiving a standing ovation from the crowd and praise from the president himself. In Vegas, McEnany asked Frank why he did what he did. "It was about the unity, the togetherness, and that's why I'm out here," he replied.

"If you could ask the president one question," McEnany said, "what would it be?"

"Who is Q?" Frank said.

"All right," McEnany said. "I will pass all of this along."

Q signs, hats, T-shirts, and even tattoos appeared at Trump rallies. The president retweeted well-known QAnon influencers, or QTubers. Trump's younger son, Eric, retweeted—then deleted—a post that featured a large "Q" and the QAnon slogan "Where we go one, we go all." The White House's press office deflected questions about the president's thoughts on QAnon and other conspiracy theories, while at the same time a senior aide to the president, Dan Scavino, shared QAnon

259

memes and another campaign representative appeared on a popular QAnon-focused podcast, Patriot Soapbox.

Trump had used conspiracy theories about Barack Obama and Benghazi to break onto the political stage. As president he had railed against the deep state, corrupt Democrats, and scheming globalists—the same enemies found in the fun-house mirror ideology of QAnon. He hadn't gone so far as to accuse the Democrats and their Hollywood backers of being pedophiles and sex traffickers, as QAnon believers did, but that wasn't necessary to convey that he valued their support.

What fueled QAnon more than Trump's tacit endorsement was the arrival of a deadly new coronavirus first identified in central China. By late March, the US and most of Europe had gone into lockdown to stop the spread of COVID-19. While QAnon's convergence with the Republican Party looked more assured than ever, its broader popularity had shown signs of petering out in the months before the pandemic. Google searches for QAnon-related words had flatlined. Tweets remained at a low ebb. Then the country went into lockdown in mid-March, most Americans were stuck at home with their phones and computers, and interest in QAnon surged in a way it hadn't before. The number of tweets using the QAnon hashtag doubled; Wikipedia page views for QAnon subjects reached peaks forty times higher than they had prepandemic. On Facebook, Q-related posts and comments spiked in the spring and summer; by August, many QAnon-themed Facebook groups included some three million members and growing.

But the clearest indication of QAnon's rapid spread and how it was breaking through in the Republican Party was the number of Q-supporting candidates running for office. Joyce Bentley had been an isolated example in 2018. With six months to go to the 2020 election, forty-eight candidates for Congress were on the record praising or endorsing QAnon. Not all of these candidates were marginal like Bentley, either. Jo Rae Perkins, an avid QAnon enthusiast, won the Republican primary for US Senate in Oregon. Lauren Boebert, a candidate and QAnon supporter in Colorado who ran a restaurant where the staff carried guns, and Marjorie Taylor Greene, a candidate in Georgia who'd espoused a slew of conspiracy theories associated with

QAnon, looked like serious contenders for the Republican nomination in their bids for the House of Representatives. Greene had also promoted one of the more obscure versions of the Seth Rich conspiracy theory when she claimed that members of the violent Central American gang MS-13 had killed him. By the summer of 2020, it looked possible that the next session of the United States Congress would feature a Seth Rich conspiracy theorist and QAnon supporter.

————◆————

The pandemic forced dozens of states to scramble and adapt their voting systems in a matter of weeks and months in an election year. Cramming voters into school gymnasiums and senior centers was no longer safe. Many local and state officials moved to implement widespread, no-excuse absentee voting. As states looked to expand mail-in voting, Trump and his supporters found a new target. Despite decades of evidence that voting by mail was safe and secure, and despite Republicans enjoying an advantage in several crucial states in the absentee voting, Trump warned that widespread vote-by-mail would be a disaster.

MAIL-IN VOTING WILL LEAD TO MASSIVE FRAUD AND ABUSE. IT WILL ALSO LEAD TO THE END OF OUR GREAT REPUBLICAN PARTY. WE CAN NEVER LET THIS TRAGEDY BEFALL OUR NATION.

This quickly became a rallying cry not only for the president but also for his top aides, the dark-money groups supporting him, and the "digital soldiers" online churning out memes and tweets and videos to help him. "The president views vote-by-mail as a threat to his election," a lawyer for the Trump campaign told *60 Minutes*, while Attorney General Bill Barr said on Fox News that vote-by-mail "absolutely opens the floodgates to fraud." The Trump campaign and the Republican National Committee filed lawsuits in more than a dozen states, many of them battleground states, including Colorado, Michigan, Wisconsin, Pennsylvania, and Florida, challenging new rules intended to make it easier to vote during the pandemic.

Many questioned this strategy because Republicans had long dominated absentee voting. It was also not a given that increased turnout would improve the Democrats' chances. In Arizona, for example, Republicans had designed and mastered the work of driving up turnout through mail-in voting. Florida's elderly population, which skewed conservative, had voted absentee in large numbers as the state's Republican Party won key races. Yet here was the sitting Republican president spreading baseless claims about absentee voting in his own election.

Trump and his allies were reprising a strategy from four years earlier: cast enough doubt on the integrity of the election ahead of time, and if you lose, your supporters believe the result was rigged. That's what his longtime associate Roger Stone had tried to do in 2016 with his Stop the Steal operation, pushing stories about voter fraud and priming Trump's supporters to expect wrongdoing on Election Day. The only hitch back then was that Trump won, which made it hard to rail against widespread fraud. (That didn't stop Trump from asserting that three million illegal residents voted for Hillary Clinton, which explained how she won the popular vote.) Now Trump was running Stop the Steal 2.0, with the ultimate aim to "sow doubt in people's minds about the process," as a Republican political consultant said at the time. Trump floated the idea of postponing the election, which by law he cannot do, and encouraged his supporters to commit fraud by voting twice—once by mail and once in person—to "test the system." Put another way, Trump's plan for winning reelection was selling the American people not on a vision for the future but on an alternate reality of the present.

The entire conspiracy-theory-industrial complex built up over the previous four years was soon amplifying Trump's claims that voting fraud would be rampant. Q drops spun an elaborate theory about how Democrats had denied life-saving cures to COVID-19–stricken Americans and had overhauled voting laws in key states as part of a desperate "power grab" to defeat Trump.

It's not what you know but what you can prove.
Q: can we prove it?
Q: can we prove coordination?

Q: can we prove deliberate action to inc death count to justify vote-by-mail, stay-at-home, bail-out-state, kill-economy, kill-P-rallies, inc unemployment, etc?
Q

More than two years into the case, Butowsky still had not produced all of the documents that Aaron's lawyers had requested. Eden Quainton, Butowsky's lawyer, explained that his client had been in and out of the hospital for procedures on a bad hip and that Quainton couldn't be expected to hound him for documents while he was on morphine laid up in a hospital bed. "I can't do it, Your Honor," Quainton said. "It violates my basic ethical sense."

Couch had insisted on withholding the name of the source who he claimed was behind his assertions that Seth and Aaron were responsible for leaking to WikiLeaks. This source, Quainton implied, could speak to Couch's claim that Aaron knew "the hit was coming" on Seth but didn't want to be named as part of Aaron's case. Judge Leon didn't buy the argument. The source hadn't taken any steps toward becoming a legally protected government whistleblower, and if Couch was going to rely on him to make his defense, then Gottlieb deserved the right to know who the source was to gauge his credibility. Leon ordered Quainton to give Gottlieb the source's name and the full, unredacted video file featuring the source talking about the Rich brothers.

Leon seemed annoyed with the slow pace of the court in Texas that was considering Butowsky's suit against Gottlieb and the other Rich family lawyers. The judge said he was inclined to do as Gottlieb had asked and freeze the other suit. "My research to date indicates that I am well within my authority to grant that kind of a motion," Leon said. "Never granted one before, and I would rather not grant one, frankly, to be quite honest with you." But he went on, "I've given them a long time down in Texas to get to the—you know, make a decision. As we say in New England, fish or cut bait."

As the hearing ended, Judge Leon told Quainton that Butowsky needed to produce the remaining four thousand pages in the next five days before he went into the hospital for another operation on his damaged hip. Couch needed to immediately hand over an audio recording that he had refused to produce or be fined several thousand dollars each day that he failed to obey the judge's order. But not long after that hearing, Leon announced he would delay the case for forty-five days in response to the COVID-19 pandemic. He said the discovery process should continue, but Governski's second deposition of Couch would be put on hold until the stay was lifted. With the various delays, a trial date in June was out of the question and not likely to happen until sometime in 2021.

Joel and Mary's lawyers were having more success prying information out of Fox. Having won their appeal, the case had returned to district court to be heard again by Judge Daniels. Fox provided 3,500 documents to the Riches' legal team, and emails offered the fullest picture yet of the many connections between Fox, Zimmerman, and Butowsky.

The newly obtained emails showed Butowsky listing off the various stories he was working on with Zimmerman and a colleague of hers. They revealed how he took credit, always behind the scenes, for Zimmerman's story. "I have and know everything," he wrote to the TV reporter Soledad O'Brien, who'd asked him about Seth. On the day Fox retracted the article, Butowsky emailed Judge Andrew Napolitano, a Fox contributor, to ask if he could share with him "a lot of information that is not known right now" about Seth. Napolitano said he'd meet Butowsky in the lobby of Fox's Manhattan headquarters. The same day Butowsky contacted Sean Hannity, offering to swing by his radio show to talk. "I'm at the center of the Seth Rich WikiLeaks uncovering," he wrote. (It's unclear if Hannity ever responded.) The emails also showed Fox distancing itself from Butowsky. When an employee in the network's PR department saw him standing by a bank of elevators at network headquarters one day in June, she sent a note to her boss, who forwarded the message to executive Suzanne Scott. "Please quietly spread the word that we should stay away from him," Scott wrote back.

Cut off from Fox, fighting multiple lawsuits while waging several of his own, Butowsky had become an embattled figure. On August 4, his wife drove him to a hospital near his house in Plano for a long-awaited hip replacement surgery the next day. During the night, however, he went into a sudden cardiac arrest and lay unresponsive for thirteen minutes. The medical staff performed CPR until his heart restarted.

———◆———

In deeply conservative northwestern Georgia, Marjorie Taylor Greene easily won the Republican primary in the Fourteenth Congressional District. Facing little competition from the Democrats, she was all but assured of victory in the November general election. Trump congratulated Greene and called her a "future Republican Star" who is "strong on everything." Lauren Boebert also won her Colorado primary race and was expected to win her general election as well. QAnon had notched two of its biggest electoral victories yet.

At a White House press briefing the day after Greene's primary win, a reporter asked Trump for his position on QAnon. "During the pandemic, the QAnon movement appears to be gaining a lot of followers," the reporter said. "Can you talk about what you think about and what you have to say to people who are following this movement?"

Trump said he didn't know much about QAnon but praised the people who supported it. "I've heard these are people that love our country," Trump said. "So I don't know really anything about it other than they do supposedly like me." When asked whether he could produce evidence to support the primary tenets of the theory, Trump responded, "If I can help save the world from problems, I am willing to do it. I'm willing to put myself out there."

———◆———

About a month later, Joel and Mary's lawyers submitted a new filing. The document spelled out a proposed schedule for upcoming depositions in the case. The names listed were some of the biggest at Fox News: Sean Hannity, Lou Dobbs, Newt Gingrich, and VP of news Jay Wallace. The depositions had the potential to open Fox up to scrutiny in a way it never had been before. The first deposition, of Zimmerman's editor Greg Wilson, was due to begin in six weeks.

28

The Blood of Tyrants

ONE MONTH BEFORE the election, Dana Nessel, the attorney general for the state of Michigan, announced that her office had filed four felony charges for a series of robocalls that "aimed at suppressing the vote." Nessel's office described the two men behind the alleged scheme as "political operatives." They were Jack Burkman and Jacob Wohl.

Nessel alleged that, in late August, Burkman and Wohl paid for nearly twelve thousand calls to go out to residents with a 313 area code, which covered Detroit. The call featured a prerecorded message from a woman who introduced herself as Tamika Taylor. She warned that anyone who voted by mail in the 2020 election would have their personal information added to a "public database" used by police departments to "track down old warrants" and credit card companies to collect on old debts. The Centers for Disease Control and Prevention, she added, was considering whether to use the vote-by-mail data to "track people for mandatory vaccines."

"Don't be finessed into giving your private information to the man," she said at the end of the robocall. "Stay safe and beware of vote-by-mail."

None of this was true. The intent of the calls, Nessel said, was to confuse and intimidate Detroit voters—"to deter them from voting in the November election." Detroit wasn't the only target: during her office's investigation, Nessel said that attorneys general in New York, Pennsylvania, Ohio, and Illinois told her that they'd received reports of a similar robocall blitz. In all, Nessel estimated about eighty-five thousand such calls were made. In each state the calls focused on cities where large populations of Black, Hispanic, and other minority voters lived. The strategy was obvious: spread frightening information about mail-in voting in the hope of suppressing the vote in Democratic strongholds.

Nessel's office found it surprisingly easy to tie the robocalls to Burkman and Wohl. The phone number that appeared when someone received the call was Burkman's personal cell phone; his name appeared if the recipient used caller ID. The voice heard on the call, "Tamika Taylor," identified herself as part of Project 1599, the "civil rights organization founded by Jack Burkman and Jacob Wohl." Legally Project 1599 did not exist: it was a bogus front group cooked up by Burkman and Wohl. Perhaps it was intended to evoke the similar sounding 1619 Project, the much-debated series in the *New York Times* that placed slavery at the center of American history. Certainly by describing it as a "civil rights organization," they hoped that minority voters would trust the message.

It was quintessential Burkman, equal parts malevolence and incompetence. But unlike in his past stunts, Burkman and his protégé faced real legal peril. Two of the felony counts they faced in Michigan came with a maximum sentence of seven years in prison; the other two came with five-year sentences. A grand jury in Cleveland also returned an indictment, accusing them of eight counts of telecommunications fraud and seven counts of bribery. In New York State, a real civil rights group, the National Coalition on Black Civic Participation, sued Burkman and Wohl in federal court on behalf of eight voters who had received a Project 1599 robocall. The suit alleged violations of the Voting Rights Act of 1965 and the Ku Klux Klan Act of 1871.

Burkman and Wohl appeared in court in the New York case on October 26, a week before the 2020 election. They had not found an attorney in time, so they represented themselves. Burkman and Wohl didn't try to distance themselves from their scheme: when the judge asked Burkman if he took responsibility for the calls, he replied, "Oh, yes, Your Honor, yes. That is our call, yes, yes." Still, he said it was "absurd" and "far-fetched" to charge him and Wohl with violating the Ku Klux Klan Act, which he called "a statute from 150 years ago, which has never been used for this purpose or any purpose even close to it." Wohl embarked on a long monologue, arguing that their robocalls were protected by the First Amendment and that everything said in them was accurate. States maintain huge databases of voter information, debt collectors use "every piece of data at their disposal," and the CDC was on the record trying to force vaccines on Americans who didn't want them, he argued.

All states held personal information about their citizens, the plaintiffs replied. How else could they issue a driver's license? How could you ever get a credit card if you didn't hand over private financial data? None of this was remotely like what Burkman and Wohl's robocall had claimed about improper use of people's data. "There is zero evidence to support that," she said. "This is an effort by defendants to discourage mail-in voting, and thereby discourage voting."

Two days later Judge Victor Marrero granted the National Coalition on Black Civic Participation's request for a temporary restraining order. Burkman and Wohl must stop running the robocall and pay for a different message with accurate information about mail-in voting. What's more, Marrero said the Ku Klux Klan Act was created for precisely such a case. Burkman and Wohl may not have used "guns, torches, burning crosses, and other dire methods perpetrated under the cover of white hoods," the judge wrote, but their campaign of "electoral terror" using modern technology served "the same deleterious ends."

————◆————

On October 30, the Friday before Election Day, Sean Hannity, the biggest name on the Riches' deposition list, was set to appear for a deposition. But on the appointed day, Hannity was nowhere to be found. There would be no deposition. Two weeks earlier, on October 12, Fox had agreed to settle the case.

The terms of the settlement were confidential. But Butowsky's lawyer Ty Clevenger, who said he was privy to Butowsky's portion of the deal, would later say that the "real issue" that prompted Fox and its lawyers to settle was the scheduled depositions for Hannity, Zimmerman, and several network executives. Fox "did not want anybody, any of the higher-up people at Fox, to have to participate in depositions," Clevenger said. Clevenger added that Butowsky "did not particularly want to settle, but Fox put a tremendous amount of pressure on him and Malia" to resolve the case. Clevenger said he pleaded with Fox's lawyers to not settle the case until his ongoing lawsuit against the FBI for records related to Seth Rich was completed, as if those records might affect the litigation. But Fox's lawyers mostly ignored him as they "strong-armed" Butowsky into settling five other cases. "We can thank Fox News for all that," Clevenger said.

In addition to allegedly pressuring Butowsky to withdraw his other suits, Fox News would pay Joel and Mary several million dollars as part of the agreement, Yahoo News would later report.

A settlement offered a sure thing; a trial was a risk no matter how strong their case, and with all the appeals that were certain to follow, it would take a long, long time to come to a resolution. It was unlikely but still possible that Judge Daniels could dismiss the case for a second time at a later stage in the pretrial phase. There was always the possibility that the jury pool could skew in Fox's favor and the Riches could lose the case on a verdict. The lawyers for both sides spent weeks finalizing the agreement. Near the end of the negotiations, Fox had one additional demand: the settlement must remain secret until after the election.

———————

The crowd spilled out of Freedom Plaza and into the streets of downtown Washington, headed for the steps of the US Supreme Court. They carried pro-police Blue Lives Matter banners and homemade signs and every variety of Trump flag imaginable. "Stop the steal!" they chanted as the procession moved down Pennsylvania Avenue. Some ten thousand people had gathered on November 14 for what was billed as the Million MAGA March. They had come to protest the result of the 2020 election, which news organizations had called for Democrat Joe Biden a week earlier, and to show their support for the man they believed was the rightful winner, President Trump. "This isn't over," said a marcher dressed in a MAGA hat and USA scarf as she marched in the street. "This isn't even close to being over."

Starting on election night, Trump embarked on a months-long campaign to convince the American public that the presidency was stolen from him. He accused "corrupt forces" of "registering dead voters and stuffing ballot boxes." He said "the corrupt Democrat political machine" had prevented Republican volunteers from observing the vote-counting process: "It's because they know they are hiding illegal activity." He took aim at one of the biggest voting machine companies, Dominion Voting Systems, calling it "horrible, inaccurate, and anything but secure," and shared a report that claimed Dominion's software had "deleted 2.7 million Trump votes nationwide." When a top government official in charge of securing American elections fact-checked this claim, Trump fired the employee. And while Trump raged against these perceived enemies, lawyers working on his behalf filed dozens of lawsuits in closely decided states alleging a litany of election-related crimes. Put it all together and what emerged was the newest iteration of Stop the Steal.

Trump also had another powerful ally in his corner: Fox News. In the two weeks after news outlets—among them Fox's own decision desk—called the race for Biden, Fox guests and hosts cast doubt on the outcome or aired conspiracy theories about the election nearly eight hundred times. Host Laura Ingraham aired an interview with an anonymous person who claimed to be a Nevada poll worker who had witnessed "rampant voter fraud." Some of Fox's most prominent hosts, including Lou Dobbs, Sean Hannity, and Maria Bartiromo, devoted airtime to Trump lawyers like Rudy Giuliani and Sidney Powell, a former federal prosecutor who defended Trump's former national security adviser Michael Flynn, as they made outlandish and at times laughable claims about how Venezuela's government had manipulated vote totals using Dominion voting machines. Another recurring guest was a lawyer named Cleta Mitchell. Trump had tasked Mitchell to run an "election integrity" task force during the campaign, and in one Fox appearance Mitchell claimed that "dead people . . . voted," some people "voted in two states" at once, and there was "illegal voting by non-citizens." Fox host Tucker Carlson said the accusations aired on Fox about Dominion Voting Systems could amount to "the single greatest crime in American history."

On November 19, Sidney Powell and Rudy Giuliani, two lawyers representing the president, spoke at a press conference at the Republican National Committee headquarters on Capitol Hill. As hair dye dripped down his face, a hunched and sweaty Giuliani offered one outlandish theory after another, quoted the movie *My Cousin Vinny*, cursed in Italian, and explained how if you threw out the hundreds of thousands of fraudulent ballots in Michigan, Wisconsin, and Pennsylvania, then Trump won the presidency. Sidney Powell veered further into delusion. She alleged that "communist money" routed through Venezuela, Cuba, and "likely" China had interfered with the presidential election by manipulating ballot-counting machines and voting software. Dominion Voting Systems, a Canadian company used by thousands of US jurisdictions, was in fact the brainchild of deceased Venezuela president Hugo Chavez to "make sure he never lost an election," Powell said, and now that technology had been used against President Trump. Powell added that Dominion was tied to George Soros, the billionaire investor and liberal donor. There were algorithms and back doors, it was all very complicated and technical, she said, but the conclusion was undeniable: "President Trump won by a landslide. We are going to prove it, and we are going to reclaim the United States of America for the people who vote for freedom." Another vocal proponent and funder of the election-fraud groundswell, former Overstock.com CEO Patrick Byrne, even claimed that Dominion had had some involvement in Seth's murder, saying that Dominion had manipulated the 2016 Democratic primary, Seth knew about it, and so Dominion "couldn't have let a guy who had the kind of knowledge that we're now talking about to walk around."

In court Trump's attempts to challenge the election went nowhere. But he had his supporters convinced that he'd been robbed of four more years in office. Standing on the steps of the Supreme Court and looking out at the Million MAGA March crowd, Rep. Louie Gohmert, a Republican from Texas and a Trump ally, said he saw a deep state conspiracy at work that had denied the president a second term in office. "This is a multidimensional war that the US intelligence people have used on other governments," Gohmert said. "You not only steal the vote but you use the media to convince people that they're not really seeing what they're seeing."

———◆◆———

There would be no Hollywood ending to Joel and Mary's years-long legal battle with Fox. No Aaron Sorkin-esque courtroom showdown. No dramatic climax that anyone outside of the parties to the case and their lawyers would be privy to. Joel and Mary had been faced with the wrenching decision of whether to take their lawsuit all the way to trial, forcing executives and hosts at Fox to take the stand and potentially winning damages in a jury verdict. But Fox had the ability to drag the case out for years if it wanted to, and even if Joel and Mary made it to trial, they could lose and walk away with nothing. A settlement would not only assure them and their attorneys of a financial payout; it would also signal that there was a price to pay for telling harmful lies, which was its own quasi precedent.

The details of the settlement would be confidential, prohibiting anyone who was a party to the agreement from talking about it. In that way, even though Fox settled, the network won. The agreement created a vacuum of information, of truth, at a critical moment in Joel and Mary's struggle to clear Seth's name. A hole that left anyone following their case with a sense of loss that sat uncomfortably next to the feeling that justice had been done.

At 1:45 on the afternoon of November 24, Joel and Mary's lawyers hit send on the settlement announcement. The agreement between them and Fox "allows us to move on from the litigation we initiated in response to Fox News' May 2017 article and televised statements concerning Seth's murder," it said. "We are pleased with the settlement of this matter and sincerely hope that the media will take genuine caution in the future." Soon afterward, Fox's PR department issued its own one-sentence statement: "We are pleased with the resolution of the claims and hope this enables Mr. and Mrs. Rich to find a small degree of peace and solace moving forward." What Fox did not offer was an apology or any admission of wrongdoing.

Aaron was facing many of the same questions his parents had to struggle with—should he settle or risk a trial? The pandemic had slowed the judicial system to a halt. Aaron's original trial date had been in June 2020. At the current rate, it was unclear whether the trial would happen in 2021, 2022, or later. The longer a court case drags on, the harder it becomes to prove. Memories fade, documents disappear, witnesses die. In Aaron's case one potential witness, the bylined author on the *Washington Times* op-ed, had already died in late 2018.

Gottlieb and Governski wanted to take the case to trial. They'd spent almost three years on it. Gottlieb sometimes let himself imagine his closing argument in the case or cross-examining witnesses on the stand. He would keep pushing for that day, but, increasingly, he wasn't sure whether that day would ever come.

———◦|◦———

Matt Couch took up the cause of election fraud with a loyalist's zeal. He produced livestreams, blog posts, and tweets at a frenetic clip on the subject.

> WOW: Outsiders with USBs and VCards Were Allowed in Pennsylvania Counting Areas with No Observers Present

> DEM MELTDOWN: Sydney Powell Reads Affidavit Revealing 'Stunning Evidence' That Votes Could Be Changed Without Detection

His tweets caught the attention of Giuliani, Michael Flynn, and eventually the president himself. When Couch tweeted out a call for prayer on behalf of Giuliani, who'd gotten infected with COVID-19, Trump shared Couch's message to his eighty million followers. For an online influencer, a retweet from the president could bring in thousands of new followers and ensure a new level of celebrity. After the success of the Million MAGA March in November, a group named Women for America First announced "March for Trump," a multicity tour through a dozen states to spread the word about election fraud and rally support for the president. The tour would conclude with a rally in Washington, DC.

The tour's organizers invited Couch to speak at their stop in Pittsburgh on December 10. The biggest draw was probably Mike Lindell, the founder and CEO of MyPillow and one of the most visible election fraud activists. "I've seen the evidence," Lindell told the crowd. "You are not going to steal this election from we the people," said Amy Kremer, a former Tea Party activist and the founder of Women for America First. Couch was one of the last people to speak.

"This right now is a revolution by ballots, not bullets, and we hope it doesn't come to that," he said. "We pray to God that it doesn't come to that."

"It might," someone in the crowd said.

"I'll let you say it," Couch said. "But yeah, I know what you mean."

At the final rally in Washington a few days later, Couch shared a stage with the leaders of the election fraud movement: Michael Flynn, the former national security adviser; Patrick Byrne, the ex-CEO of Overstock.com, who helped bankroll the election fraud movement; and Congresswoman-elect Marjorie Taylor Greene. Couch quoted Thomas Jefferson's line about how the tree of liberty "must be refreshed from time to time with the blood of patriots and tyrants," and added, "This is our 1776, right now, right here, in Washington, DC. We are not going to allow them to fraudulently steal an election."

Shortly afterward Couch launched a new website, FightTheFrauds.com, and announced plans for a rally on January 6, the day Congress would certify Biden's election victory.

———◆———

"We need to send a loud message that we need you in Washington, DC," Couch said from a hotel in Washington, livestreaming to an audience of more than 150,000 viewers.

January 6 was two days away and already shaping up to be the biggest demonstration yet since the president's defeat in November. Trump and other conservative luminaries would speak at a rally to "Save America" on the Ellipse near the White House. Smaller rallies were planned near the US Capitol. The goal of these demonstrations was to convince Congress to vote against certifying the election result, denying Biden the victory and plunging the peaceful transfer of power into chaos.

Couch assured his viewers that they had nothing to fear. "Folks, you will be safe," he said. "There are security protocols in place." The president, he went on, had called his followers to be there. "The president has never made a call like this asking you to be here. And folks, I'm here and I expect you to join me. I expect millions of you to join me." He wasn't asking much of them, he said. "I'm telling you right now we need you all in this fight. There is no other fight to be in than this fight on January 6."

On the morning of the sixth, Couch was due to speak at a small rally on the West Front of the Capitol. Jack Burkman and Jacob Wohl were spotted on the Capitol's East Front, though Burkman would later say he'd been on Capitol Hill that day for an unrelated meeting. A half mile away, speaker after speaker riled up the crowd of some forty thousand people. "Let's have trial by combat!" said Rudy Giuliani. Congressman Mo Brooks of Alabama mentioned past generations of Americans who'd sacrificed their lives for their country and asked, "Are you willing to do the same?" Trump told the crowd that they needed to "fight like hell," and if they didn't "you're not going to have a country anymore." He added that he knew "everyone here will soon be marching over to the Capitol building to peacefully and patriotically make your voices heard."

Hours later thousands of Trump supporters mobbed the US Capitol, beating police officers, smashing windows, and desecrating the Senate floor. Couch, for all his assurances about the safety of the event and the need to join the "fight" on January 6, returned to his hotel after

Trump's rally at the Ellipse and watched the insurrection on his social media channels. He fired off tweet after tweet using other people's photos and videos, claiming that "Antifa" was in the crowd that stormed the Capitol and calling Republican senator Mitch McConnell a "traitor" for voting to certify Biden's victory.

———◆———

A week later Matt Couch started a new livestream. He didn't wait for the audience to grow this time. He was back home in Arkansas, seated at a desk, Hulk Hogan photos on the wall behind him. There was none of the usual banter found in Couch's Periscopes. In a flat voice, Couch read a statement:

> In August of 2017 America First Media and I began to report that Aaron Rich, Seth's brother, was involved in transfer of DNC documents to WikiLeaks, and receiving money in exchange.
>
> Our reports about Aaron Rich were largely driven by information given to us by a single source, who we now believe provided us with false information and who, as of this date, has retracted his statements.
>
> Today, we retract and disavow our statements, and we offer our apology to Mr. Rich and his family.
>
> I take full responsibility for my actions and those of America First Media before its dissolution, and would like to apologize to Mr. Rich and his family. All references related to Mr. Rich have been removed from our websites and social media platforms to the best of our ability.

Anyone who had followed Aaron's lawsuit understood that the "single source" Couch was referring to was Ed Butowsky. On the same day, January 14, 2021, Butowsky published his own retraction and apology. "During 2017 and 2018 I made a number of comments stating or implying that Aaron Rich, the brother of Seth Rich who was tragically murdered in July 2016, had been involved in downloading and transferring emails from the DNC to WikiLeaks," he tweeted. "I never had physical proof to back up any such statements or suggestions, which I now acknowledge I should not have made." He went on to retract and apologize for "any statement I have made asserting or implying that Aaron Rich downloaded or transferred DNC emails to WikiLeaks or received payment in exchange. I take full responsibility for my comments and I apologize for any pain I have caused."

Whether Aaron received financial compensation as part of the settlement was not disclosed, as the terms of agreement were confidential. Aaron, in his own statement, said that he was "gratified" by the result of his lawsuit, which he now asked the court to dismiss.

29

Closure

THROUGH THE CROWDED lobby of the St. Regis hotel in midtown Manhattan, I spotted Joel Rich walking in my direction. He looked the same in person as he did in the many photos and the *Good Morning America* segments I'd pored over for the last four years. "Hello, sir," he said as he gave my hand a firm shake. "Mary's up in the room waiting for us."

It had been almost four years since I had first approached Brad Bauman, Joel and Mary's spokesman, with the idea of writing a book about Seth, the conspiracy theories, and his family's fight for justice. In all that time, my access to the Riches was sporadic. As long as their lawsuit was in the works or moving through the court system, their lawyers counseled the Riches to lay low and say little publicly. Now, with the Fox suit behind them, Joel and Mary were ready to talk. Bauman had called me to say the Riches were planning a trip to New York at the end of July. Did I want to meet with them in the city for a sit-down interview?

Joel and I arrived at the room to find Mary and Bauman chatting in a small living room area. On the table behind them sat a platter of fresh fruits and coffee that Mary had ordered for the four of us. "I didn't know if you'd eaten or not and I wasn't about to let you go hungry," she said by way of an introduction. We chatted about their plans in New

York, the museums they hoped to visit, whether to book a horse-drawn carriage through Central Park or a sunset harbor cruise around the Statue of Liberty. When I asked the reason for their trip, Mary said they had a meeting with the lawyers who'd represented them in the Fox suit but she wouldn't say more.

I could sense that Joel and Mary felt liberated to be done with their lawsuit. And yet it was clear that they remained on guard, conscious that anything they said could be used against them, well aware that even though they had won a settlement in court, that didn't mean the conspiracy theories about Seth would ever go away for good. "I used to think we'll go to court, we'll get the facts out, and people will finally shut up," Mary said. She was coming around to the realization that the aftershocks of Seth's murder would continue to affect her family for the foreseeable future, and there was little she could do about it. For instance, Ty Clevenger, the onetime lawyer for Ed Butowsky, had asked the FBI for any records that mentioned Seth and Aaron Rich. At first the bureau said it couldn't find any such records. After Clevenger sued the agency, demanding it look harder, the bureau came back and said that it did have several thousand pages that mentioned Seth or Aaron. In May 2021, it released a few hundred pages of the documents, some containing redactions, and the rest it withheld for either personal privacy or national security reasons. The right-wing media pointed to the documents—and the FBI's initial failure to release them—as further evidence of a cover-up. However, the documents themselves contained no new revelations and added little of major import to what the public already knew.

At the time I got together with Joel and Mary, Clevenger was fighting with the FBI to unredact the newly released documents. Mary said there was a part of her that wanted the redactions removed and the documents released. "Let it come out," she said. "Maybe it'll prove what everybody keeps saying is not true." She checked herself, realizing how naïve that sounded given what she'd just gone through. "I don't think you're ever going to change people's minds," she said. "It's not about proof; it's about what they want to believe, and that's that."

Joel and Mary had grown used to living in a state of constant vigilance, prepared to wake up on any given day to another story or lie about Seth. Every so often in our conversation, Joel's iPad let out a soft, twinkly chime sound. It was an alert from their home security system: someone or something had tripped the motion sensor on one of the many cameras positioned around the property. Joel took a quick glance. He didn't see anything to worry about. Probably a neighbor out walking their dog or a package delivery. He and Mary found it hard always to be on high alert, fearful that someone might show up at their house spouting wild theories about Seth. "If someone's there too long, I'm on the security camera," Mary said. "And if they're looking in any way suspicious, I'm not hesitant to call the police or call Joel and say, 'Hey, look at this. Do we need to call the police?'"

Joel and Mary didn't want to only talk about the heavy stuff. They also told stories about Seth that gave them hope and reminded them of the full life he'd lived. Joel said that he'd gotten an email out of the blue from a high school debate coach who had competed against Seth when they were both high schoolers. The debate coach had the idea to rename an Omaha debate competition after Seth. Joel and Mary loved the idea. Shortly before their trip to New York, Joel had gotten a call from their rabbi. Around one of the anniversaries of Seth's murder, the rabbi had wanted to pay a visit to Seth's gravestone, the one with the row of little American flags around it. As the rabbi approached the location, he noticed a small group of people sitting in chairs at the gravesite, drinking beers and talking. Joel couldn't help but smile when the rabbi shared that story. Seth's high school friends tried to visit the gravestone either on his birthday in January or on the anniversary of his death in July. "Those friends will always be with us," Joel said.

Mary, in particular, hoped that, with the lawsuit over, she could reconnect with some of Seth's friends and in that way stay connected with the community he'd built and retain some link to his life. She also wanted an audience with various parties whom she felt had played some role, however small, in her son's death. This was her Irish side coming out. She blamed the DC water utility, for instance, for the construction fencing it had put up in Seth's neighborhood, making it that much easier for whoever attacked Seth to evade the police. She blamed the DC police for not committing more resources to the search for Seth's killer. Joel tried to tell Mary that these grudges weren't going to help her, but she couldn't help herself. "I will have a chance to sit in front of them and let them know: 'You helped.'"

Our conversation lasted for more than three hours. I had to catch a train back to Washington. As I got up to leave, Mary asked me a question.

"If you were in front of Fox and got a chance, what would you ask them?"

The question caught me by surprise. I had dealt with Fox's notoriously tough public relations department many times, but that wasn't what Mary seemed to be asking. I stood there for a moment, thinking.

"Why is it so hard to say you're sorry?" I said. "That's the question I have."

"Thank you," she said.

———◆———

At the very least, Joel and Mary wouldn't have to worry about Ed Butowsky and Matt Couch. After the lawsuits were dismissed, Butowsky and Couch stopped talking about Seth and Aaron Rich. Butowsky set out to rebuild his public profile as a financial commentator, and Couch searched for his place in the post-Trump political universe.

As luck would have it, I would have a chance to see both men under the same roof. After his public retraction and apology to Aaron Rich, Couch had launched a new line of Christian right–themed clothing called Faith 'n' Freedoms. He also organized a conference at a hotel outside of Dallas that would bring together evangelical pastors, conservative activists, and online influencers. As I scanned the speakers list, I noticed Butowsky's name. I booked my flight for Texas.

When I walked into the ballroom of the hotel, no one wore masks—or, as one of the speakers called them, "facial condoms." (Let that image stay with you.) The conference felt like a mix between a Christian revival, an antilockdown protest, and a Las Vegas buffet line serving up one conspiracy theory after another—about the pandemic (overblown if not fake), about the 2020 election (stolen, of course), about critical race theory (a Marxist communist plot). There was no disagreement about who their enemies were: House Speaker Nancy Pelosi (one vendor sold toilet paper with Pelosi's face on it) and President Biden (the same vendor sold "Fuck Biden" hats), the Democratic governors of California ("Adolf Newsom") and Kentucky ("Führer Beshear"). They raged against the tyranny of mask mandates, Dr. Anthony Fauci, and employee sensitivity training. They cheered for cult figures like a Twitter personality named Catturd, who enjoyed a brief flurry of attention after Trump retweeted several Catturd posts about election fraud to the president's eighty million followers.

The through line for the weekend was a profound sense of fear and alienation. These people felt like strangers in their own land, to borrow from the sociologist Arlie Russell Hochschild, convinced, despite being white and well-off enough to spend hundreds of dollars to attend this conference, that their country was no longer their own and—here's the kicker—that elections were no longer the way to bring about change in their country. Most everyone seemed to agree that the 2020 election was one of the great crimes of all time and that Donald Trump was the rightful winner. Eric Wnuck, an Arizona conservative who had led the charge to demand an "audit" of the election result in Maricopa County, captured the mood when he claimed that a free and fair election had been "pilfered by a few deep-state politicians."

Wnuck wouldn't say what the outcome of the "audit" would be, but he did leave the audience with this message: "What I believe you will see is gut-wrenching and appalling. And you will never, ever trust an election again."

I heard similar sentiments from other speakers. A podcaster and right-wing influencer named Eric Matheny said Americans had "witnessed...a hostile takeover. An election stolen right before our eyes." The country, he went on, would not be "won with elections." Change would happen only on a cultural level, within families, in the church, with neighbors talking to neighbors. (His motto, he said, was "Always be red-pilling.")

This idea wasn't shared by all the speakers. Dr. Cordie Williams, a right-wing podcaster based out of California, urged those in the audience to run for office themselves. It was up to them to take back their communities and push back against the Marxist-socialist-communist left. "We can't wait around for a Q or somebody to come and save us," he said. But the crowd seemed to gravitate to people like Wnuck and Matheny, the ones who cried fraud and said elections couldn't be trusted. And why wouldn't they? If you believe the 2020 election was a vast criminal conspiracy, why would you ever put your trust in another election?

Butowsky was there to moderate a panel about conservative Jews and their role in the Republican Party. Onstage he showed flashes of his usual chatty persona, joking that he'd always considered himself a liberal Jew until he started watching Fox News. His panelists, two rabbis from the Dallas area, said little except that they supported vaccination, which was met with silence from the audience. As the panel wrapped up, I waited for Butowsky outside of the ballroom, hoping to speak with him. But he had already left the hotel through a different door, and when I went to the parking garage to search for him, he was gone. I quickly wrote him an email to say I was at the conference and hoped to meet with him. He never responded.

Back in the ballroom, yet another speaker was railing against masks and illegal voters. I opened Twitter and scrolled until a tweet by a well-known disinformation researcher caught my eye. A team of analysts at the University of Washington had visualized the biggest promoters and amplifiers on Twitter of the so-called Big Lie—the claim that the 2020 election was stolen from former President Trump. @RealDonaldTrump was by far the biggest. No surprise there. In the visualization Trump's presence looked like the sun, huge and central, around which an entire system of disinformation flowed. Not far away from that sun was a midsized planet that represented the tenth-largest promoter of the Big Lie. It was @RealMattCouch, who at that very moment was walking onstage to introduce the conference's next speaker.

I let this sink in. In a span of four years, Couch had gone from a nobody in northwest Arkansas, a struggling entrepreneur and regional sports radio host, to one of the biggest spreaders of election disinformation in the country. With his half million followers, his websites and apparel shops, and his livestreams that regularly drew as many viewers as a CNN news show, he had amassed a level of online influence that perhaps even he couldn't have imagined.

And then, in an instant, it was gone. In late 2021, Couch shared an article that suggested coronavirus vaccines were a ploy by Bill Gates and Elon Musk to kill off millions of people and replace the human workforce with robots. Twitter responded by suspending Couch indefinitely for violating its policy against "spreading misleading and potentially harmful information related to COVID-19." His 550,000 followers, the hundreds of thousands of tweets he'd sent—all of it vanished overnight. A few days later, Couch appeared on a friend's podcast to talk about his suspension. "This is just absolute bullshit," he said. "I haven't done anything wrong. I shared an article I didn't even write." At the same time, he said he'd known such a day might come, and so he'd "diversified" his social media presence by building up audiences on other platforms, such as Parler, which was launched with funding from the conservative billionaire Mercer family, and Gettr, which was run by a former Trump spokesman.

"I always believe that everything happens for a reason," he told the podcast's hosts. "Who knows what God saved me from? Maybe there were some jackasses that were combing through my tweets from three years ago to possibly try to sue my ass again." He added, "I truly believe that God is always looking out and has always got a plan."

———— ◦ ————

If you could go back in time, would you do it all over again?

I put that question to Mike Gottlieb on several occasions. He had taken Aaron's case because he had experience fighting conspiracy theories that few other lawyers had, and also because he believed it was the right thing to do. It was the type of case he'd gone to law school to one day litigate. But the case had taken a toll on him. It had pulled him away from his family; he'd even become part of the case when he was sued for defamation in Texas.

The first time I asked Gottlieb if he would do it all again, he hesitated. There were a lot of public interest cases he hoped to work on with his pro bono hours, but the all-encompassing nature of Aaron's case made it difficult to do anything else. But when I asked him again, this time a few months after the settlement was announced, he had changed his mind. If it was another case like Aaron's, a case that resonated with Gottlieb on both personal and professional levels because he saw elements of his own life story in Seth's and Aaron's—yes, he would do it again. "Trying to play out how I would've felt about these things happening to me, it's impossible to even hypothesize," he said. "You just can't imagine things like this happening to you. From that perspective, yes, I would do it again."

Gottlieb had learned a great deal about the law and its limitations in the past four years. For starters defamation cases like Aaron's were exceedingly difficult. They required a huge amount of time and financial resources. In all, Gottlieb and his colleagues logged millions of dollars' worth of billable hours over nearly four years. They called for lawyers who believed in their client's cause and were willing to sign up for a lengthy, winding, sometimes maddening kind of litigation.

To get a prominent defamation lawyer interested, it usually took the promise of a big payday in the form of a settlement or favorable jury verdict. In the aftermath of the 2020 election, Dominion Voting Systems, the company accused of vote-rigging and other crimes by Trump and his followers, sued Fox News for $1.6 billion in damages. It also sued Trump attorneys Rudy Giuliani and Sidney Powell, as well as several other right-wing outlets. Clare Locke, a prominent defamation firm in Virginia that was representing Dominion, could theoretically reap hundreds of millions in contingency fees.

As Gottlieb saw it, the Dominion cases were the exception that proved the rule. In those cases the plaintiff, Dominion, was a multinational company that could readily show the financial damages it suffered as a result of viral lies. And the defendants in those cases, especially Fox, were even larger corporations that had the money to pay a major settlement. But even if a defamation case had a deep-pocketed defendant like Fox, without a plaintiff who could show severe financial damages it would be hard to convince a big firm to take the case.

The more Gottlieb and Governski talked about it, they realized that two things were missing. The legal doctrine for damages needed to encompass more than just lost earnings or revenue. What if damages were quantified by figuring out what it would cost to repair someone's name and reputation? How much money would it take to run a media campaign that reached as many people as possible who had seen the defamatory statements and show them the facts? Gottlieb and Governski had gone so far as to consult with a professor at Northwestern University about designing a formula for quantifying such a debunking campaign.

What was also missing was a public interest legal group willing to bring cases not because they could prove lucrative but because they defended basic democratic values like truth, facts, and human decency. A former colleague of Gottlieb's from the Obama White House, Ian Bassin, was running a nonprofit dedicated to finding ways to shore up the country's democratic institutions and stop the spread of authoritarianism in America. Gottlieb mentioned his idea to Bassin, and after some discussions, they decided that Bassin's group would house a team of lawyers to do what Gottlieb had spent the last five years doing.

The new project would be called Law for Truth. And though Gottlieb had told himself that he would take a break from the conspiracy theory work, he changed his mind and agreed to take one of the project's first cases. The plaintiffs were a mother and daughter who had worked as election workers in Atlanta during the 2020 election and who, thanks to Rudy Giuliani and One America News and the Gateway Pundit, had become the target of a vicious campaign of harassment accusing them of manipulating the vote count and many other crimes. Strangers flooded them with racist threats. One was the target of an attempted "citizen's arrest" by a mob of angry people; the other altered her physical appearance so as not to be recognized in public. Anyone who listened to their stories couldn't help but feel sympathy for them and rage at their tormentors. Gottlieb, Governski, and the lawyers at Law for Truth got to work drafting their next complaint.

In November I flew to Omaha to spend a few more days with Joel and Mary. They had lined up interviews for me with some of Seth's friends and other people who'd known him; the Riches' rabbi invited me to pay him a visit at the temple. I would get to see the house Seth grew up in, where the Riches still lived. Joel called in a favor so that I could get a tour of Central High, which he, Seth, and Aaron had all attended. If I wanted to truly understand who Seth was and where he'd come from, I needed to visit his old haunts with the people who knew him best.

I had another motive as well. There was one final set of questions that I had yet to ask Joel and Mary. It hadn't felt right to raise it in an earlier in-person conversation with them in New York over the summer. We'd talked on the phone and traded emails and texts many times since then, but it didn't feel fair or humane to bring it up in a call or a text either. I waited until the three of us were seated around their living room, surrounded by family photos and Nebraska Cornhusker memorabilia, three sleeping Newfoundlands sprawled across the floor, to finally broach a subject I'd been turning over in my head for years: closure.

I asked Joel and Mary, "What does closure look like in all of this? Do you feel like you have had it or could have it? Is it possible?"

Mary didn't hesitate in her answer. There was no closure with the death of a child, she said. You learned to live with that loss, like a giant hole that could never be filled. You didn't pretend the hole wasn't there and simply "move on"; you adapted, shaped your life around it. "I can't ever have closure," she said. "My life, my son's life, our family life, and several of his friends—life will never be the same."

Of course, that would all be true even if her son had not become the subject of a cruel conspiracy theory. She might feel some semblance of relief if she knew that no one still believed the lies and rumors about Seth, but she knew that there was no amount of logic or facts that was going to change some people's minds. "I've already realized I'm never going to accomplish 100 percent of the population believing that my son did not do it," she said.

She held out hope that the authorities might still find who had shot Seth and bring that person to justice. The homicide investigation led by the DC police and the US attorney's office had slowed down during the pandemic, with grand juries and witness interviews all but impossible due to social distancing restrictions. The case had also changed hands several times as new detectives and prosecutors cycled on and off. Mary and Joel had stayed in semiregular contact with whoever was leading the effort. The last time they spoke with the authorities, they were assured that the case remained active.

She and Joel had ideas about ways they might get involved in shaping public policy or legal guidelines so that no one else had to go through what they did. They weren't entirely sure yet what that advocacy would look like. Should they push for the repeal of Section 230 of the Communications Decency Act, which protects websites from being liable for the content they hosted? If Twitter or Facebook could be sued for what their users said on those platforms, would that tamp down on conspiracy theories—or would it open those companies up to so much legal risk that they couldn't remain in operation?

They also thought it was outrageous that there were so few legal protections against defaming someone who is no longer alive. "There [must be] some liability to protect the people that are dead," Mary said. "They still have rights, even though they're dead."

Joel sounded more open to the possibility of closure when I put the same question to him. He understood that Seth's name would continue to appear in news stories for years to come and there was nothing he or anyone else could do to prevent it. "He'll be mentioned, or the case will be mentioned, or the lie will be mentioned," he said. "That will stay there forever." But Joel took solace from the fact that he could point to Fox News's original retraction and Judge Calabresi's opinion and the two settlements and the apologies to Aaron as evidence of the truth. "You get that kind of closure knowing that people are aware of what happened, and that it was wrong, and that there were consequences for what they did," he told me.

Seth's story was now as much a cautionary tale about the personal, legal, and financial repercussions of repeating conspiracy theories as it was about the unproven theories themselves. "There are consequences for lies," he said. "But it will never go away as an issue for us."

Epilogue

One by one the friends arrived. Most had stuck around Omaha after graduating from Creighton or had left for a few years only to return. James Perry and Kevin Z—that's what everyone called him—had married and bought their first homes. Migs and Werner had landed impressive jobs at big companies. Scott, who flew in from Minneapolis, was a new father. They were some of Seth's closest confidants from college, and, on a gray winter morning, they had offered to meet me at a coffee shop and talk about Seth.

No one was quite sure where to begin. The last five years had been surreal, they all agreed, like something out of a sci-fi show. Even this gathering felt strange to them, a reporter asking about hearing your dead friend's name in the mouth of Sean Hannity.

"Start at the beginning," I suggested. "Tell me how you met Seth."

Slowly the conversation opened up and the stories poured out. There was the time Seth wore a polar bear suit on campus to get other students interested in environmental justice. Or the time he handed out "Have a free beer with me" business cards at his senior year fraternity speech. Scott reached into his wallet and pulled out one of those cards—he'd held on to it for all these years. They remembered how Seth's interviews with new fraternity pledges, which were meant to take fifteen or twenty minutes, turned into hours-long interrogations about philosophy or politics or the meaning of life. They joked about how Seth liked to say that if he ever ran for office he'd have to hire all his friends because they knew all of his most embarrassing stories. All the stories about Seth's love of American-themed clothing were true, they said.

But his love of America was not a posture or a joke. This wasn't a Stephen Colbert routine. He meant it. He believed in democracy like it was a religion. Sometimes he was so passionate about it that his friends wondered if Seth cared more about the state of democracy in this country than he did the friends-and-family part of his life.

Seth believed in a kind of politics where you didn't demonize the other side. You didn't see people who had opposing views as villains, the enemy. And so there was something darkly ironic, not to mention infuriating, about watching Seth's name and memory turn into a convenient narrative and a cudgel to wage political combat. That was the opposite of what Seth stood for, Scott said.

For the most part, the college friends had avoided getting sucked into the conspiratorial vortex. A photo of the guys at Scott's bachelor party had spread online, which led people online to think Migs, who was of Portuguese descent, was a Pakistani IT expert who was the fixation of an entirely different conspiracy theory. With that one, all they did was laugh. James Perry said the friend group had chosen to ignore the likes of Matt Couch, Ed Butowsky, or any of the Fox News hosts. They shut out the lies on the internet. "We know who Seth is," Perry told me. "We know what he was like, his big heart. That's what we hold on to."

As I drank my coffee and listened to his friends talk, I had a realization: Seth Rich felt human again. He was not a meme to be shared. Not the leading man of some made-up tale. In that moment, he was a real person, at once remarkable and ordinary, flawed and virtuous, which is all any of us can ever hope to be.

Acknowledgments

This book would not exist were it not for the cooperation, patience, and grace of Mary, Joel, and Aaron Rich. When I first approached the Rich family with the idea of writing a book about Seth's life, death, and everything that came afterward, part of me expected their response to be a resounding no. And who would blame them? I was asking them to revisit one of the most painful and traumatic periods of their lives. To my surprise, they not only agreed to participate but opened themselves up to me in a way that still fills me with awe. Our many interviews must have felt at times like tearing at wounds that had not yet healed. And yet the Riches always responded to my incessant questions, told me their favorite stories about Seth, and assisted me in making this book as accurate and honest as it could possibly be.

I feel a deep sense of gratitude to the people who guided the Riches through the last six years and who were invaluable resources and interview subjects as I reported and wrote this book. Special thanks to Mike Gottlieb, Brad Bauman, Meryl Governski, Deb Sines, and Andrew Therriault. I also want to thank Seth's friends who generously shared their memories, photos, old emails, chat messages, and more. I tip my hat to the Central High guys and the Creighton crew. The first round of beers is on me the next time I see any of you.

I drew on the expertise of a great many scholars, academics, and journalists in the course of my research. Renée DiResta, Darren Linvill, and Kate Starbird are three of the smartest thinkers out there on the subject of social media's impact on our democracy. Melissa Ryan helped me to connect the dots between the many conspiracy theories that spring out of the far-right fringes of the internet.

As I reported this book, I often felt like a social-media archeologist. A tweet or a 4chan post or a Reddit thread that I had flagged would disappear one day without any warning. The author had deleted it, the platform had suspended the author, or the platform had purged the contents of an entire forum, as was the case when Reddit banned the notorious r/The_Donald subreddit in 2021. Suddenly evidence that I had spent months gathering slipped through my fingers like a fistful of sand. It was an incredibly frustrating experience. I learned to screenshot everything. And I made ample use of Internet Archive's Wayback Machine, which was often my last resort in tracking down long-vanished social media posts. I'm grateful to the good folks at the Internet Archive for creating and maintaining this essential tool.

Before I wrote this book, the extent of my knowledge about police work and solving homicides largely came from prestige TV and Dashiell Hammett. Retired MPD homicide detectives Mitch Credle, Mike Irving, and Darryl Richmond gave me an education on what it takes to investigate murders in the District of Columbia. I could sit and listen to those three men talk about old cases for hours. Someone give them a podcast.

This is my first book. When I set out to write it, I talked to—OK, interrogated—anyone I knew who had already written one. If there was a theme in those conversations, it was the importance of having a good team behind you. Writing can be a lonely process, it's true, but publishing a book proved to be far more collaborative than I had imagined.

I owe a debt of gratitude to Clive Priddle at PublicAffairs. From our first meeting, Clive grasped the importance and scope of this story. He pushed me to sharpen my thinking and deepen my reporting. His guidance and edits improved the manuscript enormously. Clive has surrounded himself with a talented and creative team. Anu Roy-Chaudhury, Johanna Dickson, Ruth Schemmel, and Jennifer Crane were all a joy to work with, a source of great ideas, and cool under pressure. Their excitement for this book only made me want to work harder.

Matt Giles, my fact-checker, did a phenomenal job on a tight deadline. I used to work as a fact-checker and so my appreciation for Matt's exhaustive attention to detail knows no bounds. Needless to say any errors that appear in the book are my own.

My former editors at *Rolling Stone*, Patrick Reis and Sean Woods, published several stories of mine about Seth Rich, Fox News, and the family's lawsuits. Patrick, Sean, and the great legal team at *Rolling Stone* stood behind my reporting at every step of the way.

I can still remember the exact moment when my agent, David Halpern, called to say that he and The Robbins Office would represent me. David is everything a writer could ever want in a literary agent: an advocate and a therapist, an incisive reader and a shrewd negotiator. Most of all David believed in this book when few others did. I can't thank him enough for that.

To say Kit Rachlis was instrumental in the writing of this book would be a gross understatement. He read and edited several versions of the proposal. He read and edited every word of the manuscript. He offered to talk whenever I needed guidance. He managed all this on top of his actual job editing some of the finest journalism in America and winning every major award in the business. When I sit down to write, I hear Kit's voice in my head as much as my own. *Cliché. Stock phrase alert. Ugh.* Kit is more than an editor to me; he's a mentor. I feel unbelievably lucky to call him and his wife, Amy, my dear friends.

My parents, Keith and Lisa, instilled in me at a young age a love of reading, a hunger for learning, and the belief that I could accomplish whatever I wanted if I put in the work—the essential building blocks, in other words, to make a career as a journalist. At every juncture in my life, they supported me unconditionally and without judgment, sacrificing so that me and my brother, Nick, could attend great schools and pursue our dreams. My dad was my first editor. To this day I live by the advice he's given me. Writing is rewriting, Pops.

There were many bleary-eyed early mornings and coffee-fueled late nights spent finishing this book. Thankfully George and Millie were always there to keep me company, climbing up into my lap, walking across my keyboard, or snoozing in my office chair.

This book is dedicated to Sarah, my wife. She is my true love, trusted confidante, wiser half, and partner in all things. In my low moments she encouraged me to keep going, believing that I could write this book even when I didn't. I couldn't imagine embarking on this project without her because I couldn't picture my life at all without her.

Source Notes

This book is a work of nonfiction. During five years of reporting and research, I conducted more than two hundred interviews, collected several gigabytes of social-media posts and videos, and reviewed hundreds of thousands of pages of court filings, government reports, and documents obtained via public-records requests. I drew extensively on emails, text messages, voicemails, social-media posts, and other records produced in the lawsuits *Butowsky v. Folkenflik*, *Rich v. Fox News Network LLC*, and *Rich v. Butowsky*. When I describe what a person was thinking, it's because that person conveyed those thoughts to me. When I include dialogue in the narrative, I've sought to confirm that dialogue with all parties involved in the conversation. Sources below are listed in the order in which the information appears in the chapters.

PROLOGUE

Pat Collins and Andrea Swalec, "27-Year-Old DNC Staffer Seth Rich Shot, Killed in Northwest DC," NBC Washington, July 11, 2016, https://www .nbcwashington.com/news/local/man-shot-killed-in-northwest-dc /2074048/.

CHAPTER 1: STRIVER

Pratt Wiley, interview with author, June 6, 2018.
James Perry, interview with author, November 17, 2021.
Joel Rich, interview with author, May 20, 2021.
Mary and Joel Rich, interview with author, July 20, 2021.
Jacob Cytryn, interview with author, January 20, 2022.
Manuel Roig-Franzia, "Seth Rich Wasn't Just Another D.C. Murder Victim. He Was a Meme in the Weirdest Presidential Election of Our Times," *Washington Post*, January 18, 2017, https://www.washingtonpost.com/lifestyle/style

/seth-rich-wasnt-just-another-dc-murder-victim-he-was-a-meme-in-the
-weirdest-presidential-election-of-our-times/2017/01/18/ee8e27f8-dcc0
-11e6-918c-99ede3c8cafa_story.html.

Allison Villalobos Steele, interview with author, October 12, 2021.

Former GQR coworker of Seth's, interview with author, December 1, 2020.

Andrew Therriault, interview with author, November 4, 2018.

Seth Rich LinkedIn profile, https://archive.is/01a92.

CHAPTER 2: THE LAST WALK HOME

Raphael Satter, Jeff Donn, and Chad Day, "Inside Story: How Russians Hacked the Democrats' Emails," Associated Press, November 4, 2017, https://apnews.com/article/technology-europe-russia-hacking-only-on-ap-dea73efc01594839957c3c9a6c962b8a.

Former DNC employees, interviews with author.

Pratt Wiley, interview with author, June 6, 2018.

Andrew Brown, closed-door testimony before the House Permanent Select Committee on Intelligence, August 30, 2017, https://www.dni.gov/files/HPSCI_Transcripts/2019-03-11-AndrewB-MTR.pdf.

Select Comm. on Intelligence, Russian Active Measures Campaigns and Interference in the 2016 US Election, Volume 5: Counterintelligence Threats and Vulnerabilities, S. Rep. 116-XX (2019), https://www.intelligence.senate.gov/sites/default/files/documents/report_volume5.pdf.

Dmitri Alperovitch, "Bears in the Midst: Intrusion into the Democratic National Committee," Crowdstrike, June 14, 2016, https://www.crowdstrike.com/blog/bears-midst-intrusion-democratic-national-committee/.

Robert Peston, "Assange on Peston on Sunday: 'More Clinton Leaks to Come,'" Peston on Sunday, ITV, June 12, 2016, https://www.itv.com/news/update/2016-06-12/assange-on-peston-on-sunday-more-clinton-leaks-to-come/.

I've drawn many biographical details about Julian Assange from two superb New Yorker profiles by staff writer Raffi Khatchadourian: Raffi Khatchadourian, "No Secrets," New Yorker, June 7, 2010, https://www.newyorker.com/magazine/2010/06/07/no-secrets, and "A Man Without a Country," New Yorker, August 21, 2017, https://www.newyorker.com/magazine/2017/08/21/julian-assange-a-man-without-a-country.

Zack Beauchamp, "Why WikiLeaks Hates Hillary Clinton," Vox, September 15, 2016, https://www.vox.com/2016/9/15/12929262/wikileaks-hillary-clinton-julian-assange-hate.

Frank James, "WikiLeaks Is a Terror Outfit: Rep. Peter King," NPR, November 29, 2010, https://www.npr.org/sections/itsallpolitics/2010/11/29/131664547/wikileaks-is-a-terror-outfit-rep-peter-king.

Guardian Staff, "WikiLeaks Embassy Cables: The Key Points at a Glance," *Guardian*, December 7, 2010, https://www.theguardian.com/world/2010/nov/29/wikileaks-embassy-cables-key-points.

Laura Poitras, dir., "Risk," Praxis Films Berlin, Praxis Films, May 5, 2017.

Micah Lee and Cora Currier, "In Leaked Chats, WikiLeaks Discusses Preference for GOP over Clinton, Russia, Trolling, and Feminists They Don't Like," The Intercept, February 14, 2018, https://theintercept.com/2018/02/14/julian-assange-wikileaks-election-clinton-trump/.

United States District Court for the District of Columbia, Case: 1:17-mj-00821, Document No. 29-4, application for a search warrant, November 6, 2017, April 28, 2020.

James Perry, interview with author, November 17, 2021.

Ellen Nakashima, "Russian Government Hackers Penetrated DNC, Stole Opposition Research on Trump," *Washington Post*, June 14, 2016, https://www.washingtonpost.com/world/national-security/russian-government-hackers-penetrated-dnc-stole-opposition-research-on-trump/2016/06/14/cf006cb4-316e-11e6-8ff7-7b6c1998b7a0_story.html.

Joseph Morton, "Friends in D.C. Celebrate Omaha Native Seth Rich's Generous Spirit," *Omaha World-Herald*, August 4, 2016, https://omaha.com/news/metro/friends-in-d-c-celebrate-omaha-native-seth-rich-s/article_2b231843-8166-5b52-98fe-8335827464e1.html.

CHAPTER 3: A HIDEOUS PARADE

Mark Mueller, interview with author, March 18, 2021.

Scott Roberts, "Bloomingdale: DC Highest Intensity of Gentrification Map Shows North Bloomingdale Is Hot Pink!" Bloomingdale Neighborhood Association, March 19, 2019, http://bloomingdaleneighborhood.blogspot.com/2019/03/dc-highest-intensity-of-gentrification.html.

"Two More Armed Robberies in Bloomingdale Last Night," PoPville, July 6, 2016, https://www.popville.com/2016/07/two-more-armed-robberies-in-bloomingdale-last-night/.

Peter Hermann, "Bloomingdale Residents Question Police After Killing, Robberies in Neighborhood," *Washington Post*, July 19, 2016, https://www.washingtonpost.com/local/public-safety/bloomingdale-residents-question-police-after-killing-robberies-in-neighborhood/2016/07/19/99ce212c-4dab-11e6-a7d8-13d06b37f256_story.html.

Joel Rich, interview with author, May 20, 2021.

Mary and Joel Rich, interview with author, July 20, 2021.

Aaron Rich, interview with Noah Lanard, 2017.

Aaron Rich, interview with author, July 20, 2018.

Sean Spicer (@SeanSpicer), "Despite the political difference, prayers of @gop go out to our counterparts at @TheDemocrats for their loss," Twitter, July 11, 2016, 11:13 p.m., https://twitter.com/seanspicer/status/752702295192862720.

Kurtchella, "The Death of Seth Rich," r/Conspiracy, Reddit.com, July 11, 2016, https://www.reddit.com/r/conspiracy/comments/4sejv7/the_death_of_seth_rich/.

Kurt Ramos, interview with author, July 6, 2021.

Former DNC employees, interviews with author.

"Senator Bernie Sanders Campaign Event with Hillary Clinton," C-SPAN.org, July 12, 2016, https://www.c-span.org/video/?412571-1/bernie-sanders-end orses-hillary-clinton.

CHAPTER 4: THE UNITED STATES OF SHEEPLE

Steve Vogel and Cheryl W. Thompson, "3 Employees Killed at D.C. Starbucks," *Washington Post*, July 8, 1997, https://www.washingtonpost.com/wp-srv/local/daily/march99/starbucks070897.htm.

Cheryl W. Thompson and John Fountain, "One Year Later, Starbucks Slayings Unsolved," *Washington Post*, July 6, 1998, https://www.washingtonpost.com/wp-srv/local/daily/march99/starbucks070698.htm.

Snopes Staff, "Clinton Body Bags," Snopes.com, January 24, 1998, https://www.snopes.com/fact-check/clinton-body-bags/.

"Strange Deaths Surround the Presidency," September 9, 1997, Internet Archive Wayback Machine, https://web.archive.org/web/19980203223231/http://www.ksfo560.com/Personalities/Deaths2.html.

Jodi Kantor, "Does Bill Clinton Run Murder Inc.?," Slate.com, February 18, 1999, https://slate.com/news-and-politics/1999/02/does-bill-clinton-run-murder-inc.html.

Washington Post Staff, "Full Text: Starbucks Affidavit," *Washington Post*, March 17, 1999, https://www.washingtonpost.com/wp-srv/local/daily/march99/affidavit18.htm.

Jesse Walker's *The United States of Paranoia* (New York: Harper Perennial, 2013) and Michael Barkun's *A Culture of Conspiracy* (Berkeley: University of California Press, 2006) were two of several superb books I read to better understand the broader sweep of history as it relates to conspiracy theories.

Nancy Jo Sales, "Click Here for Conspiracy," *Vanity Fair*, October 10, 2006, https://www.vanityfair.com/news/2006/08/loosechange200608.

Sander van der Linden, interview with author, June 25, 2021.

Nate Blakeslee, "Alex Jones Is About to Explode," *Texas Monthly*, January 20, 2013, https://www.texasmonthly.com/news-politics/alex-jones-is-about-to-explode/.

Elizabeth Williamson, "Conspiracy Theories Made Alex Jones Very Rich; They May Bring Him Down," *New York Times*, September 7, 2018, https://www.nytimes.com/2018/09/07/us/politics/alex-jones-business-infowars-conspiracy.html.

Sebastian Murdock, "Alex Jones' Infowars Store Made $165 Million over 3 Years, Records Show," *HuffPost*, January 7, 2022, https://www.huffpost.com/entry/infowars-store-alex-jones_n_61d71d8fe4b0bcd2195c6562.

"InfoWars: Alex Jones Interviews Donald Trump—December 2, 2015," YouTube, https://www.youtube.com/watch?v=4LeChPL0sLE.

Brooks Jackson and Eugene Kiely, "Donald, You're Fired!," FactCheck.org, April 9, 2011, https://www.factcheck.org/2011/04/donald-youre-fired/.

Russell Muirhead and Nancy L. Rosenbaum's *A Lot of People Are Saying: The New Conspiracism and the Assault on Democracy* (Princeton, NJ: Princeton University Press, 2019) is an insightful book I drew on to better understand how Trump's conspiracism fit into the broader arc of conspiracy thinking in America.

David Weigel, "Alex Jones Celebrates Trump's Takeover of the GOP," *Washington Post*, July 18, 2016, https://www.washingtonpost.com/news/post-politics/wp/2016/07/18/alex-jones-celebrates-trumps-takeover-of-the-gop.

CHAPTER 5: OUR SOURCES TAKE RISKS

Eelco Bosch van Rosenthal, interview with author, April 19, 2021.

"The DNC Leaks," Wikileaks.org, https://wikileaks.org/dnc-emails.

"The 4 Most Damaging Emails from the DNC WikiLeaks Dump," ABC News, July 25, 2016, https://abcnews.go.com/Politics/damaging-emails-dnc-wikileaks-dump/story?id=40852448.

Aaron Blake, "Here Are the Latest, Most Damaging Things in the DNC's Leaked Emails," *Washington Post*, July 25, 2016, https://www.washingtonpost.com/news/the-fix/wp/2016/07/24/here-are-the-latest-most-damaging-things-in-the-dncs-leaked-emails.

Jonathan Martin and Alan Rappeport, "Debbie Wasserman Schultz to Resign D.N.C. Post," *New York Times*, July 24, 2016, https://www.nytimes.com/2016/07/25/us/politics/debbie-wasserman-schultz-dnc-wikileaks-emails.html.

Holly Otterbein, "Bernie Sanders Delegates Mount Convention Rebellion over 'Medicare for All,'" Politico, July 27, 2020, https://www.politico.com/news/2020/07/27/bernie-supporters-medicare-single-payer-381972.

"Wikileaks Founder: We Create Maximum Ambiguity for Sources," CNN, July 26, 2016, http://www.cnn.com/videos/world/2016/07/26/julian-assange-dnc-emails-chance-interview.cnn.

"EXCLUSIVE: WikiLeaks' Julian Assange on Releasing DNC Emails That Ousted Debbie Wasserman Schultz," Democracy Now!, July 25, 2016, https://www.democracynow.org/2016/7/25/exclusive_wikileaks_julian _assange_on_releasing.

Van Rosenthal, "Julian Assange on Seth Rich," *Nieuwsuur* interview, YouTube, August 9, 2016, https://www.youtube.com/watch?app=desktop&v=Kp7Fk LBRpKg.

Aaron Rich, interview with author, May 21, 2021.

Peter Hermann and Clarence Williams, "WikiLeaks Offers Reward for Help Finding DNC Staffer's Killer," *Washington Post*, August 9, 2016, https:// www.washingtonpost.com/local/public-safety/wikileaks-offers-reward-in -killing-of-dnc-staffer-in-washington/2016/08/09/f84fcbf4-5e5b-11e6 -8e45-477372e89d78_story.html?utm_term=.de48867bd489.

Darren Linvill, a professor at Clemson University and an expert in social-media forensics, provided me with several large datasets and visualizations that show the surge in activity mentioning Seth Rich in the aftermath of Assange's *Nieuwsuur* interview.

Here is an example of one of Deplorable Dani's (@NimbleNavgater) tweets: "TWEET USING HASHTAGS #SethRich and #HisNameWasSethRich !!!," Twitter, August 10, 2016, 12:13 a.m., https://twitter.com/NimbleNav gater/status/763226635474706436.

Mike Cernovich (@Cernovich), "Was Seth Rich, the source of #DNCleaks, murdered?," Twitter, August 9, 2016, 5:15 a.m., https://web.archive.org /web/20171102120723/https://twitter.com/Cernovich/status/76316 6970569224193?ref_src=twsrc%5Etfw&ref_url=http%3A%2F%2Fwww .mediaite.com%2Fonline%2Fmegyn-kelly-corners-assange-over-recent -claims-why-are-you-so-interested-in-seth-richs-killer%2F.

Jim Hoft, "WOW! BREAKING=> Julian Assange Suggests Seth Rich - Who Was MURDERED in DC - Was Wikileaks DNC Source!," Gateway Pundit, August 10, 2016, https://www.thegatewaypundit.com/2016/08/wow -breaking-video-julian-assange-suggests-seth-rich-wikileaks-dnc-source -shot-dead-dc/.

Martin Gould, "Parents of Murdered Seth Rich Outraged After Julian Assange Reward," *Daily Mail Online*, August 10, 2016, https://www.dailymail.co.uk /news/article-3726250/Enemies-Hillary-Bill-say-27-year-old-murder-vic tim-Seth-Rich-suspected-leaking-DNC-emails-belongs-Clinton-Death -List-people-ties-couple-died-time.html.

"WikiLeaks Offers Cash Reward for Leads on DNC Staffer's Murderer," Sputnik International, August 9, 2016, https://sputniknews.com/20160809 /wikileaks-seth-rich-1044103047.html.

"WikiLeaks Offers $20K Reward in Shooting Death of DNC Staffer," Ghana News Agency, August 10, 2016, accessed via Nexis; "WikiLeaks Offers

$20K Reward in Shooting Death of DNC Staffer," FARS News Agency, August 10, 2016, accessed via Nexis; "WikiLeaks S'implique Dans l'Enquête Sur La Mort d'Un Salarié Du Parti Démocrate à Washington," *Le Monde*, August 10, 2016, https://www.lemonde.fr/pixels/article/2016/08/10/wikileaks-s-implique-dans-l-enquete-sur-la-mort-d-un-jeune-salarie-du-parti-democrate-a-washington_4980875_4408996.html.

Beimeng Fu, "This Is Why a Conspiracy Theory About the Clintons Has Gone Viral in China," BuzzFeed News, August 15, 2016, https://www.buzzfeednews.com/article/beimengfu/a-conspiracy-theory-about-the-clintons-murdering-people-has.

"Fox's Eric Bolling Floats Conspiracy Theory That Murdered DNC Staffer 'Was a Hit,'" Media Matters for America, August 10, 2016, https://www.mediamatters.org/fox-news/foxs-eric-bolling-floats-conspiracy-theory-murdered-dnc-staffer-was-hit.

Andrew Therriault, interview with author, November 4, 2018.

Brad Bauman, interview with author, August 21, 2019.

CHAPTER 6: THE FIRST GOOD SAMARITAN

Jack Burkman interview with WTTG Fox 5 DC, September 15, 2016.

"About the Founder," https://burkmanassociates.com/.

The original press release for Burkman's $100,000 reward is accessible only via the Internet Archive's Wayback Machine: https://web.archive.org/web/20160915172641/http://www.prnewschannel.com/2016/09/14/gop-lobbyist-offers-100000-reward-in-dnc-staffers-death/.

Jesse Byrnes, "GOP Lobbyist Offers $100K Reward for Info in DNC Staffer's Death," The Hill, September 14, 2016, https://thehill.com/blogs/blog-briefing-room/news/295916-gop-lobbyist-offers-100k-reward-for-info-in-dnc-staffers-death/.

Noah Lanard, "A Republican Lobbyist Went Hunting for Seth Rich's Murderer; Things Got Bizarre," *Mother Jones*, July 10, 2017, https://www.motherjones.com/politics/2017/07/a-lobbyist-detectives-strange-quest-to-find-seth-richs-murderer/. Noah Lanard's profile of Jack Burkman for *Mother Jones* was a valuable resource for my reporting about Burkman and his activities.

Megan R. Wilson, "Lobby Firms Sweep Up New Clients," The Hill, January 26, 2014, https://thehill.com/business-a-lobbying/196401-lobby-firms-sweep-up-new-clients.

"JM Burkman & Assoc Lobbying Profile," OpenSecrets.org, https://www.opensecrets.org/federal-lobbying/firms/summary?cycle=2013&id=D000075580.

Ralph Palmieri's quote comes from Lanard's story about Burkman, "A Republican Lobbyist Went Hunting for Seth Rich's Murderer."

Simon Tomlinson, "Washington Lobbyist Moves to Ban Gay Players from the NFL," *Daily Mail Online*, February 25, 2014, https://www.dailymail.co.uk /news/article-2567583/We-losing-decency-nation-Washington-lobbyist -moves-ban-gay-players-NFL-college-star-Michael-Sam-came-ahead-de claring-draft.html.

Sam Stein, "GOP Lobbyist Behind Anti-Gay NFL Bill Has a Gay Brother Who Thinks He's an Ass," February 25, 2014, *HuffPost*, https://www.huffpost .com/entry/anti-gay-nfl-bill_n_4850859.

Jack Burkman, interview with author, March 2, 2021.

Brad Bauman, interview with author, August 21, 2019.

Joel Rich, interview with author, May 20, 2021.

CHAPTER 7: THROUGH THE LOOKING GLASS

Aaron Rich, interview with author, May 21, 2021.

US Department of Homeland Security, "Joint Statement from the Department of Homeland Security and Office of the Director of National Intelligence on Election Security," DHS Press Office, October 7, 2016, https://www.dhs .gov/news/2016/10/07/joint-statement-department-homeland-security -and-office-director-national.

David A. Fahrenthold, "Trump Recorded Having Extremely Lewd Conversation About Women in 2005," *Washington Post*, October 7, 2016, https:// www.washingtonpost.com/politics/trump-recorded-having-extremely -lewd-conversation-about-women-in-2005/2016/10/07/3b9ce776-8cb4 -11e6-bf8a-3d26847eeed4_story.html.

Marshall Cohen, "Access Hollywood, Russian Hacking and the Podesta Emails: One Year Later," CNN.com, October 7, 2017, https://www.cnn.com/2017 /10/07/politics/one-year-access-hollywood-russia-podesta-email/index .html.

Stone's quote about urging Corsi to tell WikiLeaks to drop the "Podesta emails immediately" appears on page 249 of volume 5 of the Senate Select Committee on Intelligence's report titled "Russian Active Measures Campaigns and Interference in the 2016 US Election," https://www.intelligence.senate .gov/sites/default/files/documents/report_volume5.pdf.

Philip Bump, "Analysis: How the 'Access Hollywood' Incident Gave Us the Trump We Recognize Today," *Washington Post*, July 10, 2019, https://www .washingtonpost.com/politics/2019/07/10/how-access-hollywood-incident -gave-us-trump-we-recognize-today/.

Julianna Goldman, "Podesta Emails Show Excerpts of Clinton Speeches to Goldman," CBS News, October 7, 2016, https://www.cbsnews.com/news /podesta-emails-show-excerpts-of-clinton-speeches-to-goldman/.

Gregor Aisch, Jon Huang, and Cecilia Kang, "Dissecting the #PizzaGate Con-spiracy Theories," *New York Times*, December 10, 2016, https://www.ny times.com/interactive/2016/12/10/business/media/pizzagate.html.

John Herrman, "Donald Trump Finds Support in Reddit's Unruly Corners," *New York Times*, April 8, 2016, https://www.nytimes.com/2016/04/09/busi ness/media/in-reddits-unruly-corners-trump-finds-support.html.

Tyler Pager, "At Trump's 'Ask Me Anything' Questions Get Carefully Screened," Politico, July 27, 2016, https://www.politico.com/story/2016/07/donald -trump-reddit-ama-226336.

Many of the Reddit posts I cite come from my own research digging through old r/The_Donald threads. An early *Washington City Paper* feature about Seth Rich also quoted some of these Reddit comments. Will Sommer, "Mining a Murder: How Seth Rich Became a Martyr for the Alt-Right," *Washington City Paper*, November 17, 2016, https://washingtoncitypaper.com/article /193663/mining-a-murder-how-seth-rich-became-a-martyr-for-the -altright/.

CHAPTER 8: THE LIVES OF A FEW FOR THE LIVES OF MANY

James Alefantis, interview with author, September 12, 2018.

Will Sommer, "Alt Right Conspiracy Theorists Obsess over Comet Ping Pong," *Washington City Paper*, November 6, 2016, https://washingtoncitypaper .com/article/327515/alt-right-conspiracy-theorists-obsess-over-comet -ping-pong/.

Amanda Robb, "Anatomy of a Fake News Scandal," *Rolling Stone*, November 16, 2017, https://www.rollingstone.com/feature/anatomy-of-a-fake-news-scan dal-125877/. Journalist Amanda Robb's 2017 investigation is the most in-depth investigation into the origins of Pizzagate. Robb's story was a valu-able resource for me.

Adam Goldman and Alan Rappeport, "Emails in Anthony Weiner Inquiry Jolt Hillary Clinton's Campaign," *New York Times*, October 28, 2016, https:// www.nytimes.com/2016/10/29/us/politics/fbi-hillary-clinton-email.html.

Joanna Walters, "Anthony Weiner Sent Sexually Explicit Messages to 15-Year-Old, Report Says," *Guardian*, September 21, 2016, https://www.theguard ian.com/us-news/2016/sep/21/anthony-weiner-sexually-explicit-messages -teen-daily-mail.

Gregor Aisch, Jon Huang, and Cecilia Kang, "Dissecting the #PizzaGate Con-spiracy Theories," *New York Times*, December 10, 2016. https://www.ny times.com/interactive/2016/12/10/business/media/pizzagate.html.

I reported on some of the online threats and abuse Alefantis and John Podesta received in a 2018 investigation published by *Rolling Stone*. Andy Kroll,

"John Podesta Is Ready to Talk About Pizzagate," December 9, 2018, *Rolling Stone*, https://www.rollingstone.com/politics/politics-features/john-podesta-pizzagate-766489/.

Marc Fisher, John Woodrow Cox, and Peter Hermann, "Pizzagate: From Rumor, to Hashtag, to Gunfire in D.C.," *Washington Post*, December 6, 2016, https://www.washingtonpost.com/local/pizzagate-from-rumor-to-hashtag-to-gunfire-in-dc/2016/12/06/4c7def50-bbd4-11e6-94ac-3d324840106c_story.html.

Mike Gottlieb, interview with author, May 25, 2018.

Pennsylvania Democratic Party v. Republican Party of Pennsylvania, 2:16-cv-05664 (US District Court of Pennsylvania 2016), https://www.documentcloud.org/documents/20398013-2016_10_30-pa-dem-party-v-roger-stone-gottlieb-lawsuit-in-2016-for-dnc.

Heather Gerken, interview with author, October 31, 2018.

Geneva Sands, "'Pizzagate' Gunman Recorded 'Goodbye' Video Message to His Family," ABC News, June 23, 2017, https://abcnews.go.com/US/pizzagate-gunman-recorded-goodbye-video-message-family/story?id=48235100.

Welch's messages to his friends are described in the federal government's criminal complaint filed against Welch on December 12, 2016: https://www.documentcloud.org/documents/20398014-2016_12_12-edgar-maddison-welch-arrest-document.

Rachel Kurzius, "Body Cam Footage Shows What Happened During Arrest of Pizzagate Gunman," WAMU, February 25, 2019, https://wamu.org/story/19/02/25/body-cam-footage-shows-what-happened-during-arrest-of-pizzagate-gunman/.

CHAPTER 9: SHE WHO FIGHTS MONSTERS

"About Us," The Office of the United States Attorney for the District of Columbia, https://www.justice.gov/usao-dc/about-us.

"Robert S. Mueller III," US Department of Justice, https://www.justice.gov/criminal/history/assistant-attorneys-general/robert-s-mueller.

"Eric Holder: Eighty-Second Attorney General, 2009–2015," US Department of Justice, https://www.justice.gov/ag/bio/attorney-general-eric-h-holder-jr.

Deborah Sines, interview with author, March 20 and 21, 2019.

Keith L. Alexander, "Killers Fear This Woman," *Washington Post*, June 7, 2009, https://www.washingtonpost.com/wp-dyn/content/article/2009/06/06/AR2009060602147.html.

Scott McCabe, "Gang Leader to Be Sentenced for Killing Witness," *Washington Examiner*, June 4, 2009, https://www.washingtonexaminer.com/gang-leader-to-be-sentenced-for-killing-witness.

"Azariah Israel & Ronald Marquet Cheadle, Appellants, v. United States, Appellee," District of Columbia Court of Appeals, November 26, 2014, https://caselaw.findlaw.com/dc-court-of-appeals/1693641.html.

Theo Emery, "Mother Guilty of Killing 4 Girls Whose Bodies Decomposed in Home," *New York Times*, July 29, 2009, https://www.nytimes.com/2009/07/30/us/30mom.html.

Paul Duggan, "Banita Jacks Sentenced to 120 Years," *Washington Post*, December 18, 2009, http://voices.washingtonpost.com/crime-scene/paul-duggan/banita-jacks-sentenced-to-120.html.

Keith L. Alexander and Paul Duggan, "Eight Years After Pamela Butler Disappeared from Her D.C. Home, Her Killer Admits Guilt," *Washington Post*, October 6, 2017, https://www.washingtonpost.com/local/public-safety/eight-years-after-pamela-butler-disappeared-from-her-dc-home-her-killer-admits-guilt/2017/10/06/5c8134e2-aa9f-11e7-92d1-58c702d2d975_story.html.

Keith L. Alexander, "Retrial in Chandra Levy Murder Case Scheduled for March," *Washington Post*, June 12, 2015, https://www.washingtonpost.com/local/crime/retrial-in-chandra-levy-murder-case-scheduled-for-march/2015/06/12/4bb8a646-1126-11e5-a0dc-2b6f404ff5cf_story.html.

Keith L. Alexander, "Prosecutor in Retrial of Man Charged in Levy Murder Acknowledges 'Mistake,'" *Washington Post*, November 20, 2015, https://www.washingtonpost.com/local/public-safety/prosecutor-in-retrial-of-man-charged-in-levy-murder-acknowledges-mistake/2015/11/20/ab31854c-8fbc-11e5-ae1f-af46b7df8483_story.html.

Maria Sacchetti and Keith L. Alexander, "Man Once Charged in Slaying of Chandra Levy Is Deported," *Washington Post*, May 8, 2017, https://www.washingtonpost.com/local/man-once-charged-in-slaying-of-chandra-levy-is-deported/2017/05/08/e4753b1c-341d-11e7-b4ee-434b6d506b37_story.html.

Harry Jaffe, "DC's Mystifying Decision to Shut Down Vice Squads," *Washingtonian*, August 26, 2015, https://www.washingtonian.com/2015/08/26/why-did-dc-shut-down-its-vice-squads-crime-rate-cathy-lanier/.

CHAPTER 10: CODE PURPLE

Mary and Joel Rich, interview with author, July 20, 2021.

Brad Bauman, interview with author, August 21, 2019.

The Rich family's press conference with Burkman can be viewed here: https://www.facebook.com/watch/live/?v=10154903121067494&ref=watch_permalink.

Scott Roberts, "Bloomingdale: Here Is the New Seth Rich Flyer: $125,000 Reward," Bloomingdale Neighborhood blog, November 20, 2016, http://

bloomingdaleneighborhood.blogspot.com/2016/11/here-is-new-seth-rich
-flyer-125000.html.

Peter Hermann, Clarence Williams, and Ann E. Marimow, "D.C. Police Chief
Cathy L. Lanier Steps Down to Work for the NFL," *Washington Post*,
August 16, 2016, https://www.washingtonpost.com/local/public-safety/dc
-police-chief-cathy-l-lanier-leaves-to-work-for-the-nfl/2016/08/16/9d81
ae2c-63ba-11e6-be4e-23fc4d4d12b4_story.html.

Aaron Rich, interview with author, May 21, 2021.

The details about Ed Butowsky's initial outreach to the Rich family are largely
drawn from the lawsuit Mary and Joel would later file against Butowsky: *Rich
v. Fox News Network LLC*, 1:18-cv-02223, (Dist. Court, SD New York
2018).

"About Ed," https://www.edbutowsky.com/financial-services-advisor/.

Pablo Torre, "How (and Why) Athletes Go Broke," *Sports Illustrated*, March 23,
2009, https://vault.si.com/vault/2009/03/23/how-and-why-athletes-go-broke.

The emails between Butowsky and the Rich family described in this chapter are
drawn from filings and exhibits made public in two lawsuits: *Rich v. Fox
News Network LLC*, and *Butowsky v. Folkenflik*, 4:18-cv-00442 (Dist. Court,
ED of Texas 2018).

Brad Bauman, interview with author, August 22, 2019.

"'Who Murdered Seth Rich?': Billboards, Ads to Be Posted in Search of Killer,"
NBC Washington, January 18, 2017, https://www.nbcwashington.com
/news/local/who-murdered-seth-rich-billboards-ads-to-be-posted-in
-search-of-killer/17685/.

Louise Boyle, "EXCLUSIVE: Republican Lobbyist Says He Has 'Evidence'
That 27-Year-Old DNC Analyst Seth Rich Was Murdered After Discover-
ing Russian Operatives Had Hacked the DNC and Has Asked Congress for
Investigation," *Daily Mail Online*, February 27, 2017, https://www.daily
mail.co.uk/news/article-4264558/GOP-lobbyist-claims-Russia-murder
-Seth-Rich.html.

CHAPTER 11: CREATURE OF THE GREEN ROOM

Ed Butowsky with Dennis Kneale, "Wealth Mismanagement: A Wall Street
Insider on the Dirty Secrets of Financial Advisers and How to Protect
Your Portfolio," *Post Hill Press*, August 13, 2019.

Butowsky described his Ogilvy firing and other biographical details during a
deposition he gave in the lawsuit *TRNS LLC v. Ellen Ratner*, filed US District Court in Connecticut. The deposition can be accessed at https://www
.documentcloud.org/documents/21155361-butowsky-march-2017-deposi
tions-in-trns-v-ratner#document/p68/a2070418.

Zac Crain, "Ed Butowsky, Dallas' $3 Billion Money Manager," *D Magazine*, July 23, 2008, https://www.dmagazine.com/publications/d-magazine/2008/august/ed-butowsky-dallas-3-billion-money-manager/.

Billy Corben, dir., "Broke," *30 for 30*, ESPN, October 2, 2012, https://www.imdb.com/title/tt2318140/.

An internal Fox email produced in *Rich v. Fox News Network LLC* tallied Butowsky's appearances on Fox News and Fox Business. The email can be accessed at https://www.documentcloud.org/documents/7044184-2020-08-25-Discovery-Dispute-Letter-With-Emails#document/p5/a578066.

Former Fox employees, interviews with author.

Reeves Wiedeman, "The Rise and Fall of a Fox News Fraud," *Rolling Stone*, January 26, 2016, https://www.rollingstone.com/politics/politics-news/the-rise-and-fall-of-a-fox-news-fraud-240554/.

US Department of Justice, "CIA Imposter Sentenced to Prison for Fraud," US Attorney's Office Eastern District of Virginia, July 15, 2016, https://www.justice.gov/usao-edva/pr/cia-imposter-sentenced-prison-fraud.

Ed Butowsky and Ty Clevenger, email to author, May 1, 2019. In response to a sixteen-page fact-checking letter sent by the author, Butowsky declined to answer questions about his interactions with the Rich family, his help assembling Zimmerman's story about Seth and WikiLeaks, and the aftermath of that story. Clevenger, writing on behalf of Butowsky, said that Butowsky "is prohibited from answering many of your questions."

Stuart Blaugrund, interview with author, April 10, 2019. Blaugrund also shared with me screenshots of Butowsky's comments to him about Obama's birth certificate and Benghazi and provided me with a copy of the invitation Butowsky and his wife sent out for their book event featuring the Benghazi security contractors.

The clip of Butowsky's appearance on Newsmax with Mark Geist can be viewed at https://twitter.com/ATafoyovsky/status/1353055244037492737.

Butowsky deposition, *TRNS LLC v. Ellen Ratner*.

Citizens' Commission on Benghazi, "Betrayal in Benghazi: A Dereliction of Duty," Accuracy in Media, June 29, 2016, https://www.aim.org/wp-content/uploads/2016/06/AIM-Citizens-Commission-on-Benghazi-FINAL-REPORT-June-2016.pdf.

Former Fox correspondent Adam Housley stated in a declaration submitted in *Rich v. Fox News Network LLC* that Butowsky provided him with information. The declaration can be accessed at https://www.documentcloud.org/documents/6999267-Adam-Housley-Court-Declaration#document/p2/a572614.

Butowsky described first meeting Ratner in several interviews, such as John B. Wells, Ark Midnight, September 14, 2019. He also confirmed it in an email to the author.

"Speaker Series: John LeBoutillier and Ellen Ratner," YouTube, November 15, 2016, https://www.youtube.com/watch?v=gdtkACCxdnc.

Seymour Hersh, interview with author, May 1, 2020.

The transcript of the call between Butowsky and Hersh was submitted in a court filing in the case *Rich v. Butowsky*. The transcript can be accessed at https://www.documentcloud.org/documents/6881859-Hersh-Butowsky-Original-Call-Transcript.html.

CHAPTER 12: ASK ME ANYTHING

James Alefantis, interview with author, September 12, 2018.

Mike Gottlieb and Meryl Governski, interview with author, May 25, 2018.

Molly Levinson, interview with author, July 17, 2018.

Fox News, "Pizzeria Owner Targeted by Fake News Stories Speaks Out," YouTube, December 15, 2016, https://www.youtube.com/watch?v=YXApkzwKIh8.

Margaret Talbot, "Taking Trolls to Court," *New Yorker*, November 28, 2016, https://www.newyorker.com/magazine/2016/12/05/the-attorney-fighting-revenge-porn.

Giulia Segreti, "Facebook CEO Says Group Will Not Become a Media Company," *Reuters*, August 30, 2016, https://www.reuters.com/article/us-facebook-zuckerberg-idUSKCN1141WN.

Tom Kludt, "The Story Behind Alex Jones' Unlikely Pizzagate Apology," CNNMoney, March 30, 2017, https://money.cnn.com/2017/03/30/media/alex-jones-apology-pizzagate-james-alefantis/index.html.

CHAPTER 13: A NICE BUT SOMEWHAT UNCOMFORTABLE MESSAGE

Wheeler's food-safety consultancy was called the Global Food Defense Institute, https://www.myfooddefense.com.

Rod Wheeler, interview with author, April 21, 2020.

Butowsky's first text message to Wheeler appeared in hundreds of pages of text messages between the two men submitted as part of the *Butowsky v. Folkenflik* case. The messages can be accessed at https://www.documentcloud.org/documents/7006525-Ed-Butowsky-and-Rod-Wheeler-text-messages-Feb-to#document/p2/a2091637.

Wheeler described the meeting between himself, Butowsky, and Zimmerman during a November 18, 2019, deposition in Rich v. Butowsky, 1:18-cv-00681 (US District Court, District of Columbia 2018). Portions of that deposition were submitted in publicly accessible filings in the case, which can be

accessed at https://www.documentcloud.org/documents/6660039-2020-01
-16-Exhibits-60-69#document/p5/a2091640.

Butowsky's "Don't mention you know Malia" text appears in the court filing containing Wheeler and Butowsky's text-message history, which can be accessed at https://www.documentcloud.org/documents/7006525-Ed-Butowsky-and
-Rod-Wheeler-text-messages-Feb-to#document/p2/a2091637.

Malia Zimmerman, email to author, March 6, 2022.

Patti Epler, "Editor's Desk: Hawaii Reporter's Malia Zimmerman Bids Aloha," Honolulu Civil Beat, January 12, 2015, https://www.civilbeat.org/2015/01
/editors-desk-hawaii-reporters-malia-zimmerman-bids-aloha/.

Former Fox News reporter, interview with author.

Greta Van Susteren, interview with author, April 23, 2020.

Former Fox News host, interview with author.

Former FoxNews.com editors, interview with author. A spokeswoman for Fox responded to characterizations of FoxNews.com by saying the network's digital operation had dramatically expanded and improved in recent years under the oversight of Porter Berry, a former executive producer for Sean Hannity's show who now runs Fox's digital side.

Brad Bauman, interview with author, August 21, 2019.

Mary and Joel Rich, interview with author, July 20, 2021.

Louise Boyle, "EXCLUSIVE: Murdered DNC Staffer Was About to Join Hillary Clinton Presidential Campaign, Reveals Father," Daily Mail Online, August 16, 2016, https://www.dailymail.co.uk/news/article-3741754/Father
-murdered-DNC-staffer-reveals-son-join-Hillary-Clinton-presidential
-campaign-punching-hole-ugly-rumor-Wikileaks-source.html.

Malia Zimmerman, "Slain DNC Staffer's Father Doubts Wikileaks Link as Cops Seek Answers," FoxNews.com, January 10, 2017, http://web.archive
.org/web/20201111202758/https://www.foxnews.com/politics/2017/01/10
/slain-dnc-staffers-father-doubts-wikileaks-link-as-cops-seek-answers.amp.

Butowsky's emails to Joel Rich cited in this chapter were included in a court filing in Butowsky v. Folkenflik. The emails can be accessed at https://www
.documentcloud.org/documents/20400472-2020_05_08-2020_10_28-bu
towsky-v-folkenflik-exhibit-132-5#document/p11/a2017072.

The signed contract was included in court filings in Rich v. Butowsky, https://
www.documentcloud.org/documents/20400492-2020_03_23-butowsky
-v-folkenflik-118-2#document/p48/a2017095.

Zimmerman's email about the Rich family's contract with Rod Wheeler was included in a court filing in Rich v. Butowsky. It can be accessed at https://
www.documentcloud.org/documents/6776020-2020-02-10-PLAINTIFF
-S-MOTION-and-MEMORANDUM-of.html#document/p46/a551051.

CHAPTER 14: WAR ROOM

Mary and Joel Rich, interview with author, July 20, 2021.

Louise Boyle, "EXCLUSIVE: Republican Lobbyist Says He Has 'Evidence' That 27-Year-Old DNC Analyst Seth Rich Was Murdered After Discovering Russian Operatives Had Hacked the DNC and Has Asked Congress for Investigation," *Daily Mail Online*, February 27, 2017, https://www.daily mail.co.uk/news/article-4264558/GOP-lobbyist-claims-Russia-murder -Seth-Rich.html.

Noah Lanard, "DC Lobbyist Will Hire Actors to Reenact Seth Rich's Murder," *Washingtonian*, March 2, 2017, https://www.washingtonian.com/2017/03 /02/dc-lobbyist-will-hire-actors-to-reenact-seth-richs-murder/.

I obtained Doherty's early emails to Burkman and Doherty's résumé via a public-records request submitted to the Arlington County Police Department.

Rachel Kurzius, "GOP Lobbyist Now Opening 'War Room' Dedicated to Solving Seth Rich Murder," DCist.com, March 23, 2017, https://dcist.com /story/17/03/23/seth-rich-war-room/.

Jack Burkman, interview with author, March 2, 2021.

Deborah Sines, interview with author, March 21, 2019.

Using the Metropolitan Police Department's interactive "Crime Cards" data tool, I located each of the armed robberies in and around Seth's neighborhood in the summer of 2016 and plotted them on a Google Map. The number of crimes and the familiar pattern matched Sines's description of those crimes in interviews with the author. The "Crime Cards" tool is accessible at https://dcatlas.dcgis.dc.gov/crimecards/. The public incident report numbers for the armed robberies in question are CCN-16091291, CCN-16096252, CCN-16111231, CCN-16098585, CCN-16095970, CCN-16111233, CCN-16100088, CCN-16112480, CCN-16090676, CCN-16103403, and CCN-16091294.

CHAPTER 15: GIVE US A WINK

Wheeler described this phone call with Butowsky in his November 18, 2019, deposition in *Rich v. Butowsky*, which can be accessed at https://www .documentcloud.org/documents/6776020-2020-02-10-PLAIN TIFF-S-MOTION-and-MEMORANDUM-of.html#document/p51 /a551054. Wheeler confirmed the conversation in an interview with the author. Butowsky said in an email to the author that he did not remember making these statements to Wheeler.

Rod Wheeler, interview with author, April 21, 2020.

Text messages between Wheeler and Butowsky come from court filings.

Zimmerman's reporting emails were included in court filings in *Butowsky v. Folkenflik*, https://www.documentcloud.org/documents/20400492-2020_03_23-butowsky-v-folkenflik-118-2#document/p62/a2017107.

Zimmerman's emails to Wheeler about getting information from the Rich family were included in court filings in *Rich v. Butowsky*, https://www.documentcloud.org/documents/6660039-2020-01-16-Exhibits-60-69.html#document/p45/a560417.

Mary and Joel Rich, interview with author, July 20, 2021.

Butowsky's email to Wheeler about Detective Joe Della-Camera was included in court filings in *Butowsky v. Folkenflik*, https://www.documentcloud.org/documents/20400492-2020_03_23-butowsky-v-folkenflik-118-2#document/p66/a2017110.

Wheeler memorialized his meeting with Della-Camera in a memo. The memo can be accessed at https://www.documentcloud.org/documents/7012639-Wheeler-Notes-Della-Camera-Meeting-April-25-2017.

Zimmerman's early, unconfirmed draft of her Seth Rich–WikiLeaks story was included in court filings in *Butowsky v. Folkenflik*, https://www.documentcloud.org/documents/20400475-2020_05_08-2020_10_28-butowsky-v-folkenflik-exhibit-132-2#document/p2/a2017075.

Zimmerman's April 29 draft was included in court filings in *Butowsky v. Folkenflik*, https://www.documentcloud.org/documents/6660039-2020-01-16-Exhibits-60-69.html#document/p57/a551148.

Zimmerman's email asking Butowsky and Wheeler if they had "any news" about Seth and WikiLeaks was included in court filings in *Butowsky v. Folkenflik*, https://www.documentcloud.org/documents/6660039-2020-01-16-Exhibits-60-69.html#document/p57/a552813.

Zimmerman's email asking Butowsky and Wheeler to "please ask your sources" was included in court filings in *Rich v. Butowsky*, https://www.documentcloud.org/documents/6660040-2020-01-16-Exhibits-70-79.html#document/p2/a551134.

Butowsky and Zimmerman's text and phone records were disclosed in *Butowsky v. Folkenflik*, https://www.documentcloud.org/documents/6954277-20200512-NPR-filing-re-Butowsky-communications.html.

Butowsky's presence on most phone calls about Seth with Wheeler and Zimmerman comes from Wheeler's deposition in *Rich v. Butowsky*, https://www.documentcloud.org/documents/6660039-2020-01-16-Exhibits-60-69.html#document/p7/a560411.

Butowsky's mention of a "senior Trump person" comes from *Butowsky v. Folkenflik*, https://www.documentcloud.org/documents/7006527-2020-02-20-APPENDIX-TO-DEFENDANTS-RULE-11-MOTION#document/p4/a573574.

Butowsky's claim that "we are working on the case together" comes from *Butowsky v. Folkenflik*, https://www.documentcloud.org/documents/7006 527-2020-02-20-APPENDIX-TO-DEFENDANTS-RULE-11-MO TION#document/p3/a2104385.

Sean Spicer, interview with author, September 3, 2021.

Maggie Haberman, Matthew Rosenberg, Matt Apuzzo, and Glenn Thrush, "Michael Flynn Resigns as National Security Adviser," *New York Times*, February 13, 2017, https://www.nytimes.com/2017/02/13/us/politics/don ald-trump-national-security-adviser-michael-flynn.html.

Michael S. Schmidt, "Comey Memo Says Trump Asked Him to End Flynn Investigation," *New York Times*, May 16, 2017, https://www.nytimes.com /2017/05/16/us/politics/james-comey-trump-flynn-russia-investigation .html.

James Griffiths, "Trump Says He Considered 'This Russia Thing' Before Firing FBI Director Comey," CNN, May 12, 2017, https://www.cnn.com/2017 /05/12/politics/trump-comey-russia-thing/index.html.

Butowsky's emails sent to Seymour Hersh were included in court filings in *Butowsky v. Folkenflik*, https://www.documentcloud.org/documents/20400 492-2020_03_23-butowsky-v-folkenflik-118-2#document/p84/a2017109.

Butowsky's references to "D.O. or Dee O" were included in court filings in *Butowsky v. Folkenflik*, https://www.documentcloud.org/documents/7006 525-Ed-Butowsky-and-Rod-Wheeler-text-messages-Feb-to#document /p45/a574279.

Excerpt of Wheeler deposition in *Rich v. Butowsky*, which can be accessed at https://www.documentcloud.org/documents/6671280-2020-01-17-RE PLY-IN-SUPPORT-OF-PLAINTIFF-S.html#document/p61/a551104. Wheeler confirmed this exchange in an interview with the author. Kash Patel did not respond to multiple requests for comment.

Betsy Swan, "Nunes Ally Kash Patel Who Fought Russia Probe Gets Senior White House National Security Job," Daily Beast, July 31, 2019, https:// www.thedailybeast.com/kash-patel-devin-nunes-ally-who-fought-russia -probe-gets-senior-white-house-national-security-job.

Butowsky and Zimmerman's call to Wheeler with an update about Zimmerman's draft story comes from *Rich v. Fox News Network*, amended complaint filed on January 22, 2020, which can be accessed at https://www.document cloud.org/documents/6999818-2020-01-22-Rich-v-Fox-Amended-Com plaint#document/p12/a2092677.

Butowsky's voicemail for Wheeler claiming that they "have the full attention" of the White House was included in court filings in *Rich v. Butowsky*, https:// www.documentcloud.org/documents/6660040-2020-01-16-Exhibits-70 -79#document/p14/a560407.

Butowsky's text message to Wheeler about Trump reading Zimmerman's draft was included in court filings in *Butowsky v. Folkenflik*, https://www.docu mentcloud.org/documents/7006525-Ed-Butowsky-and-Rod-Wheeler -text-messages-Feb-to#document/p2/a2091637.

Zimmerman's message to Wheeler that her "bosses at Fox want her to go" with her story was described in the amended complaint in *Rich v. Fox News Network*, https://www.documentcloud.org/documents/6999818-2020-01-22-Rich -v-Fox-Amended-Complaint#document/p12/a2092677.

Wheeler's text message to Zimmerman about adding a quote to her story was included in court filings in *Rich v. Butowsky*, https://www.documentcloud .org/documents/6660039-2020-01-16-Exhibits-60-69#document /p42/a560415.

Greg Miller and Greg Jaffe, "Trump Revealed Highly Classified Information to Russian Foreign Minister and Ambassador," *Washington Post*, May 15, 2017, https://www.washingtonpost.com/world/national-security/trump -revealed-highly-classified-information-to-russian-foreign-minister-and -ambassador/2017/05/15/530c172a-3960-11e7-9e48-c4f199710b69_story .html.

Brad Bauman, interview with author, August 21, 2019.

Zimmerman's email saying she had filed her draft was included in court filings in *Butowsky v. Folkenflik*, https://www.documentcloud.org/documents/20400 492-2020_03_23-butowsky-v-folkenflik-118-2#document/p107/a2017336.

Fox 5 DC removed Marraco's story from its website. But it is still accessible using the Internet Archive's Wayback Machine: https://web.archive.org/web/2017 0516030628/https://www.fox5dc.com/news/local-news/254852337-story.

Zimmerman's text message that it "could be really bad" if Fox 5 DC scooped FoxNews.com was included in court filings in *Rich v. Fox News Network*, https://www.documentcloud.org/documents/6999818-2020-01-22-Rich-v -Fox-Amended-Complaint#document/p14/a2092697.

Butowsky's email to Fox producers and hosts was included in court filings in *Butowsky v. Folkenflik*, https://www.documentcloud.org/documents/2040 0485-2020_10_28-butowsky-v-folkenflik-exhibit-214-3#document/p217 /a2011795.

CHAPTER 16: RABBITS OUT OF HATS

Brad Bauman, interview with author, August 21, 2019.

Zimmerman's original May 16, 2017, story is no longer on Fox's website. It can still be accessed at https://web.archive.org/web/20170516113017/http:// www.foxnews.com/politics/2017/05/16/slain-dnc-staffer-had-contact-with -wikileaks-investigator-says.html.

Megan Garber, "It's Too Late for Fox to Retract Its Seth Rich Story," *Atlantic*, May 23, 2017, https://www.theatlantic.com/politics/archive/2017/05/fox -seth-rich/527850/.

The liberal-watchdog group Media Matters for America assembled a detailed timeline of Fox News's coverage of the Seth Rich–WikiLeaks story, which I drew on for this chapter. Matt Gertz, "Fox News' Seth Rich Conspiracy Theory, Two Years Later: A Timeline," Media Matters for America, May 17, 2019, https://www.mediamatters.org/seth-rich-conspiracy-theory/fox-news -seth-rich-conspiracy-theory-two-years-later-timeline.

Lois Beckett, "Newt Gingrich Repeats Seth Rich Conspiracy Theory in Fox Appearance," *Guardian*, May 21, 2017, https://www.theguardian.com/us -news/2017/may/21/newt-gingrich-seth-rich-wikileaks-conspiracy-theory -fox-friends.

Yochai Benkler, interview with author, June 13, 2020.

Yochai Benkler, Robert Faris, and Hal Roberts, *Network Propaganda: Manipulation, Disinformation, and Radicalization in American Politics* (Oxford: Oxford University Press, 2018).

Robert Costa, Sarah Ellison, and Josh Dawsey, "Hannity's Rising Role in Trump's World: 'He Basically Has a Desk in the Place,'" *Washington Post*, April 17, 2018, https://www.washingtonpost.com/politics/hannitys-rising -role-in-trumps-world-he-basically-has-a-desk-in-the-place/2018/04/17 /e2483018-4260-11e8-8569-26fda6b404c7_story.html. Sean Hannity did not respond to a request for comment sent by author.

Former Fox News host, interview with author.

Jonathan Rich's since-deleted tweet can be accessed at https://www.document cloud.org/documents/21046591-jonathan-rich-tweet-seth-rich-hannity -screen-shot-2020-07-26-at-104628-am.

Mary and Joel Rich, interview with author, July 20, 2021.

Alex Seitz-Wald, "DNC Staffer's Murder Draws Fresh Conspiracy Theories," NBC News, May 16, 2017, https://www.nbcnews.com/politics/white-house /dnc-staffer-s-murder-draws-fresh-conspiracy-theories-n760186.

CHAPTER 17: PANIC AT THE NETWORK

"Press Gaggle by Press Secretary Spicer," Trumpwhitehouse.archives.gov, May 16, 2017, https://trumpwhitehouse.archives.gov/briefings-statements/press -gaggle-press-secretary-spicer/.

Brad Bauman, interview with author, August 22, 2019.

Peter Hermann, "Family of Slain Seth Rich Says Reports That He Fed DNC Info to WikiLeaks Are Untrue," *Washington Post*, May 16, 2017, https:// www.washingtonpost.com/local/public-safety/family-of-slain-seth-rich

-says-reports-he-fed-wikileaks-dnc-info-are-untrue/2017/05/16/9b32ef9c
-3a46-11e7-8854-21f359183e8c_story.html?utm_term=.a1e4c4fc358d.

The rewritten version of Zimmerman's May 16 story is no longer viewable on FoxNews.com. It can be accessed at https://web.archive.org/web/2017051 6153020/www.foxnews.com/politics/2017/05/16/slain-dnc-staffer-had -contact-with-wikileaks-investigator-says.html.

Oliver Darcy, "Story on DNC Staffer's Murder Dominated Conservative Media—Hours Later It Fell Apart," CNNMoney, May 16, 2017, https:// money.cnn.com/2017/05/16/media/seth-rich-family-response-claims-of -wikileaks-contact/index.html.

Butowsky's text message to Wheeler telling him to "speak to no one before you talk to me" was included in court filings in *Butowsky v. Folkenflik*, https:// www.documentcloud.org/documents/7006525-Ed-Butowsky-and -Rod-Wheeler-text-messages-Feb-to#document/p59/a2051500.

Zimmerman's text message about Wheeler and CNN was included in court filings in *Butowsky v. Folkenflik*, https://www.documentcloud.org/documents /20400485-2020_10_28-butowsky-v-folkenflik-exhibit-214-3#document /p126/a2051637.

I used the Internet Archive to view the May 2017 episodes of *Hannity* that covered the Seth Rich–WikiLeaks story.

Wheeler's appearance on Hannity's show can be accessed at https://www.media matters.org/embed/clips/2019:05:07:66036:fnc-hannity-5162017-wheeler.

Claudia Koerner, "The Private Detective Who Ignited a Clinton Conspiracy Theory Says He Was Misquoted," BuzzFeed News, May 17, 2017, https:// www.buzzfeednews.com/article/claudiakoerner/the-private-detective-who -ignited-a-clinton-conspiracy.

Rachel Kurzius, "Fox 5 Clarifies Discredited Seth Rich Story, but Family Wants Full Retraction and Apology," DCist, May 18, 2017, https://dcist.com /story/17/05/18/fox-5-clarifies-discredited-seth-ri/.

Brad Bauman, email shared with author on April 22, 2020.

Fox News' internal emails about the reaction to Zimmerman's story were included in court filings in *Butowsky v. Folkenflik*, https://www.document cloud.org/documents/20400492-2020_03_23-butowsky-v-folkenflik -118-2#document/p122/a2018680. The original tweet by the Russian embassy in the UK can be accessed at https://archive.ph/DfZqr.

The Fox PR employee's internal email asking for an update about the network's response was included in court filings in *Butowsky v. Folkenflik*, https:// www.documentcloud.org/documents/20400492-2020_03_23-butows ky-v-folkenflik-118-2#document/p122/a2018680.

The Fox PR employee's email about looking foolish was included in court filings in *Butowsky v. Folkenflik*, https://www.documentcloud.org/documents/2040

0492-2020_03_23-butowsky-v-folkenflik-118-2#document/p122/a205 1612.

Zimmerman's email to Wheeler asking him to "Please call me asap" was included in court filings in *Butowsky v. Folkenflik*, https://www.documentcloud.org /documents/20400484-2020_05_08-2020_10_28-butowsky-v-folkenf lik-exhibit-132-14#document/p2/a2051609.

Butowsky's "Total BS" email to Zimmerman was included in court filings in *Butowsky v. Folkenflik*, https://www.documentcloud.org/documents/20400 484-2020_05_08-2020_10_28-butowsky-v-folkenflik-exhibit-132-14#doc ument/p3/a2017831.

The transcript of the three-way call on May 16, 2017, between Butowsky, Wheeler, and Zimmerman was included in court filings in *Rich v. Butowsky*, https://www.documentcloud.org/documents/6660040-2020-01-16-Exhib its-70-79#document/p23/a2051614.

Rod Wheeler, interviews with author, April 21, 2020, and May 19, 2020.

Butowsky's supposed Facebook response for Wheeler and Wheeler's email to Butowsky about it were included in court filings in *Butowsky v. Folkenflik*, https://www.documentcloud.org/documents/20400489-2020_03_26-bu towsky-v-folkenflik-122-2#document/p28/a2018684.

Butowsky's comment about "Putting an end to the Russian bullshit" was included in the amended complaint in *Wheeler v. Fox*, https://www.documentcloud .org/documents/21090352-2017_10_23_wheeler-v-fox-amended-com plaint#document/p36/a2061139.

Butowsky's admission that he outlined a plan to pressure Seymour Hersh by dis- tributing a recording of Hersh was included in court filings in *Butowsky v. Folkenflik*, https://www.documentcloud.org/documents/6994999-2020-06 -22-REDACTED-MOTION-for-SANCTIONS#document/p28 /a573683.

The emails between Zimmerman and Greg Wilson about an alleged NSA source were included in court filings in *Butowsky v. Folkenflik*, https://www.docu mentcloud.org/documents/20400492-2020_03_23-butowsky-v-folkenf lik-118-2#document/p114/a2051618.

Hannity would later delete these tweets. I accessed them using the Internet Archive's Wayback Machine: https://web.archive.org/web/20171102120805 /https://twitter.com/seanhannity/status/865290701306826753.

Media Matters Staff, "Sean Hannity: 'I'm Not Backing Off' the Seth Rich Con- spiracy," Media Matters for America, May 19, 2017, https://www.media matters.org/sean-hannity/sean-hannity-im-not-backing-seth-rich-cons piracy.

CHAPTER 18: NEVER SAY SORRY

Aaron Rich, interview with author, May 21, 2021.

Seth's Reddit posts about Newfoundland dogs and dating in a city can be accessed at https://archive.is/8NZjv and https://archive.is/ajxrO.

The May 19, 2017, Reddit thread on r/The_Donald about discovering Seth's account on the platform can be accessed at https://web.archive.org/web/201 70519181345/https://www.reddit.com/r/The_Donald/comments/6c4klg /since_i_found_seth_richs_reddit_account_the/.

Andrew Therriault, interview with author, November 4, 2018.

Mary Rich, interview with author, July 20, 2021.

The details about Fox executives trying to understand what went wrong with Zimmerman's story were included in the amended complaint in *Wheeler v. 21st Century Fox*, filed on October 23, 2017, US District Court for the Southern District of New York, https://www.documentcloud.org/documents/2109 0352-2017_10_23_wheeler-v-fox-amended-complaint#document/p17 /a2061138.

Tweet by Kim Dotcom (@KimDotcom), "If Congress includes #SethRich case into their Russia probe I'll give written testimony with evidence that Seth Rich was @Wikileaks source," May 19, 2017, 6:42 p.m., https://twitter.com /kimdotcom/status/865699156278484992.

Sean Hannity's "You have that evidence" tweet was deleted but can still be accessed at https://web.archive.org/web/20170520061411/https://twitter .com/seanhannity/.

Mike Gottlieb, interview with author, June 23, 2021.

Jim Hoft, "BREAKING VIDEO: Seth Rich's Parents Grateful for Assistance Finding Son's Murderers—No Indication They Want Search Stopped," Gateway Pundit, May 21, 2017, https://www.thegatewaypundit.com/2017 /05/breaking-seth-richs-parents-grateful-for-assistance-finding-sons -2-murderers-no-indication-they-want-search-stopped/.

The online posts calling Bauman a "hitman" were included in the original complaint in *Bauman v. Butowsky*, filed on May 21, 2018, https://www.docu mentcloud.org/documents/6885936-2018-05-21-Bauman-complaint-v-Bu towsky-Couch#document/p13/a572918.

Mary Rich and Joel Rich, "We're Seth Rich's Parents. Stop Politicizing Our Son's Murder," *Washington Post*, May 23, 2017, https://www.washington post.com/opinions/were-seth-richs-parents-stop-politicizing-our-sons -murder/2017/05/23/164cf4dc-3fee-11e7-9869-bac8b446820a_story .html.

Oliver Darcy, "Seth Rich's Brother Pleads with Hannity to Stop Spreading Conspiracy Theory," CNN, May 23, 2017, https://money.cnn.com/2017/05/23/media/seth-rich-family-letter-hannity-fox-news/.

"Statement on Coverage of Seth Rich Murder Investigation," Fox News, May 23, 2017, https://www.foxnews.com/politics/statement-on-coverage-of-seth-rich-murder-investigation.

Andrew Kirell, "Fox News Retracts Article on Seth Rich Murder Investigation," Daily Beast, May 23, 2017, https://www.thedailybeast.com/cheats/2017/05/23/fox-news-retracts-article-on-seth-rich-murder-investigation.

Matt Gertz, "How Sean Hannity Became the Champion of the Seth Rich Conspiracy Theory," Media Matters for America, May 30, 2017, https://www.mediamatters.org/sean-hannity/how-sean-hannity-became-champion-seth-rich-conspiracy-theory.

Sean Hannity's "Stay tuned" tweet can be accessed at https://web.archive.org/web/20171111234856/https://twitter.com/seanhannity/status/867211447901851649?ref_src=twsrc%5Etfw&ref_url=https%3A%2F%2Fwww.mediamatters.org%2Fblog%2F2017%2F05%2F24%2Fhow-murder-dnc-staffer-turned-right-wing-conspiracy%2F216644.

CHAPTER 19: THE WIDENING GYRE

Scott Taylor, "READ: Independent Group Releases New Report on Seth Rich Murder Investigation," WJLA, June 20, 2017, https://wjla.com/news/local/read-new-report-released-on-seth-richs-murder-investigation.

A video of the press conference can be accessed at https://www.facebook.com/watch/live/?ref=external&v=10155469038443734.

The Profiling Project v. The District of Columbia, Superior Court for the District of Columbia, original complaint filed on May 31, 2017, https://www.documentcloud.org/documents/21747284-burkman-profiling-project-seth-rich-lawsuit.

Doherty's emails to Burkman, his registration of Profiling Project LLC, and Burkman's responses were obtained via a public-records request to the Arlington County Police Department.

Online disinformation expert Melissa Ryan documented the protest in a series of tweets, on which I relied. See, e.g, https://twitter.com/MelissaRyan/status/884505139377311750/photo/1 and https://twitter.com/MelissaRyan/status/884505961829982208.

Jack Posobiec's Periscope broadcast of the protest can be accessed at https://www.pscp.tv/w/1lPKqyvWbLlKb.

Twitter would later suspend Roger Stone's account. An archived version of this tweet can be accessed at https://web.archive.org/web/20170710233904/https://twitter.com/rogerjstonejr/status/884526482160320512.

Mary and Joel Rich, interview with author, July 20, 2021.

Andrew Therriault, interview with author, November 4, 2018.

"Intel Vets Challenge 'Russia Hack' Evidence," Consortium News, July 24, 2017, https://consortiumnews.com/2017/07/24/intel-vets-challenge-russia-hack -evidence/.

Michael W. Robbins, "The Skeptical Spy," *Mother Jones*, March 10, 2004, https:// www.motherjones.com/politics/2004/03/skeptical-spy/.

Thomas Drake, interview with author, July 29, 2021.

Patrick Lawrence, "A New Report Raises Big Questions about Last Year's DNC Hack," *The Nation*, August 9, 2017, https://www.thenation.com/article /archive/a-new-report-raises-big-questions-about-last-years-dnc-hack/.

"A Leak or a Hack? A Forum on the VIPS Memo," *The Nation*, September 1, 2017, https://www.thenation.com/article/archive/a-leak-or-a-hack-a-forum -on-the-vips-memo/.

"Former NSA Official: Dems' Russia Hacking Story Likely Bogus," *Fox News Insider*, August 14, 2017, https://insider.foxnews.com/2017/08/14/russian -hacking-2016-election-nsa-member-says-trump-story-false.

Wheeler v. 21st Century Fox, original complaint filed on August 1, 2017, US District Court for the Southern District of New York, https://www.document cloud.org/documents/21900459-rod-wheeler-original-complaint-21st -century-fox.

Mary and Joel Rich, interview with author, July 20, 2021.

David Folkenflik, "Behind Fox News' Baseless Seth Rich Story: The Untold Tale," NPR, August 1, 2017, npr.org/2017/08/01/540783715/lawsuit-alle ges-fox-news-and-trump-supporter-created-fake-news-story.

Bill Binney, interview with author, March 6, 2021.

Chris Parker, interview with author, March 18, 2021.

Duncan Campbell and James Risen, "CIA Director Met Advocate of Disputed DNC Hack Theory—At Trump's Request," The Intercept, November 7, 2017, https://theintercept.com/2017/11/07/dnc-hack-trump-cia-director-william -binney-nsa/.

I drew on biographical details about Binney that were included in a *New Yorker* profile of fellow NSA whistleblower Thomas Drake: Jane Mayer, "The Secret Sharer," *New Yorker*, May 23, 2011, https://www.newyorker.com/magazine /2011/05/23/the-secret-sharer.

Pompeo's "The president has directed me" quote came from Binney, in his interview with author.

Deborah Sines, interview with author, March 20 and 21, 2019.

Jim Hoft, "Debbie Wasserman Schultz's Brother Steven Wasserman Accused of Burying Seth Rich Case," Gateway Pundit, May 30, 2017, https://www.the gatewaypundit.com/2017/05/debbie-wasserman-schultzs-brother-steven -wasserman-accused-burying-seth-rich-case/.

Phil Hornshaw, "The Latest Seth Rich Conspiracy Theory Is Also Why Steve Scalise's Doctor Is Trending," *The Wrap*, June 16, 2017, https://www.thewrap.com/seth-rich-conspiracy-theory-steve-scalise-doctor/.

CHAPTER 20: Q CLEARANCE

Henry Brean and Katelyn Newberg, "Henderson Man in Armored Truck on Hoover Dam Bypass Bridge Arrested," *Las Vegas Review-Journal*, June 15, 2018, https://www.reviewjournal.com/crime/henderson-man-in-armored-truck-on-hoover-dam-bypass-bridge-arrested/.

Harry Brean and Dave Hawkins, "Suspect in Hoover Dam Standoff Writes Trump, Cites Conspiracy in Letters," *Las Vegas Review-Journal*, July 13, 2018, https://www.reviewjournal.com/crime/courts/suspect-in-hoover-dam-standoff-writes-trump-cites-conspiracy-in-letters/.

Richard Ruelas, "QAnon Follower Sentenced to Nearly 8 Years in Prison for Standoff Near Hoover Dam," *Arizona Republic*, January 4, 2021, https://www.azcentral.com/story/news/local/arizona/2021/01/04/qanon-follower-matthew-wright-sentenced-hoover-dam-bridge-standoff/4134612001/.

Wright's letters can be accessed at https://www.reviewjournal.com/crime/courts/suspect-in-hoover-dam-standoff-writes-trump-cites-conspiracy-in-letters/.

Joe Schwarcz, "QAnon's Adrenochrome Quackery," McGill University's Office for Science and Society, February 10, 2022, https://www.mcgill.ca/oss/article/pseudoscience/qanons-adrenochrome-quackery.

EJ Dickson, "QAnon Followers Think JFK Jr. Is Coming Back on the 4th of July," *Rolling Stone*, July 3, 2019, https://www.rollingstone.com/culture/culture-features/qanon-jfk-jr-conspiracy-theory-854938/.

Kevin Roose, "What Is QAnon, the Viral Pro-Trump Conspiracy Theory?" *New York Times*, September 3, 2021, https://www.nytimes.com/article/what-is-qanon.html.

Paris Martineau, "The Storm Is the New Pizzagate—Only Worse," *New York Magazine*, December 19, 2017, https://nymag.com/intelligencer/2017/12/qanon-4chan-the-storm-conspiracy-explained.html.

The investigative website Bellingcat has documented and analyzed Q's "drops." See https://www.bellingcat.com/news/americas/2021/01/29/the-qanon-timeline/.

A running archive of all Q drops can be accessed at https://qalerts.app/. The first Q drop can be accessed at https://qalerts.app/?n=1.

David D. Kirkpatrick, "Who Is Behind QAnon? Linguistic Detectives Find Fingerprints," *New York Times*, February 19, 2022, https://www.nytimes.com/2022/02/19/technology/qanon-messages-authors.html.

Brandy Zadrozny and Ben Collins, "Who Is Behind the QAnon Conspiracy? We've Traced It to Three People," NBC News, August 14, 2018, https://

www.nbcnews.com/tech/tech-news/how-three-conspiracy-theorists-took
-q-sparked-qanon-n900531.

Zadrozny and Collins covered Diaz's role in spreading QAnon. Diaz also published her own blog post about Q, which can be accessed at https://steemit
.com/drama/@tracybeanz/she-stood-in-the-storm.

Mark Landler, "What Did President Trump Mean by 'Calm Before the Storm'?"
New York Times, October 6, 2017, https://www.nytimes.com/2017/10/06
/us/politics/trump-calls-meeting-with-military-leaders-the-calm-before
-the-storm.html.

Joseph Menn, "QAnon Received Earlier Boost from Russian Accounts on Twitter, Archives Show," *Reuters*, November 2, 2020, https://www.reuters.com
/article/usa-election-qanon-cyber-idUKL1N2HD00Z.

Mike Rothschild, "Why Does the QAnon Conspiracy Thrive Despite All Its
Unfulfilled Prophecies?," *Time*, June 30, 2021, https://time.com/6076590
/qanon-conspiracy-why-people-believe/.

Tracy Beanz, "Operation Justice: We The People - A March for Transparency," YouTube, February 15, 2018, https://www.youtube.com/watch?v=_cws-B_aCLw.

Daily Beast reporter Will Sommer posted tweets of the march, see, e.g., https://
twitter.com/willsommer/status/982606808404684800.

CHAPTER 21: NEVER CALL HIM BROTHER

Matt Couch's tweet "Our Teams are digging" was included in court filings in *Rich
v. Butowsky*, https://www.documentcloud.org/documents/4425381-Aaron
-Rich-complaint-v-Butowsky-Couch-America#document/p17/a572970.

Cassandra Fairbanks, "Brother of Seth Rich Works for Government Contractor
That Provides Cyber Defense," Big League Politics, August 1, 2017, https://
bigleaguepolitics.com/brother-seth-rich-works-government-contractor
-provides-cyber-defense/.

Aaron Rich, interview with author, May 21, 2021.

Couch's descriptions of himself as a "conservative truth slinger" and an "investigative journalist" were found in past Twitter bios of his. For instance: https://
web.archive.org/web/20170319141030/twitter.com/realmattcouch.

Couch's leading role in pushing the allegation that Aaron helped Seth steal
DNC emails is laid out in the original complaint in *Rich v. Butowsky*, which
can be accessed at https://www.documentcloud.org/documents/4425381
-Aaron-Rich-complaint-v-Butowsky-Couch-America#document/p21
/a2011794.

I drew on Couch's public LinkedIn profile for details about his background. The
profile can be accessed at https://www.linkedin.com/in/matt-couch-a598
a853/.

The details about Couch's personal finances are drawn from a voluntary petition for Chapter 13 bankruptcy filed by Couch and his wife at the time, Jennifer. The petition was filed in the US Bankruptcy Court, Western District of Arkansas, on April 25, 2014. It can be accessed online at https://www.documentcloud.org/documents/21578014-matt-couch-chapter-13-bankruptcy-filing.

Couch's discussion of "enlisting a group" of investigators comes from an archived version of his website located at https://web.archive.org/web/20180530 135645/https://www.americafirstmg.com/single-post/2017/08/06/Meet-The-America-First-Media-Team.

"Live from the Seth Rich Vigil in Washington D.C.," @RealMattCouch, Periscope, July 10, 2017, https://www.pscp.tv/w/1ypKdrqeZwVJW.

"Live from Lou's City Bar Part 2," @RealMattCouch, Periscope, July 7, 2017, https://www.pscp.tv/w/1ypKdrZborjJW.

"Live from Washington DC from Flagler and W," @RealMattCouch, Periscope, July 7, 2017, https://www.pscp.tv/w/1LyxBBWenjMxN.

"Breaking: Revealing known Roommate of Seth Rich, and his ties to Clinton," @RealMattCouch, Periscope, July 9, 2017, https://www.pscp.tv/w/1lPJq yMXebQJb.

"Another Seth Rich Bombshell Live from Washington D.C.," @RealMatt Couch, Periscope, July 8, 2017, https://www.pscp.tv/w/1RDGlZzBnVkxL.

"America First Media Live Tuesday #SethRich ShawnLucas," @RealMattCouch, Periscope, August 9, 2017, https://www.pscp.tv/w/1DXGyOMyQjdxM.

Other of Couch's comments specifically about Aaron were included in the original complaint in *Rich v. Butowsky*, original complaint, https://www.documentcloud.org/documents/4425381-Aaron-Rich-complaint-v-Butowsky-Couch-America#document/p17/a572970.

Butowsky's emails to Joel were included in court filings in *Butowsky v. Folkenflik*, https://www.documentcloud.org/documents/20400472-2020_05_08-2020 _10_28-butowsky-v-folkenflik-exhibit-132-5#document/p18/a2018734.

Butowsky's comments during Couch's August 15, 2017, Periscope livestream were described in *Rich v. Butowsky*, original complaint, https://www.documentcloud.org/documents/4425381-Aaron-Rich-complaint-v-Butowsky-Couch-America#document/p18/a2094359.

Butowsky confirmed this meeting in a set of interrogatories he submitted in *Rich v. Butowsky*, https://www.documentcloud.org/documents/6776020-2020 -02-10-PLAINTIFF-S-MOTION-and-MEMORANDUM-of#document/p28/a551047.

Thomas Schoenberger's deposition in *Rich v. Butowsky*: https://www.document cloud.org/documents/6671280-2020-01-17-REPLY-IN-SUPPORT -OF-PLAINTIFF-S#document/p70/a2094371. Butowsky's lawyer Ty

Clevenger responded to Schoenberger's testimony by saying that "Ed is prohibited from commenting, but Schoenberger has zero credibility. Just look at his fabulist claims."

Deborah Sines, interview with author, March 21, 2019.

Couch has since deleted the DCPatriot.com post about the witness. An archived version, with identifying details redacted, can be accessed at https://www.documentcloud.org/documents/21902038-2017_11_11-america-first-media-group-identifies-police-witness-in-seth-rich-murder-case-matt-couch.

Kim LaCapria, "DNC Lawsuit Process Server Shawn Lucas Dead," Snopes, August 4, 2016, https://www.snopes.com/news/2016/08/04/dnc-lawsuit-process-server-shawn-lucas-has-died/.

CHAPTER 22: THE WORST BEST OPTION

Aaron Rich, interview with author, May 21, 2021.

Aaron Rich's letters to Couch and Butowsky were included in filings in *Rich v. Butowsky*. Couch letter: https://www.documentcloud.org/documents/6660033-2020-01-16-Exhibits-1-9#document/p8/a546511; and Butowsky letter: https://www.documentcloud.org/documents/6660038-2020-01-16-Exhibits-50-59.html#document/p49/a546524.

Rich v. Butowsky, original complaint filed on March 28, 2018.

James Lyons, "More Cover-up Questions," *Washington Times*, March 1, 2018, https://www.documentcloud.org/documents/6660038-2020-01-16-Exhibits-50-59#document/p12/a2018772.

Meryl Governski, interview with author, May 25, 2018.

Mike Gottlieb, interview with author, May 25, 2018.

"We know for a fact": *Rich v. Butowsky*, original complaint filed on March 28, 2018.

Mark Mueller, interview with author, March 18, 2021.

Twitter suspended @ThinBlueLR, but an archived snapshot of the account can be accessed at https://web.archive.org/web/20170904165831/twitter.com/thinbluelr.

"The Matt and Blue Show LIVE," Periscope, January 15, 2018, https://www.pscp.tv/RealMattCouch/1ynJOoZVeowJR.

Doug Berlin, interview with author, March 23, 2022.

"What's New in the Metropolitan Police Department," September 6, 2013, https://mpdc.dc.gov/sites/default/files/dc/sites/mpdc/release_content/attachments/wn_130906.pdf.

Berlin's "Officer of the year" award was mentioned by a local Shaw neighborhood Twitter account located at https://twitter.com/Shawington/status/675861823736934401.

Matt Couch declined to comment on his interactions with Berlin, saying only, "I have no idea what Doug Berlin told you."

Sines's description of reporting Berlin's social-media posts to MPD matches Berlin's description of his decision to resign from MPD.

Rich v. Fox News Network, original complaint filed on March 13, 2018, https://www.documentcloud.org/documents/4410424-Rich-family-complaint-March-13-2018.

Michael del Moro and Catherine Thorbecke, "Slain DNC Staffer Was 'Murdered Again' in Since-Retracted Fox News Story, Family Says," ABC News, March 15, 2018, https://abcnews.go.com/GMA/News/slain-dnc-staffer-murdered-retracted-fox-news-story/story?id=53758753.

"Intentional Infliction of Emotional Distress," New York City Bar, Legal Referral Service, https://www.nycbar.org/get-legal-help/article/personal-injury-and-accidents/infliction-emotional-distress/.

Rich v. Butowsky, original complaint filed on March 26, 2018, https://www.documentcloud.org/documents/4425381-Aaron-Rich-complaint-v-Butowsky-Couch-America.

CHAPTER 23: RENDEZVOUS

Gary Frazier v. DNC Services Corporation and Hillary Clinton, original complaint filed on October 30, 2017, Superior Court of the District of Columbia, https://www.documentcloud.org/documents/21170594-2017_10_30-burkman-gary-frazier-complaint.

Frazier v. DNC, "Notice of Plaintiff's Non-Opposition to the Democratic National Committee's Motion to Dismiss," filed on December 13, 2017, https://www.documentcloud.org/documents/21170593-2017_12_13-burkman-drops-frazier-case.

Jeff Mordock, "Jack Burkman, D.C. Lobbyist, Offers $25K for Evidence of FBI Wrongdoing," *Washington Times*, February 8, 2018, https://www.washingtontimes.com/news/2018/feb/8/jack-burkman-dc-lobbyist-offers-25k-evidence-fbi-w/.

Burkman's interactions with the "whistleblower" are described in documents obtained from the Arlington County Police Department via a public-records request. The outlines of the story were also described in news stories at the time, see, e.g., Rachel Weiner, "Lobbyist Says He Was Nearly Killed by Man He Hired to Investigate Seth Rich's Death," March 19, 2018, https://www.washingtonpost.com/local/public-safety/lobbyist-says-he-was-nearly-killed-by-man-he-hired-to-investigate-seth-richs-death/2018/03/19/a4261e48-2baa-11e8-8688-e053ba58f1e4_story.html.

Jack Burkman, interview with author, March 2, 2021.

The attack on Burkman at the Marriott is described in documents obtained via a public-records request from the Arlington County Police Department.

Rachel Weiner, "Ex-Marine Admits He Lured Seth Rich Conspiracy Theorist Jack Burkman to a Hotel Parking Garage, Then Shot Him," *Washington Post*, December 3, 2018, https://www.washingtonpost.com/local/public -safety/disgruntled-ex-employee-of-conspiracy-theorist-admits-shooting -him/2018/12/03/e5df4478-f719-11e8-8c9a-860ce2a8148f_story.html.

Press conference organized by Jack Burkman and attended by author, April 24, 2018.

Keith L. Alexander, "19-Year-Old Found Guilty of First-Degree Murder in Shootings of Teen, Off-Duty U.S. Secret Service Officer," *Washington Post*, March 9, 2018, https://www.washingtonpost.com/local/public-safety/19 -year-old-found-guilty-of-first-degree-murder-in-shootings-of-teen-off -duty-us-secret-service-officer/2018/03/09/573f9640-2286-11e8-badd -7c9f29a55815_story.html.

Deborah Sines, interview with author, March 20 and 21, 2019.

The Special Counsel's office memorialized the meeting with Sines in what's known as an FD-302. A heavily redacted version of that document was later released as a part of a Freedom of Information Act lawsuit and can be accessed at https://www.documentcloud.org/documents/20695594-210423 -seth-rich-documents#document/p65/a2032536.

CHAPTER 24: EXTREME AND OUTRAGEOUS

Mary and Joel Rich, interview with author, November 16, 2021.

"District Judge Hon. George B. Daniels," US District Court, Southern District of New York, https://www.nysd.uscourts.gov/hon-george-b-daniels.

Jonathan P. Hicks, "The Mayor's Quiet Counselor," *New York Times*, May 8, 1993, https://timesmachine.nytimes.com/timesmachine/1993/05/08/04499 3.html?pageNumber=25.

Benjamin Weiser, "Judge's Decisions Are Conspicuously Late," *New York Times*, December 6, 2004, https://www.nytimes.com/2004/12/06/nyregion/judges -decisions-are-conspicuously-late.html.

A transcript of the oral arguments held on June 20, 2018, in *Rich v. Fox News Network LLC* can be accessed at https://www.documentcloud.org/docu ments/21171453-2018_06_20-rich-v-fox-oral-arguments-transcript.

Rachel Pereira, "Four Federal Judges Talk About Their Journey to the Bench," American Bar Association, February 12, 2019, https://www.americanbar .org/groups/litigation/committees/diversity-inclusion/articles/2019/winter 2019-four-federal-judges-talk-about-their-journey-to-the-bench/.

Mike Gottlieb, interview with author, June 23, 2021.

Ty Clevenger's application to appear in *Rich v. Butowsky* can be accessed at https://www.documentcloud.org/documents/21171860-2018_05_18-clev enger-application-appear-in-aarons-case.

Clevenger's "Will find that very interesting" email was included in court filings in *Rich v. Butowsky*, https://www.documentcloud.org/documents/21580913 -2018_06_13-gottlieb-opposition-to-clevenger-pro-hac-vice#document /p179/a2104730.

Ty Clevenger, "Why Won't Seth Rich's Brother Authorize Wikileaks to Tell What It Knows?," *Lawflog* (blog), June 11, 2018, https://lawflog.com/?p=1937.

"Opposition to Ty Clevenger's Motion for Permission to Appear Pro Hac Vice," *Rich v. Butowsky*, filed on June 13, 2018, https://www.documentcloud.org /documents/21171862-2018_06_13-gottlieb-opposition-to-clevenger-pro -hac-vice. In an email to the author, Clevenger emphasized that much of the disciplinary issues included in Gottlieb's opposition motion stemmed from Clevenger's representation of the same client, a former classmate named Wade Robertson. He said that he had sued opposing counsel in response to this litigation. He added that his application to appear in *Rich v. Butowsky* "did not hide anything."

"Memorandum & Order," *Scottie Nell Hughes v. Twenty-First Century Fox*, US District Court, Southern District of New York, June 25, 2018, https://www .documentcloud.org/documents/21903341-judges-denial-of-clevenger -pro-hac-vice-application-in-scottie-nell-hughes-case.

United States of America v. Viktor Borisovich Netyksho, et al., US District Court, District of Columbia, filed on July 13, 2018, https://www.justice.gov/file /1080281/download.

"Memorandum Decision and Order," *Wheeler v. Twenty-First Century Fox*, US District Court, Southern District of New York, filed on August 2, 2018, https://www.documentcloud.org/documents/21171690-2018-08-02 -rod-wheeler-dismissal-daniels.

"Memorandum Decision and Order," *Rich v. Fox News Network*, filed on August 2, 2018, https://www.documentcloud.org/documents/21171691-2018-08 -03-judge-daniels-order-dismiss-joel-mary-lawsuit#document/p14 /a2071670.

Brad Bauman, interview with author, August 21, 2019.

Jeff Benjamin, "Exonerated in Defamation Suits, Ed Butowsky Is Out for Blood," InvestmentNews, August 6, 2018, https://www.investmentnews.com/exo nerated-in-defamation-suits-ed-butowsky-is-out-for-blood-75434.

CHAPTER 25: A SIGN IN THE CROWD

Video footage of Trump's Tampa rally can be accessed at https://www.you tube.com/watch?v=fhF2XRWpZQQ.

Alexander Mallin, "White House Dodges 'QAnon' Questions as Conspiracy Theory Hits Mainstream," ABC News, August 8, 2018, https://abcnews.go .com/Politics/white-house-dodges-qanon-questions-conspiracy-theo ry-hits/story?id=56987934.

Asawin Suebsaeng and Will Sommer, "Trump Meets QAnon Kook Who Believes Dems Run Pedophile Cult," Daily Beast, August 24, 2018, https:// www.thedailybeast.com/trump-in-oval-office-meets-promoter-of-qanon -conspiracy-theory-that-says-democrats-run-pedophile-cult.

"August to September 2018": Edward Tian, "The QAnon Timeline," Bellingcat, January 29, 2021, https://www.bellingcat.com/news/americas/2021/01/29 /the-qanon-timeline/.

Jana Winter, "Exclusive: FBI Document Warns Conspiracy Theories Are a New Domestic Terrorism Threat," Yahoo News, August 1, 2019, https://news .yahoo.com/fbi-documents-conspiracy-theories-terrorism-160000507 .html.

Ali Watkins, "He Wasn't Seeking to Kill a Mob Boss. He Was Trying to Help Trump, His Lawyer Says," *New York Times*, July 21, 2019, https://www .nytimes.com/2019/07/21/nyregion/gambino-shooting-anthony-comello -frank-cali.html.

Eric Hananoki, "Nevada GOP-Backed Congressional Candidate Promotes QAnon Video," Media Matters for America, October 30, 2018, https:// www.mediamatters.org/qanon-conspiracy-theory/nevada-gop-backed -congressional-candidate-promotes-qanon-video.

Those lawsuits are Chapwood Capital Inv. Mgmt., LLC v. Charles Schwab & Co., 4:18-CV-548 (E.D. Texas 2019); Butowsky v. Folkenflik; Butowsky v. Susman Godfrey (District Court, 416th Judicial District, Collin County, Texas); Butowsky v. Gottlieb, 4:19-CV-180 (E.D. Texas 2020), Butowsky v. Wigdor, 4:19-cv-577-ALM-KPJ (E.D. Texas 2020); Butowsky v. Democratic National Committee, 4:19-cv-00582 (E.D. Texas 2019). The lawsuits were described in a filing submitted in *Butowsky v. Folkenflik*, which can be accessed at https://www.documentcloud.org/documents/6660031-2020-01 -16-Opp-to-EOT-Motion-FINAL#document/p15/a544315.

Butowsky's appearance on "Ark Midnight," September 14, 2019. A transcript of this interview was submitted in *Rich v. Butowsky*, https://www.document cloud.org/documents/6660037-2020-01-16-Exhibits-40-49#document /p23/a2071849.

Butowsky made similar comments in an interview on the show "America, Can We Talk?" on September 10, 2019. The interview can be accessed at https:// americacanwetalk.org/ed-butowsky-acwt-interview-9-10-19/.

Joel Rich, interview with author, May 20, 2021.

A recording of the oral arguments before the Second Circuit can be accessed at https://www.ca2.uscourts.gov/decisions.

CHAPTER 26: DEFENDANT

Deborah Sines, interview with author, March 19 and 20, 2019.

Mike Gottlieb, interview with author, June 23, 2021. Assange's lawyer Jennifer Robinson did not respond to a request for comment.

The suit filed against Gottlieb was Butowsky v. Gottlieb, 4:19-CV-180 (E.D. Texas 2020).

Washington Times Staff, "Retraction: Aaron Rich and the Murder of Seth Rich," *Washington Times*, September 30, 2018, https://www.washington times.com/news/2018/sep/30/retraction-aaron-rich-and-murder-seth-rich/.

Andy Kroll, "Pro-Trump Conspiracy Peddler Jerome Corsi Apologizes to Seth Rich's Family," *Rolling Stone*, March 4, 2019, https://www.rollingstone .com/politics/politics-news/pro-trump-conspiracy-peddler-jerome-corsi -apologizes-to-seth-richs-family-802581/.

Andy Kroll, "CNN Is Silent on Why It Gave Airtime to a Conspiracy Theorist," *Rolling Stone*, March 5, 2019, https://www.rollingstone.com/politics/politics -news/cnn-conspiracy-theory-803467/.

Order, *Rich v. Butowsky*, filed on March 29, 2019.

Special Counsel Robert S. Mueller, III, "Report on the Investigation into Russian Interference in the 2016 Presidential Election," US Department of Justice, March 2019, https://www.justice.gov/archives/sco/file/1373816 /download.

Andy Kroll, "WikiLeaks and Fox News Are Silent on the Debunked Seth Rich Conspiracy Theory," *Rolling Stone*, April 23, 2019, https://www.rolling stone.com/politics/politics-news/wikileaks-and-fox-news-are-silent-on-the -debunked-seth-rich-conspiracy-theory-825686/.

"Plaintiff's Opposition to Defendant Couch's Motion for Relief from Order Granting Plaintiff's Motion to Compel," *Rich v. Butowsky*, https://www.doc umentcloud.org/documents/21918384-plaintiffs-opposition-to-defendant -couchs-motion-for-relief-from-order-granting-plaintiffs-motion-to-compel.

"Ex-Fox News Commentator Reveals Source for Claims That Seth Rich Sold DNC Emails to Wikileaks," Rick Ungar Show, July 10, 2019; archived version can be accessed at https://web.archive.org/web/20210301214945 /https://www.rickungarshow.com/ex-fox-news-commentator-reveals -source-for-claims-that-seth-rich-sold-dnc-emails-to-wikileaks/.

CN Live!, July 26, 2019, https://www.documentcloud.org/documents/666 0037-2020-01-16-Exhibits-40-49#document/p3/a2020005.

Duncan Campbell, interview with author, January 27, 2021.

"Plaintiff's Motion for Issuance of a Letter of Request," *Rich v. Butowsky*, filed on November 8, 2019, https://www.documentcloud.org/documents/21941394 -plaintiffs-motion-for-issuance-of-a-letter-of-request.

"Plaintiff's Motion for Anti-Suit Injunction," *Rich v. Butowsky*, filed on March 26, 2019, https://www.documentcloud.org/documents/21941452-plaintiffs -motion-for-anti-suit-injunction.

Mary and Joel Rich, interview with author, November 16, 2021.

Rich v. Fox News Network, No. 18-2321 (2d Cir. 2019).

Scheduling Order, *Rich v. Butowsky*, filed on September 5, 2019, https://www .documentcloud.org/documents/6561167-2019-09-05-Aaron-Rich-Lawsuit -Scheduling-Order.

CHAPTER 27: BIRTH OF A LIE

The exchange between McEnany and Frank can be accessed at https://www .youtube.com/watch?v=MEopZYx437I.

BrieAnna J. Frank and Chelsea Curtis, "Trump Praises 100-Year-Old World War II Veteran Carried to Seat at His Phoenix Rally," *Arizona Republic*, February 20, 2020, https://www.azcentral.com/story/news/local/phoenix /2020/02/20/trump-rally-phoenix-two-carry-man-said-wwii-veteran -seat/4813284002/.

Isaac Stanley-Becker, "How the Trump Campaign Came to Court QAnon, the Online Conspiracy Movement Identified by the FBI as a Violent Threat," *Washington Post*, August 2, 2020, https://www.washingtonpost.com/politics /how-the-trump-campaign-came-to-court-qanon-the-online-conspiracy -movement-identified-by-the-fbi-as-a-violent-threat/2020/08/01/dd0e a9b4-d1d4-11ea-9038-af089b63ac21_story.html.

Ali Breland and Sinduja Rangarajan, "How the Coronavirus Spread QAnon," *Mother Jones*, June 23, 2020, https://www.motherjones.com/politics/2020 /06/qanon-coronavirus/.

Ari Sen and Brandy Zadrozny, "QAnon Groups Have Millions of Members on Facebook, Documents Show," NBC News, August 10, 2020, https://www .nbcnews.com/tech/tech-news/qanon-groups-have-millions-members -facebook-documents-show-n1236317?cid=sm_npd_nn_fb_ma.

Alex Kaplan (@AlKapDC), "Folks, we are now up to 48 current or former 2020 congressional candidates who have endorsed or given credence to QAnon. New additions are candidates from Pennsylvania, New Mexico, Maryland, & 2 from New Jersey," Twitter, May 26, 2020, 3:07 p.m., https://twitter .com/AlKapDC/status/1265358928319307777.

Marjorie Greene, "There Is a Storm Brewing That Is About to Reveal the Real Source of Evil in America!," Americantruthseekers.com, November 15, 2017, https://web.archive.org/web/20171220034057/http:/americantruth seekers.com/there-is-a-storm-brewing-that-is-about-to-reveal-the-real -source-of-evil-in-america.

Taylor Greene said during a November 1, 2018, appearance at the American Priority Conference that "Seth Rich was murdered by two MS-13 gang members." The video can be accessed at https://www.mediamatters.org/media/3889836.

Andy Kroll, "The Plot Against America: The GOP's Plan to Suppress the Vote and Sabotage the Election," *Rolling Stone*, July 16, 2020, https://www.rollingstone.com/politics/politics-features/trump-campaign-2020-voter-suppression-consent-decree-1028988/.

QAlerts.app, June 17, 2020, https://qalerts.app/?n=4477.

Status Conference, *Rich v. Butowsky*, held on March 3, 2020, https://www.documentcloud.org/documents/21174753-2020_03_11-gottlieb-quainton-hearing-re-discovery#document/p26/a2072769.

Order, *Rich v. Butowsky*, filed on March 20, 2020.

The reference to 3,500 documents produced by Fox comes from a July 20, 2020, letter sent by Mary and Joel's lawyers to Judge Netburn in *Rich v. Fox News Network*, https://www.documentcloud.org/documents/7007616-2020-07-23-Rich-Lawyer-Letter-With-Wheeler#document/p1/a2020157.

Butowsky's comment about being "at the center" of the Seth–WikiLeaks story were included in court filings in *Rich v. Fox News Network*, https://www.documentcloud.org/documents/7007616-2020-07-23-Rich-Lawyer-Letter-With-Wheeler#document/p1/a2020157.

Rich v. Fox News Network, https://www.documentcloud.org/documents/20394765-2020_09_10-jm-rich-lawyers-letter-butowsky-new-york-connections#document/p12/a2018693.

Letter to the court, *Rich v. Butowsky*, filed on August 12, 2020, https://www.documentcloud.org/documents/21942035-butowsky-letter-to-court-heart-failure.

An archived version of Trump's "Future Republican star" tweet can be accessed at https://www.thetrumparchive.com.

Katie Rogers and Kevin Roose, "Trump Says QAnon Followers Are People Who 'Love Our Country,'" *New York Times*, August 19, 2020, https://www.nytimes.com/2020/08/19/us/politics/trump-qanon-conspiracy-theories.html.

Susman Godfrey letter to Judge Sarah Netburn, *Rich v. Fox News Network*, filed on September 10, 2020, https://www.documentcloud.org/documents/21942088-susman-godfrey-fox-deposition-list.

CHAPTER 28: THE BLOOD OF TYRANTS

Ryan J. Foley, "Conservative Hoaxers Face Charges over False Voter Robocalls," Associated Press, October 1, 2020, https://apnews.com/article

/election-2020-technology-arrests-michigan-voting-rights-e0d4915
5dc8f347b1347cf779fd43812?utm_medium=AP_Politics&utm_cam
paign=SocialFlow&utm_source=Twitter.

The People of the State of Michigan v. John Macauley Burkman and Jacob Alex-
ander Wohl, Criminal Complaint filed on October 1, 2020, 36th Judicial
District, 3rd Judicial Circuit, https://www.michigan.gov/-/media/Project
/Websites/AG/releases/2020/october/Burkman-Wohl_complaint
_Redacted.pdf?rev=c72503b0e0e3437f9d922029849d1e35.

Cory Shaffer, "Right-Wing Hoaxers Jacob Wohl and Jack Burkman Hit with
Felony Charges in Cleveland Tied to Multi-State Voter Robocall Campaign," Cleveland.com, October 27, 2020, https://www.cleveland.com
/court-justice/2020/10/right-wing-hoaxers-jacob-wohl-and-jack-burkman
-hit-with-felony-charges-in-cleveland-tied-to-multi-state-voter-robocall
-campaign.html.

National Coalition on Black Civic Participation v. Wohl, 1:20-cv-08668 (US District Court, Southern District of New York 2020).

National Coalition on Black Civic Participation v. Wohl, hearing held on November
2, 2020, https://www.documentcloud.org/documents/21175897-2020_11
_02-burkman-wohl-hearing-new-york-robocall-case#document/p12
/a2072981.

Ben Smith, "Fox Settled a Lawsuit over Its Lies. But It Insisted on One Unusual
Condition," New York Times, January 18, 2021, https://www.nytimes.com
/2021/01/17/business/media/fox-news-seth-rich-settlement.html.

Clevenger's comments about the settlement negotiations between Butowsky and
Fox came during an appearance he made on "The Whistleblower News-
room," December 31, 2020, https://www.youtube.com/watch?v=9M59Vs
FRo94. Clevenger confirmed those comments in an email to the author.
Lawyers for Fox News declined to comment on Clevenger's descriptions of
the settlement negotiations.

Michael Isikoff, "Fox Paid Seven Figures to Settle Lawsuit over Bogus Seth Rich
Conspiracy Story," Yahoo News, November 24, 2020, https://www.yahoo
.com/video/fox-paid-seven-figures-to-settle-lawsuit-over-bogus-seth-rich
-conspiracy-story-003236858.html.

Andy Kroll, "Seth Rich's Parents Settle Their Blockbuster Lawsuit Against Fox
News," Rolling Stone, November 24, 2020, https://www.rollingstone.com
/politics/politics-news/seth-rich-wikileaks-fox-news-sean-hannity-donald
-trump-russia-1094896/.

Jason Slotkin, Suzanne Nuyen, and James Doubek, "4 Stabbed, 33 Arrested
After Trump Supporters, Counterprotesters Clash in D.C.," NPR, December 12, 2020, https://www.npr.org/2020/12/12/945825924/trump-support
ers-arrive-in-washington-once-again-for-a-million-maga-march.

Eric Kleefeld, "How Fox News Helped to Spread Right-Wing Groups' Efforts to Undermine the 2020 Election," Media Matters for America, https://www.mediamatters.org/voter-fraud-and-suppression/how-fox-news-helped-spread-right-wing-groups-efforts-undermine-2020.

Patrick Byrne's comments about Seth were included in the original complaint in *US Dominion Inc. v. Patrick Byrne*, 1:21-cv-02131 (US District Court for the District of Columbia 2021).

Luke Mogelson, "Among the Insurrectionists," *New Yorker*, January 25, 2021, https://www.newyorker.com/magazine/2021/01/25/among-the-insurrectionists.

Mike Gottlieb, interview with author, June 23, 2021.

Archived versions of Couch's DCPatriot.com website show content focused on amplifying supposed instances of election fraud, https://web.archive.org/web/20201117114224/https://thedcpatriot.com/.

Craig Silverman, Jane Lytvynenko, and Pranav Dixit, "How This Pro-Trump Bus Tour Led to the Capitol Coup Attempt," BuzzFeed News, January 25, 2021, https://www.buzzfeednews.com/article/craigsilverman/maga-bus-tour-coup.

"Watch LIVE: March for Trump Bus Tour in Washington, DC," YouTube, December 12, 2020, https://www.youtube.com/watch?v=6ltfrJ7MCW8.

See archived version of FighttheFrauds.com at https://web.archive.org/web/20201230181920/http://fightthefrauds.com/.

@RealMattCouch, "Live in Washington, D.C. and Events are NOT CANCELLED," January 4, 2021, https://www.pscp.tv/w/1jMJgplqpMlxL.

Andy Kroll, "'We Retract and Disavow Our Statements': Seth Rich's Brother Wins Apology from Conspiracy Theorists," *Rolling Stone*, January 14, 2021, https://www.rollingstone.com/politics/politics-news/seth-rich-wikileaks-conspiracy-theories-fox-news-1114700/.

CHAPTER 29: CLOSURE

Mary and Joel Rich, interview with author, July 20, 2021.

Clevenger's FBI FOIA case is Huddleston v. Federal Bureau of Investigation, 4:20-cv-00447 (US District Court, Eastern District of Texas, Sherman Division).

Kate Starbird (@katestarbird), "Top 10 most-retweeted accounts in our Stop the Steal Twitter data (Nov 3, 2020 to Jan 7, 2021)," Twitter, May 15, 2021, 4:22 p.m., https://mobile.twitter.com/katestarbird/status/1393663112218169347.

"Twitter Suspends Account of Matt Couch for Sharing Article on Dr's Advice on Covid-19," The DC Patriot, December 8, 2021, https://thedcpatriot.com/twitter-suspends-account-of-matt-couch-for-sharing-article-on-drs-advice-on-covid-19/.

Mike Gottlieb, interview with author, June 23, 2021.

US Dominion, Inc. v. Fox News Network, LLC, N21C-03-257 EMD (Del. Super. Ct. December 16, 2021)

US Dominion Inc. v. Powell, 1:21-cv-00040 (D.D.C. Aug. 11, 2021)

Law for Truth, law4truth.org.

EPILOGUE

Miguel Huerta, Werner Nelson, Scott Peak, James Perry, and Kevin Zientarski, interview with author.

Index

Andy Kroll is an investigative reporter at ProPublica, where he covers voting, politics, and threats to democracy. He is the former Washington bureau chief for *Rolling Stone* magazine, where he wrote extensively about the Seth Rich case. He has also written for *Mother Jones, National Journal*, and the *California Sunday Magazine*. He lives in Washington, DC. This is his first book.

PublicAffairs is a publishing house founded in 1997. It is a tribute to the standards, values, and flair of three persons who have served as mentors to countless reporters, writers, editors, and book people of all kinds, including me.

I. F. STONE, proprietor of *I. F. Stone's Weekly*, combined a commitment to the First Amendment with entrepreneurial zeal and reporting skill and became one of the great independent journalists in American history. At the age of eighty, Izzy published *The Trial of Socrates*, which was a national bestseller. He wrote the book after he taught himself ancient Greek.

BENJAMIN C. BRADLEE was for nearly thirty years the charismatic editorial leader of *The Washington Post*. It was Ben who gave the *Post* the range and courage to pursue such historic issues as Watergate. He supported his reporters with a tenacity that made them fearless and it is no accident that so many became authors of influential, best-selling books.

ROBERT L. BERNSTEIN, the chief executive of Random House for more than a quarter century, guided one of the nation's premier publishing houses. Bob was personally responsible for many books of political dissent and argument that challenged tyranny around the globe. He is also the founder and longtime chair of Human Rights Watch, one of the most respected human rights organizations in the world.

•　　•　　•

For fifty years, the banner of Public Affairs Press was carried by its owner Morris B. Schnapper, who published Gandhi, Nasser, Toynbee, Truman, and about 1,500 other authors. In 1983, Schnapper was described by *The Washington Post* as "a redoubtable gadfly." His legacy will endure in the books to come.

Peter Osnos, *Founder*